Stars in the Sky bring the Summer right back to me

A Collection of Stories
Celebrating Camps for Seriously-ill Children

Stars in the Sky,
Bring the Summer Right Back to Me:
A Collection of Stories Celebrating Camps for Seriously-ill Children

Meera Ramamoorthy, MD

in collaboration with Former Campers, Parents, Counselors and Medical Professionals

Doer.Dreamer.Doctor. & Company
2015

ISBN-13: 978-0692307526
ISBN-10: 0692307524

Doer.Dreamer.Doctor. & Company
8355 Wetherfield Lane
Cincinnati, Ohio 45236

https://www.facebook.com/CampStoriesBook

To place a bulk order at a discount or sell it in a camp store, please contact:
campstoriesbook@gmail.com

This is an independently orchestrated book of camp stories. This project is not affiliated with or endorsed by any specific camp. All names of campers have been changed to protect their privacy.

Cover design by Erin Hood and Kate Otte @ the1017.com

Photography by Nigel Bibler

Dedication

To the campers - You are the heart and soul of camp. You continue to inspire us with your courageous attitude, positive spirit and joy towards life! Thank you for teaching us how we can be our best selves! You will always be a part of camp - you have left your imprint on the grounds and in our hearts.

To the parents - How can we possibly thank you enough for sharing your children with us and entrusting us with their care? You amaze us everyday with your determination to advocate, love and provide your children with the best life possible. You serve as an example of what unconditional love looks like.

To the counselors - The moment you walk into camp, you dedicate every waking moment "for the kids!" You encourage friendships and teamwork within the cabin, role model camp spirit and help campers have the best week of their lives. You are the backbone of the camp and the reason why the kids want to play at the crack of dawn, everyday. Your energy is contagious!

To the medical professionals - Camp would not function without you. From dispensing medications to providing comfort to homesick kids, you are an integral part of camp and its safety and success. Thank you for volunteering your time, knowledge and skills with us to ensure that our campers are healthy enough to enjoy their camp experience.

To the donors - Because of your generosity, camp programs are provided year-round across the world to seriously-ill children and their families, always free-of-charge. Thank you for your continued help and support.

Thank you.

Contents

In the summer of 2003, I was a 17-year-old junior counselor in Clarksville, Ohio. The camp partners with Cincinnati Children's Hospital to offer illness–specific sessions: Cancer, Hemophilia, Sickle Cell, Heart Disease, Arthritis, Diabetes, Tuberous Sclerosis, among other illnesses. For the first time, my passion for camp and the outdoors included my pediatric medical interests, something I didn't know was possible. The executive director pointed to the poster of the legendary Paul Newman hanging in her office and said that's where I was meant to be. I'm a little embarrassed to admit that, at that time, I wasn't too familiar with his Hollywood or philanthropic work. I didn't even know the color of his eyes, even though one of my favorite musical artists wrote a song about them! He was just the salad dressing guy! Nonetheless, as my mentor, I respected her input and took her word for it. On May 16th, five days after I turned 19, the minimum age to volunteer, I found myself at summer staff training. I had just finished my first year of college as a pre-med Biopsychology and Spanish major, and was ready to make a difference in the life of a seriously-ill child, not realizing that they would change my life.

On the morning of the arrival of the first session of campers, my cabin nurse casually said to me as they arrived, "By the way, Bellamy, one of your kids this week, doesn't speak English." If my nerves were not going crazy before, they certainly were now. Why had I studied Latin instead of a more useful language?! My co-counselor and I quickly practiced how we would act out the schedule like a game of charades. Swimming, check. Boating and fishing, check. Horse barn, check. But how would we act out woodshop?

Despite my worries, my first group showed me what the camp is about. Kids had fun with each other even though they did not speak the same language and came from different cultures. Bellamy, a leukemia survivor facing heart failure caused by the chemotherapy, fit right into the cabin, participated in everything, and had a wonderful time despite being out of her country for the first time in her life. I tried to realize the amount of trust her family must have had in the camp to send their sick child to another continent for seven days. As a diverse community, there were many experiences to share, and we encouraged each camper to take full advantage of the unique opportunities. Everyone was able to recognize the communal respect and affection in a supportive environment with other campers to whom they could relate. And, most importantly, it was an opportunity to be heard and understood, inspired by individuality and experiences and honored for courage. The children left camp with a sense of accomplishment, a feeling of control over their own lives.

I fell in love with celebrating life that first summer, and felt committed to serve medical-specialty camps at local, national and international levels. It's said, "You can leave camp, but camp never leaves you!" What began as a single camp in Connecticut grew to a global community of 30 camps and programs serving over 30,000 children with serious illnesses and their families every year, always free of charge. I seized the opportunity to serve sick children at the camps located in my home state of Ohio, and as far away as Ireland, Israel, and India. The songs, activities and the languages spoken may be different. They may be called a pride, unit, bale or cottage, but camp is camp. To the campers  (and counselors), it's the best camp on earth!

I could not have predicted that a mere four years later during my second year of medical school, I would begin a battle with a terminal illness. Suddenly, I had been cast in contradicting roles of the physician-to-be and patient. Although this has presented me with many unexpected challenges, my experiences at camp have inspired strength to let nothing hold me back from my wildest fantasies, wishes, and aspirations, including this book! At camp, kids discover a world full of possibilities, not limitations. In a safe, respectful and loving environment, everyone, campers and counselors alike, is given a chance to safely challenge their limits, and succeed. This mindset allowed and challenged me, despite my illness, to graduate from medical school and become a doctor.

Even though I know the reality of my situation, camp creates and inspires hope, and to me, hope is that feeling that better and beautiful days lie ahead, despite how challenging life seems now. Hope is that little extra push that gets you out of bed each morning to face the day. Hope is in the way I continuously celebrate life; eager to praise all accomplishments, compassionate positivity, high-fiving friends, silliness without reservation, and active listening and validation to others' needs, thoughts, and fears. Hope is a feeling that, no matter the odds, anything is possible. I have also been given the gift to see the beauty in all aspects of life. While a positive attitude isn't going to "cure" my illness, it certainly will make it easier to overcome the daily challenges that I encounter. I still have occasional periods of doom and gloom, but I try to let them pass as quickly as possible. Uncertainty may be in the equation, but creating balance is important. The mind is a powerful tool, and I must use it to my advantage.

It's hard to explain what we do at camp. To spend time at camp is a rare opportunity few people experience, yet once you have, you wish all could. What we did was give of ourselves -- but it was far from an act of charity. What we got in return was priceless. I played with kids. I cheered. I sang. I counseled. I listened. I laughed. I cleaned. I got messy. I taught and learned. I got up early. I went to bed late. I encouraged. I planned events. I ate with no hands. I dressed in costumes. I danced. I took naps from 2-3pm. I cried. I held little hands. I gave love. I received even more. I've been to the stars and back.

Several years ago, we surprised our cabin of 13-year-olds girls with a spa night. In between avocado yogurt masques and pedicures, five words casually popped up that were immediately understood. The question? "What kind do you have?" That's it. Five words were all that were needed for a fellow camper to know that the subject was cancer. It wasn't the intended purpose of the activity. Yet, the girls felt so safe and supported to talk through their fears, insecurities and strengths in a way that was natural for them.

And THAT is the magic of the camp—not the horses, pool, archery, boating and fishing, or the theater. It is an opportunity to share scars as badges of belonging and victory. It is an opportunity to watch a child's eyes light up as they celebrate achievements. It is an opportunity to laugh with friends harder than you ever have

 before. It is an opportunity to help a child know and believe they make a difference. It is an opportunity for kids to escape any hardship they may face in their everyday life. It is an opportunity to inspire hope for themselves and their future. Most of all, camp is a place for children to love and be loved. And that is the best experience of all.

We - campers, counselors, parents, medical professionals- come to camp and are forever changed. It is these shared experiences - the fun, the laughter, the tears, the magic, the community, friendship, and love - that resonate in our heart. Regardless of where we went to camp, whether California, Colorado or Cambodia, we've  been touched by the power of camp. I believe by sharing our experiences at camp, we share a bit of our heart and breathe life into memories. What we do with our stories ultimately speaks to how we love and care for ourselves. It reflects how we understand what we have been through, how it affected us in the past, and how it makes us who we are today. How you handle your story is how you handle your heart in this world. Our stories are linked, yours and mine, and they are linked with countless others, both in our pasts and in our futures. These stories too shall live, for we are all one and they become a part of us. For that, I thank you.

Thank you for sharing a piece of your heart.

Meera Ramamoorthy, MD

Doer. Dreamer. Doctor.
Cincinnati, OH

Stars in the sky, stars in the sky
To bring the summer right back to me
Tell me you'll try, tell me you'll try
To think about me whenever you see those
Stars in the sky

We went away when we were very young
To find the person who we would become
To find the person who was hidden somewhere inside
What we discovered these it still holds true
The memories you make become a part of you
The memories you make will return to you like the tide

Stars in the sky...

Chapter 1

CATCH THE SPIRIT

A Camper Meets Mr. Spivey

Salutations! My name is Mr. Spivey. I was born approximately 104 years ago. There were no hospitals or doctors nearby when my mom gave birth, but a midwife was in attendance. At that time, there were no birth certificates. All births were recorded in the family bible along with other family information. Years later, there was a fire in our cabin. Although the cabin survived the fire, the family bible did not, so I was never sure of my exact day of birth. I'm told the weather was cold, so it must have been January or February. I think of myself as a survivor, living off the land and giving back to the land. I think this is why I have such a connection with the campers; they too are survivors!

Since I live so close to camp, I try to visit whenever possible. Once, at an opening campfire, I welcomed the campers and counselors. After I finished the talk, I proceeded to go back up the hill for the trip around the lake back to my cabin. As I walked alongside the benches, a counselor approached me with a camper. The counselor said that this particular camper really wanted to meet me! We chatted briefly, shook hands, and the camper and counselor returned to their seats while I continued my walk up to the waiting golf cart. Later that week, that same counselor sent me a telegram. The young camper had just lost his beloved grandfather two days before camp started, and he saw a remarkable resemblance between his grandfather and me. The counselor added that after the campfire, the camper revealed that after shaking my hand, he didn't feel so sad anymore.

At a different opening campfire years ago, a little girl approached me and said, "My grandma says you aren't real." I was in a particularly testy mood that evening, perhaps because I had run out of prune juice. To her I replied, "Well, I'm standing here, ain't I?" She looked up at me and responded, "Oh yeah,"and sat down.

Mr. Spivey
Eustis, FL
Camp Friend

All Piper talked about as soon as I met her was how she had just joined a wheelchair basketball team. She was over the moon about her new activity that she wanted to practice shooting the basketball every waking moment. We shared our love for the sport (and admittedly, Justin Bieber) over our two morning manatees in the gym. We spent all morning preparing and practicing for Piper's official debut at the Big Game.

That afternoon was one for the books. As I received the last inbound pass of the game, I scanned the court for Piper's wheelchair adorned with sparkly, purple Bieber paraphernalia. I locked eyes with Piper's intense glare. Our team was racing down the court to get back on offense as the seconds ran down. I passed Piper the ball, and before I knew it, she scored the winning basket. As the buzzer sounded, the crowd erupted in a loud and unified, "Piper! Piper! Piper!" Amid the overwhelming excitement, I could only focus on one thing: Piper's gleaming smile. I was so proud of her for working so hard to make her first basket.

Piper is no ordinary basketball player; instead, she is a wheelchair-using 11-year-old living with Spina Bifida. I saw Piper again this summer, and as she hurried down cabin row to come say hi, she excitedly told me how she had recently made her first 10-foot basket. She even asked me if I remembered when she made her first basket at camp those many years ago in 2010. Of course, I did. It was one of the most memorable, pivotal moments that made me fall in love with our campers, their families, and the spirit of camp and want to return again and again.

Over the years, Piper has grown into a beautiful, independent young lady with such a strong spirit, and I am so grateful that camp allowed me to be a part of her journey through this wonderful life.

Nicky Cadiz
Weston, FL
Counselor

Barnaby

Outside of the Dining Hall, there is a wooden bear that was carved by former campers named Barnaby. During my last year as a camper, my friend Ian and I would leave handfuls of Corn Pops and Fruit Loops at Barnaby's feet along with some sugar packets and coffee creamers. We joked with each other that we were making sure Barnaby got breakfast, and it was just something we did because Ian and I were a couple of goofballs.

One day, another camper from our unit saw what we were doing and asked us why we were leaving Barnaby food. Without missing a beat, Ian and I started weaving an improvised, Abbott and Costello style, ball of yarn about how the camp just tells people Barnaby was carved by a group of former campers to cover up the real story. In reality, those former campers actually encountered Barnaby in the forest. Barnaby spoke to them and told them that he was an animal spirit that symbolized the essence of goodness, happiness, and fun, and that if they made a statue of him and made sure he had breakfast everyday that camp would never run out of goodness, happiness, or fun. So they built the statue and put it outside the Dining Hall, and every morning since, it has been the duty of campers to bring Barnaby breakfast.

When we were finished with our story, the camper looked at us and said, "Okay then," and walked away. I don't know if he believed our tall tale or not, but I will say this: The next day, when Ian and I smuggled out our gifts for Barnaby, there was already a pile of food at his feet.

Ross Gipson
Chicago, IL
Former Camper

Climbing

Standing below the 40ft tower watching Damian climb was excruciating, not because of the heat of midday summer, but because the feeling of helplessness I had watching him struggle. I racked my brain thinking of things to tell him to give him the strength to stand up and reach for that fourth rung on the giant's ladder. Having exhausted my repertoire of traditional cheers, I thought back to the last two days I had spent with Damian trying to think of our conversations in hopes of discovering a nugget of motivation from what he had told me: "Damian does this... Damian does that... If I had a rapper name, it would be 'Third Person.' I started referring to myself in the third person a while back now... It makes me feel special, it's my own thing."

Third person... Damian, Damian... what does Damian do? His shirt... "Nike: Do Work"... Do Work... "DAMIAN DOES WORK!" DAMIAN DOES WORK! DAMIAN DOES WORK! I screamed it at the top of my lungs, I ran around rallying the other campers and counselors, "DAMIAN DOES WORK! DAMIAN DOES WORK! DAMIAN DOES WORK!" Everyone was yelling, screaming. I looked up at Damian, he looked down at me. He stood. He reached... He threw his leg over, struggling, but found his balance and made it! Damian... DOES WORK! DAMIAN DID WORK!!!

Kirollos Barsoum
Indianapolis, IN
Counselor

It was Camp University (CU) week of Summer 2007; a week of spirited fun celebrating the wonderful camp, its traditions, and its cheers. My pride during the staff planning meeting on volunteer arrival day wanted to put a twist on CU; we decided to devote our week in the yellow pride as CCU, Camp Clown University. The ideas soared from wearing clown wigs to painting our faces every day, to having our campers earn their red, clown noses at the end of their week at camp.

I grew with excitement to tell our wonderful campers the exciting news that they would learn to be clowns during their week at camp. Our entire pride was gathered at the gym porch playing back pocket and name games, learning the rules of the camp, and discovering a secret only we could share with them.

Kneeled on the ground, in one of the tightest huddles I have ever been in with 30 campers, I unveiled to them that their counselors and myself were not just counselors, but professional clowns, and it had come time for us to retire from the business. I told them their week at camp would not only be filled with fun and new adventures, but also clown training and the right to earn their red, clown nose at week's end.

It was at that moment, the eyes of these precious 7 to 9-year-olds lit up with pure joy and excitement. And then, peering from the huddle, a beautiful, soft-spoken girl exclaimed, "We get to learn how to create magic just like you!"

Holly Miller Carter
Nashville, TN
Woodshop Specialist, Pride Leader

Don't Let It Go

There are not many occasions where it is socially acceptable for people to sing together in public, outside of religious gatherings and karaoke. I just find it so beautiful for people to lift their voices together in song. And that is why one of my favorite times at camp is when we sing together after lunch. Often, it's the time when the campers are close to a dreamlike, rest hour soon, induced sleep. Today, this was not the case.

This past summer of 2014, EVERYTHING revolved around the Disney movie "Frozen". So, fittingly, one of our youngest campers requested that we sing "Let It Go" at lunch one day. Lydia, age nine, had stolen most of her counselors hearts with her festive and challenging demeanor. We took a chance. As the introduction to the song began, two things happened. One precious cabin of youngest boys covered their ears as the rest of the dining hall chattered with excitement. Lydia had the microphone and as soon as the crescendo hit, the entire camp erupted in full chorus. You can only imagine the joyful noise that filled our dining hall! Campers approached the stage, and Lydia graciously passed the microphone around so each of the campers could have their time to shine. Campers sang, danced, and beamed with excitement. Our entire camp lifted Lydia's spirits as she shined and as she shined, she allowed others to do the same as she passed the spotlight to them. Seven-year-old campers to sixteen-year-old campers alongside their counselors sang their hearts out, with the exception of 6 seven-year-old boys who physically clutched their ears.

And it didn't end there because the campers and counselors both started chanting "one more time, one more time, one more time…" and we all know that you have to give the people what they want!

The cold never bothered me anyway…

Kimmy Lamborn
Smyrna, DE
Assistant Camp Director

23

It was my first family weekend camp, and it was one of the best times of my life. I was there for the Rheumatic illnesses session. What was so great; you literally got a full week of fun in just two and a half days. Also, you got to know all the kids and parents pretty fast.

One of the kids I worked with had parents who, like my dad, loved the rock-n-roll from the 70's and 80's. I worked woodshop and that was all this camper, his dad, and I would talk about. I'd set the IPod up with that music, and we'd work on their project and talk music. Todd was a quiet camper, but he was always excited about ACDC, Led Zeppelin, the Rolling Stones, and so on.

On the last breakfast, Journey's "Don't Stop Believin" came on in the dining hall. I began to sing, "Just a small town girl" only I wasn't alone. Todd was right next to me singing along. And for the next four minutes, he and I sang every last word of that song at the top of our lungs, dancing, and air guitaring. We would have made Steve Perry proud.

Levi Dix
Murrieta, CA
Counselor

Finding My Human Side and My Other Half

I initially found my way to camp as a third-year medical student. I had been convinced by a friend to volunteer for a family weekend. It was a time when I was physically tired and emotionally drained from long hours on clinical rotations in the hospital learning how to diagnose diseases and prescribe medicine. I found camp to be a rejuvenating experience. I had the opportunity to see the other side of chronic medical conditions; the human side. The laughing, playing, giggly, messy side. I found my way to camp as many times as I could that year.

My favorite camp memory was when I was volunteering as a cabin counselor with a group of older girls. We were at opening campfire for the S.T.A.R. skit: Learning to Stay safe, Try new things, Always build up and to Respect one another. The girls in my cabin were veteran campers and had little attention span for the standard opening skit; far too busy chatting and giggling to pay close attention. Therefore, my focus was on trying to keep them quiet through the skit. From what I could catch of the skit, it was the story of a time-traveling romantic searching for his one true love (a standard far fetched S.T.A.R. skit with elaborate costumes). The fact that I was engaged in trying to quiet the girls made it all the more surprising when I was pulled from the audience and into the skit. The traveling romantic happened to be my boyfriend, the camp music director, who I had met at camp several years prior. Much to my surprise, he got down on a knee and proposed to me in front of the entire camp!

When I would return to the hospital and see children and adults who were at their sickest, I would try to imagine their lives outside the hospital and channel that human side back into what was all too often clinical and cold. Camp made me a better doctor, and I still strive to carry it into my daily practice of medicine.

Kari Foulke, MD
Santa Rosa, CA
Counselor

Each day I secretly crave that someone will ask me about camp because selfishly, I want an excuse to relive the memories.

The theme of the week was Kings and Queens so what better way to celebrate this than a midnight tea party with the king and queen as our special guests. Throughout the day, we kept telling the girls that we had a big surprise for them. This created a lot of excitement and curiosity amongst the campers.

As the sun set, you could hear rehearsals taking place on the porch of each cabin as it was stage night. As we cheered our way down to the dining hall in anticipation of the acts, I took a quick detour to set up for the tea party later on that night. We set up a corner of the room to resemble a Den with fairy lights dangling around the edges and blankets placed on the ground. We baked a cake and made lots of hot chocolate to add to the sugar rush of the evening and planned to hide the king and queen in the closet so the campers wouldn't see them upon entering.

After stage night, instead of returning to the cabin, we sneaked up the dirt path. By now, the children were hyper from the anxiety of "breaking camp rules." We added to that excitement by exaggerating the enormity of getting caught. The sheer look on the children's face as we introduced the King and Queen was enough to put a smile on your face. As we ate cake, we heard noises coming from outside. The camp director was looking for our cabin!

As we waved goodbye to the king and queen, we all formed a line and agreed to hold hands on the way back to the cabin so that if anyone spotted us on our journey, we would be identified as a wall and not people! On returning, each camper was exhausted but elated at the experience of having a private tea party with the king and queen. As I said goodnight, one camper whispered in my ear, "I will remember this night forever, thank you."

Orlagh Reilly
Cortown, Ireland
Counselor

Maisy and The Car on Fire

There was a little girl in my cabin that was much quieter than the other girls. It appeared that Maisy was too shy to make friends and was struggling to keep up with the group. That is until we had free time in the woodshop.

All week, she had been talking about making a wooden car to race at the Gator Grand Prix. Maisy took my hand and started explaining her plans, and they were quite specific! She needed spikes on the tires "to knock out the competition," a bubble machine for distraction, but, most of all, she wanted fire. She insisted that we find a way to make flames come out of the back of the car to make it go turbo speed! After much discussion, we compromised on flames made from orange, yellow, and red pipe cleaners. From an arts and crafts perspective, they looked quite authentic.

The day of the Gator Grand Prix, the gym was filled with a buzz of excitement. Children anxiously waited on the sidelines of the gym to push their car down the track, the pit crews were standing nearby, and Maisy couldn't wait to get in line with her car. She knew she would win the race!

To begin the show, the camp director dimmed the lights and cleared the race area. Much to my disbelief, they had lit the back of one of the cars on fire and sent it down the track. Children cheered with delight. Maisy looked at me with wide eyes and exclaimed, "How did THEY get fire!?" To say I had some explaining to do would be an understatement!

After the excitement of the race ended, she began talking about our next project; a helicopter with skis, lights, and a real camera! At the week's end, I bragged to her parents about how incredible she was in the woodshop, it all made sense when her dad told me he was an engineer!

Amanda Taylor
Daytona Beach, FL
Counselor

During Cerebral Palsy week at Camp, I had youngest campers. We decided that it would be a really fun surprise to have a sleepover for our girls so we got it ready while they were finishing up an activity. We hung sheets from the fan and pulled mattresses onto the floor. The cabin looked like a really cool pillow fort for their sleepover.

One of our campers, Sydney, required total care for activities of daily life. At home, Sydney often trades the classroom for the hospital room and friends her own age for doctors and nurses. When Sydney is in school, she is accompanied by an adult to ensure her needs are met. Making friends can be challenging as she is unable to join in the playground games. When we transferred Sydney onto her mattress on the ground with all of the other girls, her whole face lit up as she told us it was her very first sleepover. Camp allowed her to do something that seemed so simple but realistically wasn't, and she said it was the highlight of her week.

Stephanie Burkart
Boone, NC
Counselor

In the summer of 2005, I was responsible for playing music for campers and staff. Most of the time that meant acting as mealtime DJ, spinning kid-friendly radio hits over and over. When I wasn't blasting the timeless 2005 Songs of Summer (Ciara's "One Two Step" and Kelly Clarkson's "Since U Been Gone"), I was learning a repertoire of 20 camp songs.

One tradition that I quickly mastered was the end-of-lunch nap sendoff. After singing a few camp songs, campers were released to their cabins to take naps. There was music for this called "The Goodnight Song." The kids would sing it as a lullaby to themselves, and, while they shuffled out of the dining hall, I would continue the song, gently, in a folksy manner not unlike Snuffy Walden's version of "A Little Help From My Friends" during the closing credits of The Wonder Years, until everyone had left the hall.

One week, a fellow counselor asked me to come to their cabin at bedtime. The campers refused to go to sleep, and their counselors were at wit's end. They were hoping I could recreate the post-lunch nap-inducing magic. At first the campers, in their bunk beds, appeared skeptical. They requested I play "One Two Step." They requested country songs I hadn't heard of. Overconfident, I breezed through my repertoire only to find bright eyes staring back at me, mockingly. I started my set over. The campers noticed: "YOU PLAYED THAT ONE ALREADY!"

Scrambling, I played anything I could remember, including "Blackbird", "Free Bird", "No Woman No Cry", "The Sweater Song", and, inexplicably, 50 Cent's "Candy Shop," all slowed to near-dirgelike tempos, for almost two hours. When I finally reached a point of stillness that I assumed meant everyone was sleeping, I tiptoed towards the door. "THANKS!!" a few kids yelled, and I shuddered.

Nick Homenda
Bloomington, IN
Counselor, Music Specialist

Before even introducing himself on the first day of the camp session, a camper asked me, "Do you like Born in the USA?" It took me a second, but when I thought about the Bruce Springsteen song he was referencing, I answered with an obligatory "sure" and didn't think much about it.

However, over the course of the next week I would learn what true devotion to "Born in the USA" and the American flag was. This camper would spend his time at arts and crafts making American flag crafts and would write "Born in the USA" on them. He would constantly request that the director play "Born in the USA" during the mealtime and when the director would oblige, he would spend the entire song yelling the lyrics and bopping his head.

It's no surprise that this camper had the perfect rock show in mind. We created American flag jean vests with "Born in the USA" written on them and found guitars for the camper and his supporting band members. After lunch one day, the camper had the performance of his life. He took the stage and the rest of the campers stood in front of the stage. Once the opening notes of the song came on, I'm not sure if I'd ever seen a bigger smile on a person's face than this camper while he belted out "Born in the USA" at the top of his lungs.

For the rest of the week, when the camper continued to request "Born in the USA" to be played at all meal times, you could tell that he was reliving his performance every time he heard the song. I imagine he still does so today.

Matthew Cocanougher
Danville, KY
Counselor

Sacrifice

It was Thursday, and there was a slight chill. All of camp was gathered at Newman's Nook for Kid's Choice Campfire. Every cabin comes up with a skit or song to show the entire camp. Red 8, popularly known as "Rojo Ocho," was up next and, as the cabin of boys sauntered to the stage, the crowd was readily anticipating the name of their skit. "The Rojo Ocho Initiation," they proclaimed, needed a volunteer from the audience. After scanning the crowd for a few seconds, they called on Mary-Kate, the Red Unit Floater. She was a little apprehensive about going up there so they started chanting her name. Soon the entire crowd was chanting "Mary-Kate! Mary-Kate! Mary-Kate!" Face flushed and head down, she made her way through the crowd and joined the boys on the grassy stage. And, in the space between Rojo Ocho starting their skit and the last sounds of applause, I heard it.

Out of the crowd, I heard a faint high-pitched voice, no louder than a whisper, floating through the air, chanting. It was hard to decipher what was being said, but when the words finally reached my ear, I realized he was chanting "Sacrifice! Sacrifice! Sacrifice!" After scanning the crowd, I located who it was coming from.

The 8-year-old camper no bigger than a large teddy bear was on his feet chanting "Sacrifice," right fist in the air, and fire behind his eyes. He was drenched with determination and his voice only grew stronger as the crowd faded into complete silence. And horror.

Nobody knew whether to be disturbed or amused or just pretend we didn't see/hear anything. It took a good 30 seconds of silence (Sacrifice chanting) until the staff started nervously laughing and redirecting the crowd. It took some time to convince him that they weren't going to sacrifice Mary-Kate and roast her over the fire. Overwhelmed with disappointment, he melted back into his seat.

Dera Eneh
Houston, TX
Former Camper, Program Staff

31

I had youngest boys, all of whom were first-time campers with Hemophilia. This particular session is dominated by male campers, so many of the boys' cabins had female staff. I was the only male counselor in my cabin. The counselors devised a "secret mission" that would end in an initiation to bridge the divide between the male campers and female counselors in our cabin.

The theme of the week was robot invasion and the "invasion" of camp consisted of robots seeking to steal our personalities because they were jealous of all the fun we were having! Nighttime rolled around, and it was time to put our secret mission to work. I painted this elaborate vision for the boys that from the moment they entered camp, they were selected as shadow recruits for a special division of the Guardians of the Galaxy known as the Cowbots, and our job was to stop intergalactic time-traveling criminals. With the recent invasion of camp, our girls had fallen victim and were really robot impostures. The campers were informed that we were no longer training, and this was the real deal! I hastily gave them their final 3 lessons before we were to ambush the robot impostors as they recharged. I taught them the tree pose for stealth, game face for ultimate focus, and gave them their ammunition which were ridiculous cabin chat questions.

Overconfident and underprepared, we crept into the cabin where the robot impostors were recharging and bombarded them with cabin chat questions. The impostors put up a good fight but, in the end, our bravery paid off and the campers saved our girls! With victory in the air, we marched back to our cabin and proudly initiated them into the prestigious task force.

The secret mission sums up how invested we were in being completely outlandish to make it the best week of their lives. Next challenge: Calming them down enough to go to sleep!

Zane Schultz
Jacksonville, FL
Counselor

My summer as a PFD (Personal Flotation Device) brought about the strongest of snapshots. Seeing my campers return and realizing how much energy they brought to us that week, every week. Having the opportunity to experience every single Bale closing, night out, cabin prank, cabin chat, silent ball, talent show, and more. Singing "Stars in the Sky" and making S'mores on a weekly basis. Watching former campers come back as LITs and counselors. Impromptu cabin birthdays, celebrating ropes course challenges, Silly-O and dancing in the punishing spray of the fire truck hose and, yet, still finding pudding and paint in my hair, ears, and nose hours after the event. Speeding around activity areas to AMP IT UP because "There's not enough time!" For those of you who did not experience "AMPed," it was an activity that involved visiting every single area of camp: throw flour into a mixing bowl, hammer a nail into a block of wood, splash paint on a t-shirt, dip our feet into the pool, wave to Pun at his magic show, shoot a basketball in, near, or around the hoop (remember, There's Not Enough Time!), and whatever else that was going on. Hands down, it was the loudest and craziest of activities!

Camp is not where I met my husband, but it's because of camp that we started talking. Most of my favorite memories of camp involve Nick, whether it's dancing together in the dining hall, sharing a camper story, singing about Boa Constrictors and Magic Wizards, or seeing who could create the most ridiculous outfit from the costume shop for Carnival. Camp made us who we are and shaped us into stronger, brighter, and wiser versions of ourselves. I count myself as blessed for having had these experiences, to get to know so many of the young campers and families that have walked through those gates, and the friends that I have made along the way.

Robin Brandehoff
San Francisco, CA
Counselor

33

During a family weekend, one family arrived wide-eyed, but a little nervous. They were ready for camp. They had packed all of the right things but they just weren't sure if it was going to be the right place for them or if camp would give all that they wanted, and truly deserved. They tentatively greeted the exuberant counselors who had been awaiting their arrival all afternoon, trudged up to the cabin and took in their surroundings. All the while, when the children were buzzing around, sussing everything out, one child who wore a hat instead of pigtails stood back from the buzzing excitement.

Finally that evening, after dinner and some hesitant dancing, it came to the welcome event: a skit night orchestrated by the counselors for the families to enjoy. Part of this involved family challenges; one such challenge was to disguise a family member using toilet paper. When this was over, one of the children, who wore a hat instead of pigtails, decided to gather up all of the toilet paper. She carefully packed it all as tight as she could within her small grasp. Finally, when she was satisfied that she had gathered every last piece that she could reach, she stood up and with great gusto released the pieces into the air. She looked up and beamed at the falling toilet paper and shouted out, "It's snowing!"

This continued over and over and, for a few minutes, all of us just stood back and watched the joy of childhood make its way home.

Anna O'Leary
Dublin, Ireland
Counselor

Being my first big trip overseas, by mid-summer homesickness was kicking in, and the summer was starting to lag. At the start of Skeletal Dysplasia camp, I was placed with a girls' cabin as their activity counselor. Now I know what you are thinking, that's a little unorthodox for a guy. Well, I thought so too, and I was a little unsure of how it was going to work. But this cabin of girls changed my summer from being great to absolutely magical.

On camper arrival day, we had more training on the High Ropes course scheduled and returned a little late to the cabins to meet our campers for the week. I walked into the cabin for the first time to meet the youngest girls for the week where they then declared that they were my little "princesses" for the week and that was how I was to address them. Who am I to argue right?

Violet definitely took my heart. She not only had Skeletal Dysplasia, but also Downs Syndrome and sleep apnea. Violet had me wrapped around her little finger from day one. Walking to activities with her standing on my feet, playing monster and roaring all the way down cabin row to just holding her hand until she fell asleep at night. Even now when I think of that magical week, it brings a smile to my face and a warm fuzzy feeling in my heart.

It makes it all worth it, right?

Trav Jack
Melbourne, Australia
High Ropes Instructor

The Special Wig of Captain Jack Sparrow

Nellie's Catwalk is one of the highlights of Hematology and Oncology camp. It is an evening program of celebration and empowerment where the campers get to be in the spotlight by dressing up and walking down a runway like models! During this particular week, there was a camper who chose a mermaid costume to wear during the catwalk. The bright, sequenced, colorful mermaid costume, which Arielle adored, was completed with a Captain Jack Sparrow wig. When Arielle put on the big, pirate wig full of dreads over her shiny, bald head, she said, "This wig makes me feel like I don't have cancer anymore. I feel invincible."

That touched my heart because it was an expression of how a simple wig and camp can help campers not worry about being sick. They can be in the spotlight for something other than their illness. They can briefly escape to a land of mermaids and pirates! No matter what illness you have, where you come from, or where you've been, people look past the things that set you apart. Unique traits are embraced because you are special the way you are. They are superstars at camp! This powerful memory will stay with me forever.

Maddie Farmer
Oakton, VA
Counselor

They rolled up in a giant bus wearing vibrant yellow family shirts. It. Was. Awesome. Picture those shirts at Disney that help you find your kid in a crowd, only it really served as a depiction that they took up almost half the camper populous for that weekend. I was assigned to a group of kids within the family, with one in a wheelchair who had limited mobility in his arms and legs. His siblings made sure he felt included in every activity. The adaptiveness of tools made it impossible to give the excuse of "I can't do it." No matter the illness, they are always able to play at camp, and Jordan was no different.

We rolled up to Archery one morning. Approaching the platform, we found a bow stuck in the ground with a pipe, and the activity staff instructed Jordan to sit behind the bow as I fitted the arrow in place. Jordan rolled up, hooked a finger around the string, rolled his chair back, and let the arrow go. It flew up and over the targets way back in the woods. When I looked at him, his eyes were wide and his jaw dropped open. He had completely prepared himself to watch the arrow fumble into the dirt without coming close to a target. The look of surprise and disbelief was as if to say, "Did YOU see THAT?!" We laughed over and over as we continued cranking back arrows and letting them fly into the targets while occasionally sending the activity leader running back into the woods to retrieve an arrow.

I hadn't prepared myself to get so attached to these strangers who had turned into family in only a few days. I cried as I hugged them goodbye and wished them well. I drove home wondering if I made the same impact on them as they had on me. I never imagined volunteering at a camp would fill me up like it did and leave me thirsty for more. Four summers of camp later, Jordan represents just one of the many kids that foster hope and encourage the heart.

Sandra Kay Dowd
Birch Run, MI
Counselor

37

It was early in the morning, and the rest of camp was just waking up, but our girls had already been up and ready to go for hours. Today was the day they were finally getting their chance to complete the high ropes course. Several of our campers had tried the course in previous summers, and, though, they were excited and maybe even a little bit nervous, they had an idea of what to expect. But, for one first-time camper, all Annabelle could talk about throughout the week was how excited she was to "fly" on the zipline. Now that the time had come, Annabelle could barely contain herself.

As each camper climbed the rope ladder, her voice could be heard over everyone else's, building her cabin mates up and cheering them on as they conquered their fears. But when her turn finally came, her confident smile was replaced by a look of sheer panic. "I can't wait!" turned into, "I can't do it!" and it took a few minutes of reassurance before Annabelle was ready to go.

Knees knocking, Annabelle slowly approached the base of the ladder, and with the encouragement of everyone around, began to climb. Every few seconds, she'd stop to recollect herself before continuing, but eventually she made it to the top and stood proudly 30 feet above us. All fears forgotten, Annabelle completed the course. As a member of the A-Team hooked her harness into the zipline, Annabelle peeked over the edge and yelled down to the crowd below, "Everybody, look at me! I did it! Give it a... three! Three thumbs! Give it three thumbs up! Give me THREE THUMBS UP!"

Without hesitation, I stuck both thumbs in the air, and another counselor rushed to complete the "three thumbs up" for one very special camper as she finally flew.

Cory Keffer
Baltimore, MD
Counselor

This past summer during cancer week, one little guy in my cabin, Logan, decided he'd like to go to the pool for free choice. We got there and everyone was in their bathing suits except Logan. I went over to him and asked why he wasn't in his bathing suit, Logan replied, "I just want to play card games." A bit confused I mentioned that he can play those anywhere. He simply said without even looking at me, "I know, but I like being outside."

So, Logan and I played UNO poolside the entire time. At first I took it easy on him, holding on to draw two and skips, but then he became the world's greatest UNO player and beat me four times straight. He, of course, did it in amazing fashion with a grin on his face from ear to ear. He was so proud of himself that he told everyone for the rest of the day that he beat me four times in a row. Logan then had me help him in the woodshop make a UNO Champion name tag with actual UNO cards glued on.

Kyle Santo
Winter Haven, FL
Counselor

My favorite festive camper attended the first session of the summer. This kid could chant, and who else, but a loud-mouth Aussie to team up with him! I tagged in with him as his one-on-one. We chanted this song everywhere! From "We've got bacon, yes we do! We've got bacon, how 'bout you?!" to "We've got woodshop, yes we do! We've got woodshop, how bout you?!" to "We've got ketchup, yes we do! We've got ketchup, how bout you?!" to "We've got ice cream, yes we do! We've got ice cream, how bout you?!"

Well, you get the picture!

Erin "Bella" Bell
Mornington Peninsula, Australia
Assistant Activities Director

In 2010, I volunteered with a cabin full of organ transplant recipients who simply exemplified camp spirit. Despite their young age, they participated in a way I have rarely seen, knowing well that kindness, respect and acceptance made camp run successfully. They cheered loudly, made friends with campers in the other cabins too and strived to be positive role models.

During Cabin Chat on the last night, a topic was "What did you like most about your week at camp?" One of my beautiful campers responded, "I like camp because it makes me braver. I wish I could stay here all year! Everyone here shows me that I shouldn't hide because of my illness. Everyone here has the same problems I do, and we are all friends and have fun together. When I go home, I won't be scared to show my scars because there is nothing to be scared of. I'll miss everyone here and can't wait to come back next year because I feel safe here."

If anyone needed to hear her testimony, it was myself. It seemed that every day at camp gave me a new grasp on the "magic" of camp. Camp helped me see the world in a different light and appreciate what I've been given. They showed me how even serious medical issues don't hold them back and how to remain optimistic about life. I'm sure my campers thought they needed me that week, but it was I who needed them to show me what bravery truly looks like.

Ashlee Crabill
Heath, OH
Counselor

41

The camp that I have worked at for the past six summers is extremely non-competitive. Our philosophy is that there are many areas in life where our campers don't feel like they're winning and we don't want camp to be one of those areas. The phrase "the campers always win" reigns supreme at this particular camp. However, there is one area where friendly competition is not only allowed, but highly encouraged: the Cleanest Cabin Awards.

Every day, our campers clean their cabins in the hopes of winning one of six coveted awards: Best Made Beds, Tidiest Porch, Best Environment, Most Intentional Acts of Kindness, Cleanest Bathrooms, and the grandaddy of them all, The Overall Cleanest Cabin Award. The judges of this competition are not counselors, or leadership team members, or even nurses...they are the cabin fairies. Cabin fairies are constantly talked about but NEVER seen, and they have very high cleanliness standards.

One week, we told our cabin of girls that a cabin fairy had a special surprise for them but only if they did a good job cleaning their cabin every single day. Our campers rose to the occasion, and on Grand Finale night, we followed a map that glowed in the moonlight that lead us to a trail of silver fairy dust. We were invited into a cabin fairy's nest and each of our campers was allowed to ask the cabin fairy two questions via walkie-talkie, of course, because cabin fairies are notoriously shy creatures.

Our campers worked very hard that week and definitely earned their surprise from the cabin fairy. But the real prize was watching the wonder on each of our campers' faces as we celebrated their childhood and the magic within their hearts.

Catherine Johnson
Eustis, FL
Activities Coordinator

Chapter 11

LET YOUR LOVE SHINE

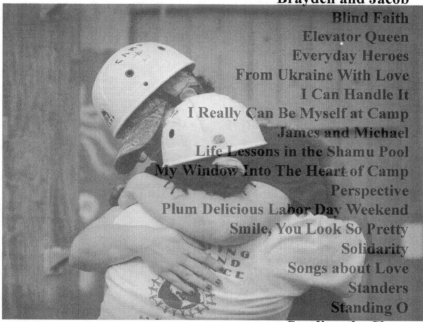

I was checking campers in when Gabriel arrived, but he wasn't responding to anyone throughout the process. I immediately knew that he was deaf, and, therefore, I was assigned to his cabin to provide ASL interpreting. Although Gabriel was deaf, he was more challenging since he was not born deaf and still new to learning ASL. Gabriel didn't have much of any language to communicate with. The "sign language" that he used was mostly things that he made up, which made it tricky to communicate at all. His cabin mates were confused by him and found it hard to relate to him because they were unable to communicate beyond "yes, no, stop, please, hello and goodbye." However, I will never forget the evening of Stage Night.

Gabriel had learned how to do a simple rope trick and when it was his turn, he stood in front of everyone (with me by his side to interpret) and performed his trick without any error. As soon as he was finished, the crowd threw their hands up in the air and all did the sign for applause (waving your hands in the air). As soon as Gabriel saw this, his face beamed with excitement and he went on to do his trick two more times. Each time, he received the same support and applause as he did the first time around. The smile on his face was incredible. The entire night throughout cabin chat, he kept signing, "trick, me, applause, happy" over and over.

The impact that camp had on Gabriel was immeasurable. I had the pleasure of being his interpreter/counselor during the five summers that he came to camp, and it was amazing to see how much he grew throughout those years. No matter how old he got, Gabriel would always ask me if I remembered stage night his first summer and would always have a smile from ear to ear when re-telling me the story about how he made the crowd go wild!

Mandy Melton
Salem, OR
Counselor

44

Brayden and Jacob

They looked like Abbott and Costello. Brayden was long and lean; his brother, Jacob, short and plump, a consequence of the medicines and steroids used to combat his cancer. They were twins, nonetheless, bonded more firmly than other siblings I had seen. They displayed just how close on the last night of camp.

At the closing campfire, campers were invited to share their favorite moments. When it was his turn, Jacob ambled front and center. Other kids spoke one word or a phrase: "Dancing," "I caught a fish," "S'mores." Despite an inherent shyness, this fragile boy gingerly took the microphone, stared straight ahead and began.

"I was at the courage course with my cabin and it was my turn to climb. All the boys were cheering me on, especially my brother. A little way up, I froze, and I turned to look at them. I said to my brother, 'Brayden, I can't go any higher. I think I might fall even with the helmet and harness.' My brother was holding onto the rope along with the counselor. He looked up at me from the ground and he said, 'Jacob, have I ever let you down?'" Then he smiled. I turned around, took a deep breath and climbed even higher than I had planned to go."

On that balmy June evening, standing in front of one hundred campers and almost as many counselors, it took Jacob longer to tell his story than it took him to climb. As he recounted his triumph, his emotions rose in intensity. Each sentence was punctuated by giant sobs, followed by the silences needed to regain some composure.

As this adolescent boy sobbed openly and unashamedly, he was not met with derision nor laughter. Instead, two hundred sets of eyes watched him with adoration. Two hundred hearts filled with elation. When he was done, all of us stood spontaneously to cheer this brave boy and his equally brilliant brother.

Pun Forphun
Studio City, CA
Counselor

From the very first day, these oldest girls stole my heart. I use the word "heart" reflecting the dichotomy of my own heart aching and growing with love at the same time because all these girls had heart disease. Their stories were rich with strength and perseverance, but one camper, in particular, told me hers and I was consumed by her encouragement. Caroline had been through so much that it was hard to imagine she had any fears, but during our first candlelight chat, she admitted climbing the wall would be challenging for her.

Four days later, it was time to climb the wall. Her hesitation was apparent, but to our surprise, as Caroline clipped into the last carabineer, she boldly blurted out that she wished to climb blindfolded. Blindfolded?! To reiterate, her goal was to ascend a 60-foot wall without a seemingly vital aspect of climbing: sight, while I supposedly was to instruct her on where to place her extremities. I was honored, but nervous. Caroline had placed her trust in me to help her conquer her fear. Even through the nerves, we all welcomed the challenge with optimism and were excited to watch.

As I coached Caroline up the wall, her confidence grew and her doubts were shattered by the awe and support of the girls. When she reached the top, I felt camp magic and was so happy to witness and be part of her success. When she zip-lined off the other end to safety, she gave me the biggest hug. Through her contagious grin, Caroline declared, "See! With faith, I can do anything I set my heart to."

Her words still impact me today and I continue to admire her faith when times get tough. I will eternally remember that even when you are scrambling up a steep and endless mountain, blind to the obstacles ahead, always have faith that you, with the help of loved ones, can accomplish something great.

Kenzie Grant
Eagle, CO
Counselor

Many of the oldest campers look forward to climbing a 42 foot beast of a tower. The voices of encouragement at the tower still echo in my soul as campers conquered obstacles together that they thought were insurmountable.

"You're almost there, Maya! You can do it!" Maya had a severe heart condition that required special attention by the staff. One of the nurses, who knew Maya well from clinic, watched scrupulously as Maya trusted her fellow campers and counselors to hoist her up the tower on a system of ropes and pulleys called the elevator. Maya was safely attached to the elevator with a harness system. She carried an oxygen tank on her back, but she also carried a heart full of grace, love, optimism, and perseverance. The intensity of Maya's determination was apparent, as she gently overcame moments of fear and doubt with confidence and courage.

Finally, the last few inches! "Step back!" she commanded those holding the elevator ropes on the ground 42 feet below her. I was waiting at the top of the tower to greet and secure Maya. I took a sigh of relief. I was so proud of Maya! She conquered her fears while modeling another way dreams can come true at camp.

At the top of the tower, we could soak in the love of camp from a new perspective. We could see and hear a group of younger campers singing songs and leading cheers on the cabin row below. Those same campers would look to Maya and her cabin mates with eyes of admiration when their feat was recognized later that day at the dining hall. Maya signed the top of the tower, next to all of the other names of campers who shared her accomplishment. The look of pride and joy on Maya's face was unforgettable!

Katie Rozofsky Payne
Fultondale, AL
Adventure Staff

In the summer of 2012, I played at Shamu's pool house and witnessed the celebration of courage, bravery, and persistence as campers attempted their swim test. During the week of Immune Deficiency, the beautiful gift of Noah came into my life. Despite his illness and fight to remain healthy, this 11-year-old boy put everything aside to fully embrace camp. Throughout the week, he tried multiple times to pass his swim test, making it farther each time. At the closing banquet, it touched my heart when he thanked me for helping him "try to pass his swim test."

The next summer, I was impatiently waiting for Noah's arrival at Shamu's poolhouse. As soon as he came through camp's gates, he found me and gave me the biggest welcoming hug. At this moment, my heart was full, and I felt complete again. During the first morning manatee rotation, Noah was there before me waiting to get into the pool. He was the first camper to take the swim test; however, this year his strength had lessened from chemotherapy. He was extremely disappointed in himself since he could only swim a couple feet, and I could physically feel the pain in my heart.

The very next day, there Noah was; before I could even say hello, he told me that he was not going to attempt his swim test that day. To his surprise, I had something better planned—to make him my assistant! I gave him my whistle, a rescue tube and pulled a lifeguard chair over by me. Noah's eyes lit up and smiled from ear-to-ear when I gave him cues to blow his whistle and inform the swimmers how much time was left to swim. He came to the pool every single day.

At the end of the week, he wrote me a letter that said not only was I his best friend, but also his hero. To this day, you will find my hero, Noah, with that lifeguard whistle hung around his neck.

Jesslynn Withey
Park Falls, WI
Pool Specialist, Counselor

Ivan was a 16-year-old boy with Spina Bifida, who had been adopted from Ukraine six months prior. He had been placed in a facility because of his cognitive age and illness, and some programs in other countries do not have the resources to properly support those with cognitive delays or psychological issues. Ivan had spent the majority of his life within 100 feet of his bed and had bed sores to prove it. He had never ridden in a car until he was picked up from the airport in the US. His legs were fractured during a standard reflex test about four months before he arrived at camp. With broken English, an underdog story and the most inspirational attitude, Ivan arrived ready to change our lives.

At mealtimes, he would look at us counselors eating and yell, "Eat too fast!" to which the only response was to stuff your face with whatever you had on your plate, regardless of temperature. During his peritoneal dialysis, my beard got the love and admiration of this young man who insisted on rubbing it while the solution was being sent into/out of his abdomen. We made the mistake of losing his bubble wand one afternoon; this was a mistake. But between the noise-canceling headphones for the cafeteria, changing the clothes of a 16 year-old boy whose legs were like glass and the photo montage that's still on my camera from when I let him use it for the day, my life has been changed forever.

Later in the summer, I was fortunate enough to discover a medical volunteer who works with Ivan regularly in the hospital. I mean, there can't be many sweet Ukrainian boys with Spina Bifida, who blast Russian techno music and have as memorable personality as our Ivan. I will remember Ivan for the rest of my life, and I sincerely do hope to run into him again.

Collin Rodino
Stafford, VA
Counselor

Volunteering for Epilepsy week was coincidentally perfect timing as I had just learned about all the different types of seizures, how they present and their treatment regimens in pharmacy school. I was excited to see what the camp had in store for me, but I must admit that I was a very nervous first timer.

On that first night before camper arrival day, all the cabin counselors sat down in a circle to go through our campers' profiles. One particular profile stood out to me. Phrases like "uncomfortable around large crowds" and "gets anxious with loud noises or clanking of dishes" worried me a little because I anticipated camp to have large crowds and loud noises.

I found myself keenly awaiting the arrival of that particular precious camper. It was already dinner time, and my hopes were diminishing by the minute as Kennedy had not arrived yet. We took the rest of the campers to the dining hall and before dinner began, we received word that she had finally arrived! I could barely contain my excitement!

I met Kennedy outside the dining hall and warned her that it was about to get really loud with lots of cheering, clamoring and banging. I offered to sit outside with her until it was calmer, but Kennedy looked at me bravely and said, "I can handle it."

As the week progressed my heart was filled with happiness and my face lit up with smiles as I watched Kennedy engage in all the activities more and more each day. She was a very smart and hilarious introvert who taught me more than I expected to learn. Words cannot express the powerful impact camp has on individuals; be it campers, counselors, parents or healthcare professionals!

Bella Mogaka
Nairobi, Kenya
Counselor

I Really Can Be Myself at Camp

Some of the best moments from my camp experience have come during the times that I least expected it. During a session for children with heart transplants and cardiac conditions, I had the pleasure of playing with the most incredible girls I've ever met.

For this week's "Cabin Night," we wanted to focus on inner beauty and strength. Each one of our girls had some sort of scar from a surgery, and we had a counselor who had a back surgery scar. She shared her story to the girls about how it took time for her to be proud of her scar, but now she realized it is a part of who she is and how her experience has shaped the person she is today. It was incredible to see these girls hear a story from an adult and role model whom they respected so much and see the "light bulb" click how each one of them could also be proud of their scars and how that scar could be a part of their individual stories instead of something to be ashamed of.

We went on to have a "fashion show" in the cabin and each girl chose a dress that showed her scar as they proudly walked the runway! One of the girls had never been to camp and was so excited to try everything that she had never experienced before. As such, we expected that her greatest memories from camp would be about riding a horse for the first time, climbing a rock wall, or zip-lining, as most new campers often share with us.

However, this camper melted our hearts when she stood on the "runway" in a fancy gown and stated very enthusiastically, "Wow! I really can be myself here at camp!" That moment was a defining one for me because, as a counselor, our goal for each camper is to feel accepted, loved, and free to be themselves.

Devon Lehman
Fort Collins, CO
Counselor

James and Michael

During my first summer working as a counselor in Arkansas, I was sitting in our cabin one-night playing cards with a couple of my campers, James and Michael. This was the second session of the summer, and it was for individuals with Muscular Dystrophy. I had 14-16 year-old boys in my cabin. In the early 1990's life expectancy for these guys was young adulthood at best. James and Michael used electric wheelchairs to get around, and while they still had enough muscle control to drive their wheelchairs, they did not have enough strength to lift their hands to their mouths to feed themselves or provide for any of their own basic needs.

James and Michael asked me about the campers who had been there the previous week, and I told them that all of those campers had Spina Bifida. They asked what that was, and I explained that their spinal columns hadn't completely formed before they were born, and that all of the campers in my cabin were paralyzed from the waist down – that they couldn't feel their legs to know when they were too hot, too cold, or in a dangerous or uncomfortable position, and that they couldn't tell when they needed to go to the bathroom or control those functions.

James looked at Michael and said, "Wow. Think how lucky we are. We may not be able to move our legs, but at least we can feel them and let someone else know when we need them to be moved," and Michael agreed.

Looking back, that was a defining moment that helped shape my career path. I saw resilience, optimism, and compassion in the words of someone who was facing serious challenges of his own. James did not return to camp again because complications during spinal surgery cut his young life even shorter. Still, his words of inspiration live on, and I can only hope my service to others continues to honor him.

Brandon G. Briery, Ph.D.
San Antonio, TX
Executive Camping Director

This summer, I witnessed one of the most beautiful and pure moment at camp. All week long, I had been working diligently with Daniel, a 7-year-old boy, trying to teach him how to swim. During each encounter, we practiced floating and the doggy paddle.

At the last pool rotation of the week, his camp buddy who was an oldest camper asked if he could help. This made me extremely nervous as Daniel was not capable of swimming on his own yet. Because Daniel was within an arms reach of me, I agreed. His camp buddy reached his arms out and patiently waited for little Daniel to swim to him. As soon as Daniel and I took some practice strokes and blew a few bubbles, he felt ready. He took a long deep breath, pushed off my legs and kicked with all his might into the waiting arms of his buddy. In that moment, I watched Daniel hug his friend and excitedly announce to the entire pool that he did, in fact, swim for the very first time!

As we all smiled and cheered, I couldn't help but think how lucky I am to work at camp. Not only did I observe a little boy smile triumphantly over his accomplishment of swimming on his own for the very first time, but I also witnessed his buddy take the first steps toward adulthood by taking on a great responsibility and handling it with such ease and compassion.

I am the lucky one. Love grows here.

Brittany "Mama Bear" Gann
Fort Myers, FL
Counselor

I worked the front desk in The Well Shell and was exposed to an amazing array of campers and counselors. I would hear things that would stop me in my tracks on a regular basis - some beautiful, some startling, and some things that brought me to my knees.

I overheard a driver telling her experience with picking up a camper that had missed the bus. As they drove up the canyon roads, they heard squeals of delight as this sweetheart of a boy said he'd never been on a "curly road" and oh how he loved it! We all knew at that moment that this child had likely never been more than a few blocks from his home and hospital.

Counselors would talk of how their campers would duck when they saw butterflies because they'd never seen them, or how they didn't know how to sleep with the lack of noise, light, and helicopters flying over. Some of these kids had never seen stars. On one hand, your heart ached for them. On the other, what a privilege to be there as they experienced these things for the first time.

I saw a camper learn that she would be the recipient of a new kidney, and an ambulance was on its way to collect her. It would finally be a chance at a new life.

I loved watching the campers interact with their physicians and nurses at camp and build relations outside of the hospital. You'd see the wheels turning in their little heads: there's doctor so and so in SHORTS INSTEAD OF A WHITE COAT!

Mostly, what I came away with was admiration for the camp staff and volunteers. These people gave with all of their hearts, and it was heartwarming beyond words. So many struggled with medical conditions of their own, but they were driven to provide a life-changing week for these campers. So humbling and beautiful to watch. It was my privilege and honor to work with such amazing people!

Claire White
Lake Hughes, CA
Medical Center Receptionist

It was my first summer as a cabin counselor. During Special Diagnosis week, I was working in a cabin of pre-teen boys. At this point, I was just getting the feel for what camp was and what "living the camp magic" actually felt like.

One day I was walking Samuel, a camper, down to the Well Shell for a routine check. He started talking about normal things- school, friends, extracurricular activities, etc. and then he mentioned that his best friend in the whole world was at camp. Samuel went on to say that during his first year at camp, he was very nervous and didn't know anyone when one of his cabin mates asked him if he wanted to play Uno. Their friendship continued beyond camp, with both families becoming involved with each other and support groups for the conditions their sons faced. They ended up going to the same school and were both very excited to be back for a week of summer camp! Samuel then went on to say, "You know what? I'm glad I have Mitochondrial Disease. Sure it's hard sometimes but it's what allowed me to meet my best friend and means I can come to camp. I wouldn't trade that for anything!"

I don't quite remember how I responded because I was so taken back by the mature perspective of this 12-year-old. It was very humbling to see someone so young face something so hard, yet carry himself with an optimistic view on his medical condition and life.

Lee Garver
Santa Monica, CA
Counselor

During my first session at a camp for heart patients in 2001, I was one of three counselors in a cabin of nine to eleven-year-olds, on Catalina Island. We'd just settled in and were organizing our living space for the week ahead. Amelia, a vivacious nine-year-old who had already proven her social skills on the boat ride over, had an idea. From her top bunk, center of the room she said, "I know… How 'bout if we all show our scars? I'll go first." Lifting her shirt, she said, "See, it's a "T" where they did my heart operation and the little smile over here is where they put in my pacemaker."

"Next?" Amelia beamed, invitingly.

"Rainbow girl," was up next, then the "tree girl," the "straight line girl," and several other configurations of scars where each of these beautiful young women had submitted to the knife for life-saving surgeries. Here we were, all together. Each girl was a member of a very special club, which no one would or could voluntarily join. What Amelia did in the very first hour, and what camp is so good at doing, was to normalize the experience of being different. In life, in school, at church, temple or Girl Scout activities, each of these beauties is the odd one out. Here at camp, each is unique, yet part of a very select club. They all have this one thing in common: a surgical scar.

"Which one do you like best?" they wanted to know of us two adults and one adolescent Counselor-In-Training. "Well, it's hard to choose," we opine. "Each is so beautiful and tells of a different experience, doesn't it? Together they weave a similar story line." Amelia and the others seemed pleased with our answer. We went on to make up a cabin name, "Cat Boat" and create a cheer uniquely ours to share at the all-camp meeting before dinner.

It was a Labor Day weekend to remember.

Melinda Maxwell-Smith
Studio City, CA
Counselor

Being a cara, or counselor, provides you with the unique opportunity to meet the most inspiring people. Staff training teaches you how to work together to make this place so special, and campers give you life lessons.

When Elena first arrived at camp, she was willing to participate in every activity and we could tell she was enjoying every bit of the experience. Despite being sick, Elena was the most cheerful person I had ever met. She laughed, smiled and sang all day long at camp, and being around her was such a pleasure. For her, giving up was not an option. Instead, fighting with an amazing optimism and a constant smile was her way of facing the illness.

However, Elena never wanted to pose for a picture, and she did not want to participate in the show her cottage was preparing for cabaret night. She just said she did not look good enough to do it. Her cottage group, full of Spanish girls, became closer each day. They were extremely supportive with each other, and they all encouraged her to go up on stage and enjoy the dance. As the days passed by, Elena stopped thinking of herself as a sick child and started feeling more comfortable with herself.

On the last day of camp, Elena decided to go up on stage with her cottage group and perform an amazing dance in front of every camper and all the staff. She felt very proud of herself and said that only a few days ago she couldn't have pictured herself being able to do something like that. After the show, Elena took some photos with her friends and feeling both impressed and happy said, "Wow, I look pretty in this picture. It's been a very long time since I looked good in a picture."

Isabel Puente Mingo
Madrid, Spain
Counselor

Solidarity

It was the third week of camp. My cabin was packed with eight campers, all of which were girls between the ages of twelve and fourteen. Despite the things they all had in common, such as age and illness, pre-teen girls will be pre-teen girls, and cliques were formed among them. We noticed that one of the quieter girls in the cabin, a petite redhead with diabetes named Hannah, didn't immediately find her place in the cabin and stuck to herself for the beginning of the week. We tried and tried to get her to open up, but she mostly responded with one-word answers and smiled politely.

On the second full day of camp, I accompanied Hannah down to archery for a special project time she'd chosen. Hannah hit a moving target and won almost every challenge the archery instructor gave her. When I told her how impressed I was with her shooting, she said she had started in school about six months earlier. She said it was one of the only things she felt really good at. While we sat on the bench and waited for the next round of campers to shoot, she told me about being bullied in school because she was clumsy and a slow talker. She said that having diabetes on top of it didn't help matters.

It just so happened that it was Nascarnival Night, and there were Nascar pit crew members touring all of camp. While Hannah was sharing her story with me, one of the pit crew members stopped beside us and asked, "Can I see your pump?" pointing at the insulin pump sticking out of her pocket. He pulled out his and they compared features and styles. He asked her about her diabetes and watched her shoot for the rest of the turn.

Through it all, Hannah kept a shy smile on her face but when we left, she whispered, "That was pretty cool." It seemed like she finally felt special, important, and able to accomplish her goals. That, to me, is the beauty of camp.

Paige Townsend
Pittsburgh, PA
Counselor

In the summer of 2014, we had a great group of young boys, including Elijah, a festive camper with a kind heart, who did not nap during Rest Hour. On the second day of camp, a storm left Elijah, Chris (my co-counselor), and I stuck in the dining hall. I asked Elijah what he wanted to do, and he picked up a song book and said, "Songs about love." We all sat on the stage and started to sing each song containing the word "love." When we sang "The World's Greatest," Elijah's eyes lit up; he was fascinated by the sign language that accompanied the song. From that day forward, Elijah asked for "songs about love" for each Rest Hour.

On the last night, following closing activities, it took a while to get the boys ready for bed. Once things had settled down, the counselors spread out across the cabin. We opted for two at the head of Elijah's bed, one on each side; I was on one side of him, but he had his back to me. I kept hearing whispering, followed by a request for him to close his eyes and go to sleep. Eventually he rolled over, looked at me, smiled wide and then flopped down on his back. After a moment, I heard him whispering again. I could see he was moving his hands as well.

Suddenly, I recognized something he said, "Marching band." I leaned in closer to get a better listen. I heard, "Star the sky," followed by, "I a lion." Sure enough, sweet Elijah had taught himself "The World's Greatest," and was now singing and signing himself to sleep. His version of the song was fragmented, the words were out of order, and his signs did not always match the words he paired them with, but it was all there; and I have never heard a more beautiful rendition of that song. I am so thankful for this festive camper, who took the time to slow down and let love in.

Kyle Nicole
New Milford, CT
Counselor

During my second summer at camp, I had the pleasure of meeting a camper with Spina Bifida named Liam. That week, an extravagant fireworks show took place after Stage Night. Liam wasn't concerned with the thousands of dollars of controlled explosions going on in front of him because his focus was on singing to the music playing in the background. It was like the Forth of July scene from The Sandlot. I felt truly blessed to be able to sing songs with a thirteen year old boy who had the courage to plow through songs even when he did not know the lyrics, which was about 70% of the time. The session ended and Liam left camp until we were reunited again in 2014.

The gym was my responsibility during Early Bird, and I spent that time being challenged by Liam to various 3-point bets. For every shot he made, I agreed to do 10 pushups. Well, I was quickly 300 push-ups in debt by the end of the session. After watching me struggle to support my limp body off the ground after thirty pushups or so, Liam slid out of his wheelchair and offered to split the rest with me, easily banging out and completing the task that I had just struggled with.

We sat on the ground after, me completely out of breath and him unfazed, when we began to discuss what his life outside of camp was like. As he climbed back into his chair, he explained that he traveled around the country for para-olympic events. I asked him if there were any other kids who used wheelchairs at his school. He looked down at me and with a smile said, "Nope, only standers." I laughed, a little taken back by his bluntness and replied "Standers? Is that what you call people not in chairs, Liam?" He just continued to smile while fiddling with his chair, locking himself into his most comfortable wheelie position and said, "Yep, I call them that, but I also call them friends."

Charisse Taylor
Houston, TX
Outdoor Fun Specialist

For many reasons, Stage Night is my favorite camp activity. There is something so inspiring about watching a camper perform on stage, perhaps for the first time. The look of pride and accomplishment on their face when they take a bow is incredible. And, of course, where else would one get a standing O, literally, from an audience?

The amount of creativity and talent is astonishing. The type of pieces seen at Stage Night range from campers dressing up in silly costumes and lip singing the latest hit song to campers singing original songs leaving few dry eyes in the audience to whole families performing a choreographed number together on a Family Weekend. Plus, at camp we have a few classic stage night numbers that are always a crowd pleaser: Cha Cha Slide, Invisible Bench, Test of the Emergency Broadcasting Network, to name a few.

Genevieve was a mature 13-year-old with HIV and Cerebral Palsy and, as a result, could not use the right side of her body. I spent a lot of time with Genevieve and was more impressed with her each moment we were together. She was willing to share so much of herself, like when she told me about her recent surgery in which doctors took a little muscle out of her left leg and put it on the right side of her face so she could have a full smile.

Genevieve had decided to play the piano for Stage Night despite having only one hand with which to play. I wanted it to go well so badly for her. She began to play; the crowd went crazy and gave her a standing ovation. As she walked off the stage, I pointed at the crowd to show her how wildly they were cheering for her. That night, as I lay in bed, I realized she had shown me what determination and taking a chance is all about. It did not matter how well she played the piano; she had won simply by walking out on the stage.

Amie Conner
Wetherfield, CT
Counselor

61

One session, we had a media event that required filming during campfire. Campers who were not photo released were given seats in a "VIP" section to ensure they were out of the camera shot. Though most of the campers didn't notice a difference, one camper, Sophia, asked her counselor if she had to sit away from the cabin so she could be closer to a nurse if a need arose. Her counselor and I couldn't stomach her feeling like she was being singled out for a medical reason. That's just not what camp is all about. Instead, I asked her if she would like to host the show with me.

We planned out the show together, I taught her some cheers and she picked out the lineup. Sophia carefully considered each cabin and tried to put them in an order to make everyone feel "the least nervous." We also planned a grand entrance. We found some towels to use as capes on a golf cart and hid under them in the back of the amphitheater until it was our turn. When we were introduced, we ran down the aisles with our capes flapping in the wind. Though she was a bit reserved at first, Sophia got more and more confident throughout the show and, by the end, had stole the show! She introduced acts, led cheers, and even added a bit of sass!

The next summer Sophia came back and asked if she could host with me again. This time we entered in full snorkel gear, and Sophia stepped right back into the role with the same confidence and attitude she had at the first campfire. I was so impressed!

Later that year, I coincidentally met Sophia's child life specialist during an interview. When she found out about my involvement at camp, she gushed on how much Sophia talked about being able to host the campfire and how she now feels like she runs the place. I feel so blessed to have been a part of her camp experience.

Melissa Pigden
New York, NY
Entertainment Director

The Bear Wedding

"Our bears should get married!" suggested our beautiful seven-year-old girls on camper arrival day.

During cabin time, the counselors turned Red 6 into a magnificent wedding venue full of lights, streamers, a red carpet and alter. Our girls invited all of camp to attend this glorious event; especially their oldest camper buddies. The nurses and doctors came and dressed up all the bears from the Patch in homemade bridesmaid dresses. They even brought milk and cookies for the reception!

One by one, our campers walked each bear down the aisle to the traditional wedding march where another camper, the minister, greeted them at the altar. Following the ceremony and ring exchanges we had a reception! Milk and cookies were served, the bouquet was tossed, Mr. and Mrs. Bear had their first dance and our campers performed "Jar of Hearts" and "We Will Rock You."

Mr. and Mrs. Bear spent their honeymoon at camp and have settled in sunny Florida as they live happily ever after.

Kelley Kilpatrick, RN
Tampa, FL
Counselor, Camp Nurse

The Big Finale

The Three Compares had planned this night since camp last year, now that they'd turned 17 and would be too old to return as campers. Before The Three Compares' Secret Finale, the audience enjoyed performances from every camper, which turned out to be superb and filled each volunteer with pride. But then came a dip in the show. A 14-year-old boy, Aiden, settled himself at the piano ready to play. I was nervous for Aiden. Not only was he visibly shaking, I remembered last year's Talent Night where a barely noticeable mistake caused Aiden to cut short his performance and spend the rest of the night crying outside the theatre. I held my breath as he started his performance. All was going well, and then, almost imperceptibly, Aiden stumbled, froze up and ran out in tears. I was heartbroken.

Towards the end, Aiden returned to the theatre with his team leader to see his friends perform, as it was time for The Big Finale. But there was an unexpected pause. The Three Compares, slick and cool as anything, whispered amongst themselves. As one, they turned to face us. "I know you were all expecting The Big Finale, but we think we've got something even better for you..."

What happened next was truly wondrous. The Three Compares sacrificed their Big Finale to welcome Aiden back to the stage, to take his seat again at the piano, and play us out with his composition. Aiden was hesitant at first, but the incredible cheer from the crowd practically carried him to the piano, where he gave a flawless performance. The instant he played the final note his hands flew up to his face in shock, tears flooding from his already reddened eyes. My mind flashed back to the lyrics from the opening act: the youngest camper present (8 years old) singing Coldplay's 'Fix You' on his guitar. "Tears stream/Down your face/And I will try to fix you."

Thom O'Neill, MBBS
Inverness, Scotland
Counselor

The Dog Show

One of the most important lessons that working at a medical camp taught me is that, no matter what challenges life throws at a child, a child's heart is full of magic that adults should learn to embrace! One particular camp memory embodies this sentiment clearly in my mind, and in my heart. It was the summer of 2006, and our unit had a group of youngest campers for this particular session. As we began to plan our unit afternoon activities, a fellow counselor suggested we put on a dog show for our campers.

We embraced this activity with enthusiasm, despite the fact that we didn't have any actual dogs to work with! This is where the fun and magic really began. The counselors and I on the planning committee agreed to play the role of the dogs for our campers to train, feed, groom, and then show off in the "dog" show. Only at a camp that is completely absorbed in bringing laughter and joy to children will you find college-age counselors willingly dress up like dogs, walk around on their hands and knees, and only speak with barks for an afternoon!

I could not have anticipated the incredible interactions that took place that afternoon between the doggie counselors and our campers. One of my favorite moments was when our campers helped us into giant trash cans of water to be "groomed" for the dog show! One camper, in particular, Precious, seemed to light up with pride as she washed my hair and talked to me as she would a beloved puppy! In that moment, when all disbelief was suspended and 100% of my focus was on acting like a dog purely to bring one child laughter and fun, I was blessed to participate in something so rare and, yes, precious in the real world: boundless joy. Now, years later, the laughter and joy of that one afternoon of silliness lingers in my heart to remind me not to forget to embrace joy in life. My world is better because of camp.

Amber Ryman
Indianola, WA
Former Camper, Counselor

I'd like to live in a Land of Empathy, Kindness, and Respect.

I'd like to live in a land where differences are not considered disabilities or special needs. In this land, everybody's quirks and uniquenesses and differences are celebrated. The only thing important in this imagined land is a person's heart. And his empathy. And his ability to treat all with respect.

The best part? This land exists. It's called camp.

After lunch, the whole camp sings songs together, and campers are given a chance to publicly appreciate someone for the nice things that they've done at the Web of Kindness. I remember watching one of our quieter campers, Scarlett, wait in line, fidgety, as she listened to each person ahead of her say into the microphone what he or she was thankful for. It was her turn next. Scarlett approached the microphone, and the camp director kneeled to her height. This camper, who was living with Epilepsy, Cerebral Palsy, and significant developmental delays, had only spoken a few words all week. I could tell Scarlett really wanted to say something but was nervous. The audience waited in pure silence, so eager and supportive to hear her. Slowly, the words slurred out, "I'd like to thank my cabin for making me feel like somebody," and the camp cheered her name!

Camp allows you to see a person for who they are; their illnesses don't define them. I couldn't imagine it any other way.

Meera Ramamoorthy, MD
Cincinnati, OH
Counselor

She came to camp shy and timid. We comforted her. She wanted to spend hours making mud pies. We made them. She wanted to play Twister, using her head, eyeballs, toes, and belly. We played. She spoke Furbish (the language of Furby's) and wanted us to speak it too. We spoke. She wanted to "marry her horse and have its babies." We laughed. She wanted to sing Twinkle Twinkle to the stars at night time. We sang. She had blinking contests with everyone, blinking first meant you won. We played. A lot. She wanted to sing a One Direction song for stage day. We practiced. She wanted to make mud smoothies for all of the dads that weekend. We delivered. She said she was going to drop out of first grade to stay at camp forever. We smiled.

What Riley took away, and what we took away from the weekend was so different, but such the same. The bliss of the weekend overcame anything else on my mind. Her innocence proved that camp is for any child of any ability. Riley was blind, young, and full of energy and hope. Her aptitude to love camp in a whole new perspective was enlightening. Riley is what camp is about. She is love, she is hope, she is our future, and she is Riley.

Becky Giallella
Fort Myers, FL
Counselor

The sun was setting, and I darted from tree to tree with nine eager campers scampering along behind me. We were on a mission to discover a chest of popsicles that had been "abandoned" by the camp director. Upon entering the gymnasium, we struck popsicle gold and began to distribute the booty.

After enjoying the spoils for only a few minutes, my co-counselor (and partner-in-crime) sounded the alarm to warn us that someone was approaching. Keeping up with the excitement and illusion of the "heist," I began to feign concern for the punishment that I, as the leader, was about to receive.

While contemplating my fate, I was approached by two young campers with severe Asthma. Through worried expressions, they reassuringly told me, "Don't worry. If we get caught, we'll say it was our idea." Then, the younger one added, "I don't care if I'm never allowed to come back to camp again; I just don't want you to get in trouble." That is when I realized how much of an impact we make as counselors at camp.

Michael McFadden
Akron, OH
Counselor

Chapter III

WHERE MAGIC HAPPENS
AND THE SOUL DANCES

A Kid Again
A Sneak Out of Confidence
A Somewhat Tall Tale
Adventure in Sherwood
Beyond the Sickness
Blake Faces His Fears
Come On and Dance
Fairy Tale
Feel the Spirit
Golden Memories
If You'd Be My Girl
It's Magic
Magical Ponchos
My Favorite Tea-Party
Parker at the Gator Grand Prix
Size Doesn't Matter
The Day We Made It Rain
The Power of Camp
The Tiger, The Wizard, and The Cupboard
Unseen
Walkie-Talkie Powers
Walking on Water
Where Horses Fly
Wish Upon a Starfish
Yes, Yes, Yes

It was camper arrival day of the Cancer and Hemophilia session. The families had started to pour through the gates when a mother came up to me to introduce her daughter, Grace. She warned me that Grace was very shy and would rather be with counselors because most kids just don't get her.

The week progressed, and Grace and I become inseparable. One day I was wearing a shirt that said "Stay Strong 31" in support of my friend who had been diagnosed with a brain tumor. Grace asked a thousand questions like usual and suddenly her face lit up. This was the first time she had heard a survivor story of someone with her same diagnosis. The rest of the week Grace had a little extra spring in her step and was more social with the other campers than ever. The week faded and so did the year.

The following summer, Grace raced up to me and whispered, "When you tell that story about your friend, tell mine too because I am healthy and cancer-free." I saw her mom standing behind her with tears in my eyes and they both had these enormous smiles. Doctors had cured her illness, and camp had treated her soul, filling her with new confidence to be a kid again. That is the magic of camp.

Becca Mowad
Pittsburgh, PA
Counselor

A Sneak Out of Confidence

It was the last night of the session. Throughout the week, our cabin of second youngest boys had embraced being the "Sigmas," our group name for the theme. We told them stories of the Sigmas that had come before them, and all that was left to make this tale complete was Sigma initiation. It's no surprise that the Sigma initiation happened to be their favorite activity—archery. But for initiation, we did...night archery!

We walked these campers out to the archery range and told them the tale of how Sigmas over the past hundreds of years had bonded over their love of archery, and that this tradition was now being handed down to them. It was difficult to calm them down and get them ready to shoot, but during this time we noticed that one of our campers, Dominic, wasn't exactly thrilled about the activity.

Dominic was one of my favorite campers, always laughing, joking and helping me learn Spanish. Dominic also had limited mobility in his right hand, and as it turns out he hadn't hit the target once during the camp due to this.

The counselors quickly scrambled to come up with a solution and decided to use a special bow that went into the ground as the Sigma ceremonial bow. The extension that held it in the ground allowed Dominic to focus on just shooting the bow without holding it, and for the first time hit the target.

As the night drew to a close, Dominic talked about how he sometimes feels left out because of his disability. He also spoke of how much he loved camp, and how this was the first time he was able to do everything, even hit the target with an arrow. His confidence was sky high. It was such a great happiness to feel, knowing this camper could do anything.

Marty Dunning
Oxford, OH
Counselor

A Somewhat Tall Tale

For reasons that seem obvious, yet somewhat ironic, Camper vs. Counselor basketball during Skeletal Dysplasia camp is the highlight of that week. The "Dwarf" team as the campers call themselves gear up to "crush" the counselors who are older and are of "average" height.

I remember one year when something extremely meaningful occurred on the basketball court of that important game. On the camper team was a boy named Dylan whose immense skill and love of basketball eclipsed the fact that he was 3 feet tall at the age of 12. On the counselor team was Isaac, the 4-year-old son of one of the camp's professional staff members. Isaac was really tall for his age (5 feet tall at the age of 4) but had never played basketball.

From the outset of the game, the counselor team dished the ball to Isaac, who would promptly have the ball stolen from him by Dylan. After the 5th time this occurred, Isaac became distraught and left the game crying. He ran to his mother on the sidelines, burying his face in her shirt.

Despite being the star of the game, Dylan walked off the court to Isaac and his mother. Fortunately, I was sitting within listening distance to hear Dylan's words to him. "Isaac, you can't be good at everything right away. Look at me. Do you think I could play basketball the first time I tried? No, I was terrible, but I loved it. I had to practice…and I did, every day, because I wanted to be able to play just like the other kids. That's why I can play basketball today. All you need is practice, Isaac. If you keep playing and practicing basketball, you are going to be so much better than I could ever be. So, will you come back and play?"

Isaac decided not to rejoin the game, but he did stop crying, sat courtside, and drew a heroic picture of Dylan dribbling down the court with a smile on his face.

Ben Meisel, MD
Valencia, CA
Medical Director

I woke up one morning in the middle of the summer to the electric ring of the rooster that beckons us to morning manatee. I donned my green hood and quiver as I did every morning and wiped the sleep from my eyes.

I walked out the door and was welcomed by the humidity of a camp that surrounded Sherwood Forest, where I ran activities for budding archers. Camp was waking up to sounds of laughter and song, and I knew I had to hurry to set up the activity before smiling faces meandered through Sherwood to the Archery range. I had to remember to set up extra "adapted" bows; I always called them "power bows" because I didn't want anyone to feel like they needed anything different and that they resulted in more arrows being lost over the range and into the depths of the forest.

I cleared my throat. There were only five more minutes until I had to completely lose the New England marble-mouthed accent that came so naturally for my preferred accent-confused Englishman, who believed in unicorns, but not giraffes. "But unicorns are real." "What sound does a giraffe make anyway?" and other nonsensical questions to ensure my archers that I, in fact, did believe in unicorns and was thus probably from England.

The archers and their counselors arrived and lined up. I tried to subtly imply that less mobile campers may like the power bows, but I was rebuffed. And I had never been happier.

My band of merry morning manateers once again illuminated the strength and the magic of camp – the campers. A place where you can convince yourself to believe in unicorns and still be befuddled and awestruck by the everyday ingenuity, courage, and joy that campers seamlessly employ daily.

Joel "Robin Hood" Kruger
Hartford, CT
Archery Activity Staff

It was the summer of 2008 when I took a left turn onto Brantley Branch Road, unaware of what would meet me there. I pulled up to the gate where I was met by a guard who told me I would love it. I hoped she was right. I was nervous, but I was excited to play with the kids too. After a week of training, we prepared for the first campers of the summer. I was thrilled when I heard the buses and the cars coming, and even more-so when our campers exited their vehicles. Some campers knew each other, and so it was like a family reunion.

There was one camper, Emma, who seemed kind of lost. It was her first experience at this camp. She was quiet and looked sad most of the time. I didn't know it then, but she wore a wig. A few days went by, and Emma slowly started to open up. There was one night during the week I was not able to hang out with the campers, but when I returned the next morning, Emma was smiling and laughing with the other campers in our cabin. It was like a barrier had been completely removed.

What moved me most; the wig Emma wore at the beginning of the week had disappeared. It was powerful for me to see someone proudly walk around without a wig that was probably worn to conceal a bald head caused by chemotherapy, as well as shame and judgment that comes from being a teen and different from the others. This was someone who was finally able to be herself with kids who could look beyond the sickness and see her true spirit. Kids like her. Kids who understood. Emma played hard that week, and I think I started to realize that this would be the most magical summer I had ever had.

Brittany Harmon
Jacksonville, FL
Counselor

Blake Faces His Fears

In the late 90's, a seven-year-old boy came to camp for the very first time. It was Cancer week, and we had 8 excited little boys in our cabin who had never been to camp. They came together as a cabin quickly and shared their excitement of all the week's activities. We were not scheduled to go to the pool until the third day of camp, so this anticipation grew as the time approached. One of the boys was pretty "beefy" and talked a lot about his ability to do the perfect cannonball in the pool. It didn't take long before every camper talked of out-doing one another with their cannonballs.

Pool day finally arrived and after lathering up with sunscreen, the boys lined up close to the lifeguard stand for their time to shine. The first in line was the "beefy" camper. He made an impressive cannonball, and the campers followed with their versions of that dive. Blake was at the end of the line. When he got closer, I noticed he had a life vest on plus a floatie on both arms. I told him that it would be too dangerous to attempt a cannonball with all of that on. He said that he was afraid of water, but I reassured him that I would catch him the moment he hit the water. He looked pretty dejected and walked away towards the shallow end of the pool.

The rest of the campers continued queueing up for their dives when I noticed Blake in line without any floatation devices on. When he finally got to the edge, the look on his face was sheer terror! I again promised him that I would catch him as he hit the water. With that, he jumped higher than the other campers and landed in the water right where I was standing. You couldn't possibly paint a bigger smile on his face than the one during the leap. It still brings a smile to my face when I think of the courage and determination this young boy had to face his fears.

Mista Bill Vessier
Orlando, FL
Counselor

Come On and Dance

Everyone has a happy place, and I am no exception. My happy place is nestled in rural Florida, close enough to the outside world so as not to endure complete isolation but far enough removed to make it your entire world. It's where the magic happens.

One of my campers, Jonathan, was an 8-year-old boy. I had begun to notice that he would often stare at me, intently, seemingly fascinated by my dancing and cheering. During one of those times, I extended my hand. "Want to join?" I offered earnestly.

Face drawn, eyes fastened to the ground, he lamented, "I can't." Most of the other campers were dancing, singing, jumping around and having an excellent time...why couldn't he? He explained that people would judge him or, worse yet, laugh. Jonathan doubted that he was strong enough to endure such hardship. He was wrong.

"Don't let what other people think stop you from doing what you want to do. It doesn't matter what other people think of you as much as what you think of yourself. Come on and dance!" I flashed him a warm smile and extended my hand a second time.

This time, he took it.

By the end of the week, Jonathan interacted with his fellow campers, took more chances and danced like nobody was watching. By judging his actions by his own standards and not worrying what other people thought, he was able to live life a little more fully.

This sort of magic, the magic that can alter the trajectory of a life, is too rare not to be treasured. Perhaps Jonathan would've found another way to learn how to be comfortable in his own skin. All I know is that I got to be part of a particularly powerful and transformative moment for this one particular little boy and that this camp is awash with such moments. That is why Camp is my happy place: because it's where the magic happens.

Tily "Spud" Stanley
Sicklerville, NJ
Counselor

76

Fairy Tale

Camp is the perfect opportunity for creativity, imagination and fun. While walking around the campgrounds with two young male campers, we came across the fairy house in The Secret Garden. Immediately, the boys were mesmerized by the thought of magic fairies living there. All they could talk about was meeting the fairies. I saw the opportunity to create a magical adventure for the boys that they would enjoy and remember.

For the following few days, I had them follow a treasure hunt which I organized with the help of fellow counselors. They had the task of finding clues around camp to lead them towards the fairies. Their interest didn't fade, and the excitement on their faces every time they discovered a clue was contagious.

They continued to search each day and finally found all the clues which led them back to the fairy house where a leader dressed up as a fairy sprinkled fairy dust over them, chatted with them and gave them fairy buns. They were speechless!

When I returned to camp a year later, I was told that the same boys had been back and were asking about the fairies! A little imagination and creativity can go a long way.

Zita McAlister
Dublin, Ireland
Counselor

Feel the Spirit

Camper arrival day is often a challenge; emotions run high through counselors, parents, and campers. Olivia was a shy girl. Her eyes were shining with unshed tears, and she was hesitant to let her mother leave, so I asked Olivia to take a walk with me.

As we walked up cabin row, I asked Olivia about her favorite books, activities and anything that seemed to interest her. Her answers were short, so I started telling her about what we would be doing at camp. As we walked up the grassy hill I explained what my job was at camp; I had the privilege of working at the horse barn. Our barn held the most well-behaved horses I had ever met. When I mentioned the word horse, for a second, her face lit up.

As we neared the pasture, the horses were far away grazing on grass. Olivia put her hand over the fence and very quietly called out to the horses. I didn't think that any of them would come because of the distance when one of the horses looked up. It was Spirit, one of the smartest and gentlest horses in the barn. He walked over and put his head over the fence right next to Olivia. She asked me what his name was and, as I told her that his name was Spirit, she reached out and touched him on the head. Spirit turned into her hand like he was telling her that everything would be okay. Olivia then put her arms around Spirit and hugged him. Spirit didn't move. He just let her hold on and shed a couple tears.

When she was ready, she dried her eyes and held out her hand to me with a smile. We walked back to our cabin, and Olivia had one of the greatest weeks of her life.

Spirit and Olivia remind me why every summer I go back to the barn; even though it's mentally and physically exhausting, horses heal. Spirit changed that week for Olivia and on departure day, Olivia cried because she didn't want to leave.

Patricia Ortiz
Kissimmee, FL
Counselor

Camp challenged me, elevated me, educated me and pushed me to be *my* very best. I met my wife at camp, I proposed at camp and I forged forever friendships at camp. I dressed as a princess, a dinosaur, a slinky, an owl, a genie, and a pirate. I've had makeovers and manicures, french braids and mohawks and starred in more ridiculous skits than I can count. I know all the songs, I eat spaghetti with my face and can do the Cha Cha Slide with my eyes closed. I still believe a third of my brain is dedicated to back pocket games and answers to all those riddles.

As my time away from camp grows longer and my years as a counselor begin to blur, a few golden memories remain. Those moments are ingrained in me forever and change the very fabric of your being. Ryan was seven years old and spending his first night away from home. In fact, it was his first night alone since his new family had adopted him. Unlike his cabin mates, his diagnosis was severe enough that Ryan had to spend the night in the Well Shell, isolated from his friends. As the nurses and doctors prepped him for bed, Ryan reached out for my hand, something his parents had said he might do for comfort before bedtime. As the long day of camp caught up with us, we both fell asleep. Later, I awoke, his hand still in mine; his eyes were closed and fast asleep.

Beyond all the laughter, the fun and games, all the skits and costumes, it is that single moment that defined for me what it meant to be a camp counselor: To comfort a child at their most vulnerable moment, to support them, to propel them to have the time of their lives at camp, to help them be their very best.

I live in the real world now, away from that beautiful bubble that we call camp. I'm no longer in skits and rarely dress like a dinosaur but on occasion, one of those golden memories will float into my consciousness and I'll catch myself humming a camp song.

Colin Foulke
Santa Rosa, CA
Counselor

79

Magic moments can happen at any time, but you don't realize it until the situation is going on. I was ready to spend another beautiful and amazing day at my favorite camp. I went to wake my girls up, help them get dressed and encourage them for the new adventures. Suddenly, Naomi, a beautiful and blonde girl looked at me with her glittering eyes full of pride. Naomi took a small picture out of the back pocket of her jeans and said, "Look! This is my little sister. She's five years old, but she has been very sick since she was two. She is very beautiful with her pink headscarf, isn't she?"

All the other girls wanted to see that picture like it was gold. At one point, Naomi was very anxious because it seemed the treasure was lost. When we found it, she kissed the picture and put it in the right place, her jeans pocket. I recommended that she keep it in the cottage to avoid getting lost during activities, but she told me she always had to have it with her to feel closer and to pray for her sister. When we were having breakfast Naomi told me the reason she was at camp; her little sister wanted her to have an amazing time, something special to call her own.

I had the feeling Naomi also needed one of her dreams to come true, so we organized an incredible princess night for our cottage. We lead them to the castle, where we prepared hot chocolate with marshmallows and painted their nails in shades of pink. We went upstairs and the magic began when they saw the princesses' costumes. My pretty girl was amazed like she couldn't believe her eyes. Naomi picked the Cinderella one and we looked each other; that kind of glance where there is no need to say anything. I was her prince. We took our shoes off and danced the night away.

As the night came to an end, Naomi said, "Please, can I take this costume home?"

Patricia Sánchez Martín
Madrid, Spain
Counselor

In the moments of our lives
Both the joyous and the tragic
If the truth is to be told
We are all pursuing magic,

And the magic that we seek
As we're sure you have discovered
Can be found in certain places
Far more easily than others...

When I was a child, I was always fascinated by magicians. Every trick made me wonder where the assistant had disappeared to or where the coin had come from. I rarely worked it out but enjoyed the challenge nonetheless. I think most people are them same. They're impressed and want to know "how did they do that?"

During fairy tale week, magic was happening every waking minute of every single day; horses into unicorns, sticks into powerful wands, glitter into fairy dust. The campers had their wands in hand ready to cast a spell at any given moment. Each counselor was expected to react to each spell in the correct manner, whether it be walking in slow motion or flying through the air. For one whole week, the campers lived in a completely magical world. I first "worked" there nearly a decade ago, although it seems unfair to label it so considering how much I loved it.

That summer I touched the lives of more children than I can recall and, in incredible and magical ways, they touched mine. They were magic and so was everyone and everything around them. This was no illusion; it was real. The barriers created by illness outside of the camp realm. had been cast away. They believed, and we believed in them.

Alena Troutman
Tallahassee, FL
Counselor

Magical Ponchos

One summer during a Cancer session, our cabin was filled with vibrant, pre-teen girls. Most of our girls were in remission; however Allison had just recently relapsed which meant more chemotherapy. When Allison's mom dropped her off, she tearfully explained how although they still physically had their daughter, they felt like her spirit had left once the doctor gave them the terrible news.

Allison was required to keep her IV site completely dry while at camp, which limited her involvement in certain activities. A few times a week, there is an "aquatic activity" which is basically a water extravaganza with hoses and buckets. It was the first aquatic activity of the session, and I volunteered to sit out with Allison on the porch. Allison was depressed, not only by her diagnosis, but also by hearing that, yet again, she would have to miss out on something thanks to her cancer. As we sat there and watched the chaos, I desperately tried to distract her from what she was missing out on. However, I looked up just as tears fell down her face.

Camp is blessed by generous people that donate all sorts of items, and our cabin had been gifted with a plethora of rain ponchos. The next aquatic activity I told a story about these magic rain ponchos passed down through the ages that deflected all water. Allison and I suited up in a few of these ancient magical ponchos, came up with a poncho dance and waited anxiously for the siren with the rest of her cabin.

The siren went off, and for the first time, we got to see Allison smile, laugh and be a kid. Thanks to those ponchos and a little camp magic, not only was Allison impenetrable to water, but also to her cancer diagnosis. Allison's mom cried when picking her up after the session ended because her daughter's spirit had returned.

Caitlin Freaney
Denver, CO
Counselor

My Favorite Tea-Party

I was a counselor in 2013 with the youngest girl's cabin, who were some of the most imaginative girls I have ever met. Each week of the summer, counselors try to think of something new and fun to make the campers' week extra special; after having met them we knew a tea-party would be perfect.

As the week ensued they became fascinated with cabin fairies, which can only be found at Camp. The cabin fairies inspect cabins and pick the cleanest one each day. They come when we are away and sometimes leave gifts behind including notes, glitter, and even candy. Of course, the girls wanted to meet the cabin fairies, and the perfect night for this was during our tea party.

Our tea party was all set to include twinkle lights, glass tea cups, cookies (which we called crumpets), and blankets spread out on our front porch. We lead the girls out, their eyes closed and hand-in-hand, onto the front porch, and they all squealed with excitement. The tea party included conversations about the proper way to have a tea-party, the proper way to drink your tea, and, of course, we talked about the cabin fairies!

All of a sudden we all heard this high pitched voice coming from a walkie-talkie; it was a cabin fairy joining us for our tea party. The cabin fairy told us she had to be up early in the morning to begin her fairy duties, but she wanted to talk with us before she went to bed. All the girls had a chance to talk to the cabin fairy, and they were all so excited.

Once we had all finished our tea and the last crumpet had been eaten, the campers went back into the cabin where sprinkled all over the floor and walls was fairy dust which glowed for us all to see. Another chorus of squeals followed! It was a long time until the girls went to bed, but it was a night that I will never forget!

Savanna McGhghy
Gainesville, FL
Counselor

Parker at the Gator Grand Prix

Parker was one of my campers in the summer of 2012. He had been through the gamut of treatments, as evident by the IV pole he slept with, the loss of hair he suffered, and the aversion he had developed to food. He had been fed through IV tubes so long that, psychologically, he had to work with specialists to help him, albeit slowly, eat solid foods again.

At meals, we would serve him a small plate. He would never eat it, but he could, if he chose, smell the food, touch the food and, if he felt moved to, kiss the food. It was all part of reintegrating solid food into his life, and it had been a long process for him. Parker had come to camp with no expectation of being comfortable enough to eat a thing.

When the Gator Grand Prix, a showcase for wooden cars the kids had made, arrived our cabin sat with the rest of camp and enjoyed cotton candy and popcorn as they watched the cars race down the track. I was busy taking photographs as part of my job that summer when one of my co-counselors, Mike, walked over and said "Andy! Parker JUST ATE COTTON CANDY."

It took me longer than I'd like to admit to figure out what he meant. The idea that Parker could feel comfortable and loved enough to do what he was struggling to do even at home barely made sense to me. But then I saw him. Chomping on tiny bits of cotton candy with his cabin-mates. Maybe it didn't seem like a big deal to him, or to the other campers, but the counselors knew that our work had manifested in a very tangible and powerful way.

Andy Gattis
Jacksonville, FL
Former Camper, Camp Photographer

When they had finished their trail ride, I walked the three nine-year-olds down to the paddocks to spend time with the horses. With helmet-hair ponytails and glittery horse shirts now covered in dust, the girls could not wait to get their small hands on the horses. While the tallest of the three girls did not reach as high as my hip, their passion dwarfed my own. One by one I brought out the horses: a black, a bay, a paint, and a chestnut. I explained each of the horses' histories including their age, their jobs before coming to work at camp, as well facts about their breed.

The chestnut mare I brought out last, because I knew she would be a crowd favorite. As I knelt to talk to the three girls, I could still rest my arm across the mare's short back. The small horse looked the young girls straight in the eyes, and they squealed in excitement to see a horse that matched their own unique heights. I explained to them that the little mare's name was Ladybug and that her parents were a Standardbred and a Haflinger – both fairly large breeds. Despite having "average" size horse-parents, Ladybug is considered a pony based on her size. Though she turned out a bit shorter than her siblings, she remains an incredible horse and one of the favorite horses here at camp.

One of the girls had been resting her hand on Ladybug's shoulder throughout this talk, and at the mention of Ladybug's parents she straightened and looked up at me. Her eyes shimmered with revelation, and the five words she spoke shook my soul, "My parents are tall too."

Claire Wilkins
Kula, HI
Counselor

The Day We Made It Rain

As soon as you enter the gates of camp, you can feel the magic that is in the air. There is just something special about camp and though sometimes it is difficult to put your thumb on exactly what it is, you can easily tell that the moments that take place at camp are something that you will remember for many years to come.

One camp session it was apparent that the camp gods wanted to add a little more magic to camp and make it an unforgettable experience for our campers. The Red Lodge took great pride in blowing up theme and spirit for our campers each week. During this particular session, we decided to make our lodge into a tribe and work on building attributes such as trust, loyalty, courage and love. To add to the fun, we created a rain dance that we could perform to help instill lodge unity. We performed the rain dance several times throughout the week. We didn't really expect it to rain but did it anyways because it was fun.

The last night our girls wanted to perform the rain dance one more time. As we chanted and stomped and smiles spread across our faces, we heard a boom of thunder. We turned to see the rain. Our Red Lodge rain dance had made it rain! This was one of those magical moments that no amount of work or preparation could have made it happen. It was a matter of perfect timing and the camp gods wanting to make camp a little more special that night for a group of girls.

Erin Harris
Campbellsville, KY
Counselor

I will never forget the day the "Girls of G1" during Spina Bifida week CONQUERED THE TOWER!

This beast called "The Tower" that I'm talking about happens to stand 42' tall, and only has 3 ways to get to the top: a rock wall, a giant's ladder or trusting your cabin to hoist you up one step at a time by a pulley system. Once at the top, your harness is attached to a cable system allowing you to drop off the edge into a free fall and down a zip line. Whaaaaat?

Every activity has an element of challenge, and it is the choice of the camper of how far beyond their comfort zones they would like to go. One by one, these amazing young ladies made their way to the top, and then went right down that zip line back to the ground. The sun hadn't even risen.

Are you kidding me? Just five minutes before, they had rolled down a thick sand trail through the woods using various degrees of assistance (wheelchairs, walkers, canes). Now, they had scaled up a 42' tower and zip lined off the top 50+ yards to the ground.

Words cannot describe how this day made me feel. The amount of courage it took, the amount of trust, the amount of strength, and most importantly the size of their beautiful smiles when they "CONQUERED THE TOWER!"

This was my moment. This was when I realized why these camps exist. This was when I realized how special these kids really were. These girls defied all barriers, physical or psychological, standing in their daily lives and soared.

This was when I realized camp changed my life.

Clint Cobb
Murray, KY
Activity Staff

Slowly, Caleb opened the cupboard door. Sure enough, there veteran camper Owen sat, wearing a wizard's hat on his head, and Caleb thought he might just be magic after all. Owen told Caleb that, at camp, he could do whatever he'd always dreamed of doing. All he had to do was ask, and the adults would somehow make it happen. Together, they painted each others' faces. Caleb drew round glasses and a lightning scar on Owen, and then Owen asked Caleb what he wanted to be. Without hesitating, Caleb replied, "A tiger!"

That week at camp, Caleb went rock-climbing, horse-riding and even learned how to swim – something that he had never been able to do before because he couldn't go to the public pool whilst he was sick. When they weren't out abseiling off walls, shooting laser rifles across the sky or making messy porridge-and-cucumber facials for the adults, the campers would sit together, playing with toys, eating sweets, and telling each other all about their illnesses. They even had competitions to see which of their hospitals had the best play room!

Each night, whilst drinking hot chocolate with whipped cream AND marshmallows, the boys would sit round with the counselors (called "Team Mates") and say what the best bits of the day were. On the last night, each Orange team mate, including the adults, got to tell everyone their favorite bit of the whole week. Caleb wanted to say everything, but the very best bit was definitely the Talent Night, where all the campers did something on stage in front of the whole camp. He had brought his set of magic tricks with him, but he had been a bit nervous about showing everyone at camp! Just as Caleb was about to go on stage, Owen had produced the wizard hat from behind his back and placed it on Caleb's head and said, "Now you're a real wizard, Caleb. Go show them your magic!"

Thom O'Neill, MBBS
Inverness, Scotland
Counselor

The session was a blended session; campers with a variety of illnesses would enter the gates. Unlike other sessions which hosted a single illness, this week would be different. Attempting to unite ten adolescent girls with no common ground was going to be the biggest challenge of the summer... Or so I thought.

The campers arrived, the days flew by, and the Sisterhood rolled right up to the last night of the session, where bittersweet feelings hung in the air. The counselors had planned a nighttime adventure, but, to our surprise, the evening took on a plan of its own. We arrived at the theater and circled up on the stage. Counselors and campers sat amongst each other; some holding hands, others laughing, all smiling. A cabin chat was planned but when the mood is easy-going and the campers are connecting, holding off on planned activities is inevitable.

One of our campers had mentioned her love for music and playing guitar; we asked her if we found a guitar, would she play for us? Before long, the circle of girls were swaying back and forth, singing all of Taylor Swift's lyrics, to the sound of beautiful guitar notes. Each and every mouth sang along. When the songs ended, a moment occurred that I will never forget.

Beside the guitarist sat a camper who was blind. This camper loved camp with her whole being,-despite the fact that she had never seen camp through her eyes. She turned to the guitarist and said, "May I feel that?" The guitarist reached out for her hand and pressed it on the strings. She showed her how to pluck each string - each note singing into the open air - then how to strum across all of them. Time froze; every girl on the stage sat and stared as this pure moment unfolded. At that moment, there were no disabilities, no illnesses, no unhappiness. It was the purest, realest love.

Jenny Abney
Owensboro, KY
Counselor

Walkie-Talkie Powers

I spent the summer of 2011 as a Bale Leader. Secret Missions seemed to be taking place left and right, and counselors were calling upon me and Lee, the PFD, to play along and really get involved with their cabin's surprise. One of the younger cabins decided to let the boys stay up past "lights out," play some music, and bring out a few dodge balls to toss around, rather than actually leave their cabin to "sneak" off to another area on camp. We were asked to wait for a counselor's call to make our visit to their cabin that night. By doing so, they had a chance to turn the music off, quiet the boys down a bit, and remind them that, if we asked, they were by no means having a party and they were sorry for being awake a little later than normal. What Lee and I didn't know, is that the counselors also emphasized to the boys the importance of the coveted walkie-talkie; "the people around camp wearing those have connections to the camp director, so we have to be very careful."

Lee and I walked into the camper bedroom to see the lights on and all the boys wide awake. I calmly asked, "What's up, boys? Shouldn't you already be asleep by now?" One of the campers apologized profusely while the rest of them nodded in agreement. That is, everyone except for Connor. He was sitting on his top bunk directly to the right of the door, and we could tell something was eating at him. Connor kept staring at the walkie-talkies on our hips like they held special powers. I already was having a hard time keeping a straight face...and clearly so was he.

A moment later, Connor pulled at his hair and shouted, "I can't take it anymore! We were having a party!" The excitement in his voice thinking he had us fooled was such a beautiful thing. There it was – a simple moment became one of the happiest memories of this guy's week at camp.

Devon Page
Los Angeles, CA
Counselor, Bale Leader

Being a young adult should be an exciting time in your life. You are filled with energy, enthusiasm, and new ideas as you embrace your new found independence. During this time, you also experience many life changes such as graduating high school, entering college or a new career, getting married or starting a family. To also deal with a life-threatening illness at this important junction in life seems unfair.

This unique session of camp was designed to help maturing young adults with life-threatening illnesses briefly escape their complex lives and medical problems to prepare for the transition from adolescence to adulthood. It was an environment where illness could be overshadowed by love, group support, and fun.

One summer, there was a girl in her twenties who had been in a wheelchair all her life due to her illness. It was pool day, so I asked Isabella if she would like to get into the pool. Isabella said she had never been in a pool but was willing to give it a shot. We tied wet towels around her ankles, and I lifted her out of her wheelchair. Together, we entered the pool. Isabella was delighted to be in the pool for the first time in her life. I asked her if she had ever stood up before and she said no. So I asked her to hold on to my neck, and she straightened her legs.

For the first time ever, Isabella stood up. Tears of joy were flowing from her face as she said she would never forget that day, energized by the realization that her illness couldn't limit her and that anything was possible.

Joe Hildebrand
Westlake Village, CA
Counselor

It was my fourth and final week as a cabin counselor. Every previous session that summer there had been one girl who would follow me around almost everywhere that I went, cute and a little bothersome at times. This week was no different. I had my favorite age group, the middle girls who were the sweetest and sassiest little nuggets that you could ever meet. The group of 9 amazing girls were energetic, loving, silly, brave, wild, and beautiful; inside and out. I had a different relationship with each of the girls, but one of them was my shadow for the week.

My shadow demanded she sit by me at every meal, walk with me and hold my hand to every activity, swim with me during pool time, and basically everything else. Savannah was a regular camper, a normal kid with normal needs. The first night when she asked if she could have a different night time routine from the other girls, I complied. Each night before she went to bed we would sit on the porch of the cabin and talk about our day. Savannah would just talk about what went well, her rose, bud, and thorn, what she enjoyed, and the new things that she tried. At times, Savannah would talk about the bugs, the sunset, her mom or sister. They were very basic stories, like her talent show that she performed in that year, and everything else that was on her mind.

One night she got very quiet and began to look around. I gazed off into the distance simply enjoying the silence. "You know what I think...?" Savannah said to me looking over. "What?" I asked. "This camp is so magical even the horses can fly." She couldn't be more right.

Brittany Huff
Harmony, PA
Counselor

I was invited by the G4 Starfish to help create a magical starfish fairyland for cabin closing with the youngest campers. I recruited some of the other nurses, and we raided the entertainment office as well as arts and crafts. We transformed the on-call room into a magical fairyland! Since the campers knew me from medication pass as well as playing with them throughout the week, I had the receptionist dress up as a fairy, Oceania. We created a glitter trail from the cabin to the Patch. The counselors had the campers "go to bed" early, and Oceania came in and surprised them. One of the campers jumped out of bed and ran to her and gave her the biggest hug. They danced their way back to the fairy land. The campers asked Oceania questions as well as crafted a starfish. They each made a wish upon their starfish.

One of the campers was beyond excited and constantly sitting next to the fairy smiling up at her. At the end of the party, the counselors asked the campers what camp was to them over the past week. This camper said that "To me camp is Disney. We are very poor, and I know we will never make it to Disney. This is my Disney. I have always wanted to meet a fairy and now my dream has come true. I have met the best fairy ever!"

Each camper left with a container of magic fairy dust to continue dreaming at home. The camper said that it was her best present ever!

Debbie Kipp, RN
Kissimmee, FL
Camp Nurse

The boys were young, wild, and way beyond what I thought I could handle. It was my first summer and, though, there were only four kiddos in my cabin that session, they were six years old, had never been to camp before, and wanted to play with Legos during the pre-dawn hours. Our camper-to-counselor ratio was high, but so was our collective level of exhaustion. During one particularly trying moment, I told my camper that no, the impossible thing he wanted to do was not going to happen. My word choice didn't resonate with me at that moment; I had simply thought of how I could de-escalate the situation quickly.

At the end of the week, a veteran counselor shared his approach to handling tough moments like the one I'd encountered. "Camp is a place of yes," he said. "For the boy who can't play contact sports for fear of sustaining a life-threatening injury, and the girl who sits through 12 hours of hemodialysis treatments each week, 'You can't, you won't, you shouldn't, no' is a constant refrain. At camp, we want to give the power of choice back to each kid; with them in the driver's seat, we strive to create a safe, magical experience in which they can go beyond the limitations others have set for them."

From that week onward, I focused on eliminating "no" from my vocabulary and, during the subsequent three summers I've spent at camp, I've sought out ways to make "yes" happen. Yes, you're upset but this is what we can do and then we'll go to our next activity. Yes, you can dance, swim, climb, and I'll help you. Yes, you can draw a "tattoo" on my arm (in non-permanent marker).

It's a mantra I now strive to incorporate into my professional life, as camp has led me to pursue my Master of Social Work degree. Yes, yes, yes – three words I hope will lift them up, and three words that will always remind me of home.

Kristin Drouin
Ann Arbor, MI
Residential Life Coordinator

Chapter IV

M-E-S-S-Y, MESSY

While some cabin themes are flashes in the pan, some of them take on a life of their own. One week brought this to a head. What do fraternity guys do with cabins? You guessed it – secret societies. We spoofed "It's Always Sunny in Philadelphia" to produce the "Secret Society of Sun Warriors." To keep our identity concealed, the task was to be the B16 Olympians. Easy peezy, lemon squeezy...

It turns out that other cabins had somehow infiltrated the Sun Warrior ranks. What at first seemed like a lost cabin theme became an opportunity. The kids bought into the society when we thought we had lost it.

As camp progressed on, we encouraged silence and secrecy, but, to no avail, the inevitable loud children at night brought the Pride Leader to our door. Our cover was blown.

As "punishment" for their "late night activities," the Olympians were punished to go down to the rec field to clean up the remainder of the Silly Olympics mess. We marched the kids down in complete silence all the way down cabin row like a work detail to the field. The kids could sense our "frustration."

What in reality was happening was that we had glow in the dark paint and were setting up evening capture the flag and a paint slip and slide. We all obliterated each other with paint and got the messiest that I have ever seen campers get. We got them back to B16 (keeping the melancholy illusion of the work detail for the rest of camp), cleaned them up, and went to bed.

We stormed back in to wake them up for our special cabin game. They had the night of their lives – all that over a work detail for some kids who couldn't keep a secret...

M-E-S-S-Y...Messy! Messy!

Matt Dube
Old Town, ME
Counselor

96

Bathroom Explosion

My relationship at camp began as a camper in 2005. Like many, this was the first time when I finally felt like I could be me. It was the first time that I didn't have to explain my medical condition, what the tubes attached to me were for, or that I'm not contagious. Everyone just knew because they were going through the same thing.

In 2012, I knew I needed a boost of camp in my life, so I applied to become a cabin counselor. During my first week as a counselor, I had a camper in my cabin that had such a contagious smile, she was known all over camp. Ava had more challenging physical limitations than the other girls in the cabin that week and required total 1:1 care. It was a long, challenging, but rewarding week that will forever remain in my heart.

On the night before departure, Ava had an accident in her bed. In an effort to not draw attention to the situation, my co-counselor and I quietly helped Ava into a wheelchair and went into the bathroom to get cleaned up. At camp, I learned quickly that there are always bathroom accidents and helping campers clean up just becomes part of the daily routine. Once in the bathroom, we discovered that the shower would be the best area to clean up this situation. Clothes and all, the three of us stood under the water trying to make light of the reality that we were soaking wet and cleaning up poop. With an embarrassed camper on our hands, my co-counselor came up with the right combination of words to make Ava realize it was going to be okay. She looked at this teary-eyed, apologetic girl and said, "You know what, Ava, sometimes 'sh*t happens,'" and shit had literally happened that night. We looked at each other, and all three of us couldn't help erupting in laughter. That night set the tone for a summer that I will always remember.

Kelly Morning
Mammoth Lakes, CA
Former Camper, Counselor

97

In the summer of 2006 I was an oldest camper, and I had the most amazing campers and counselors in my cabin. One afternoon, the counselors surprised us with an awesome activity! We walked into the cabin to find all of our beds pushed back toward one wall and our mattresses were lining the other wall. We were all very confused and then our counselors told us we were going to do human bowling! Human bowling is where you put one person on one of those small square scooters and push them as fast as you can down the "lane" to try to knock down the plastic pins and run right into the mattresses lined up on the opposite wall. We started playing, and it was one of the most fun times I have ever had in my life! We shouted so loud, people outside could hear us and laughed until our bellies hurt!

After enjoying the shenanigans of human bowling, it was time for a snack but not just any snack, a pancake burrito snack. To make a one, you take a pancake and fill it with ice cream, chocolate syrup, and sprinkles and roll it into a burrito. It was delicious! All of us campers made such a mess that our faces looked like a walking ice cream sundae.

Then we sat there laughing at ourselves and having memorable conversations about all the wonderful things we do at camp. I didn't have to worry about what if I have a seizure because I knew that we all had Epilepsy. It wasn't something that made me different, it was something that united me with everyone else. At that moment I knew this memory would last forever.

Heather Good
Boca Raton, FL
Former Camper, Counselor

Chocolate Pudding

You know you are in deep trouble when you hope to remain clean at an event named "Silly Olympics." Being a first-time counselor, I had no idea what to expect and so I decided to inquire about what takes place at this event. After speaking to several campers, it became clear that their favorite activity at camp was "Silly-O!" Each of them was so eager to explain in their own words, making me slightly anxious. I thought to myself, "I just had my hair braided, maybe it's not a good idea to partake in this event. I'll accompany a camper who wants to sit out."

To begin with, NO camper wanted to sit this event out, absolutely NONE! And as if that were not enough, they all looked up to me with beautiful eyes and pouty faces begging for me to lie on the table. I totally caved but not without confirming that they were not going to touch my hair! When the time came, a countless number of tiny hands were all massaging my head and hair with thick chocolate pudding. The laughter was priceless, the happiness was contagious, and their victory dance was so worth it.

I thought I was done for the day only to be summoned once again. This time it was the "barf chair." A mixture of oatmeal, milk, and an assortment of cereals had been sitting in the sun all day in order to create the perfect barf. This particular challenge was to aim a scoop of barf at your counselor. I think that every camper who aimed at me did not miss! I was the perfect target, so the line grew longer by the minute. At one point, I opened my mouth to scream, and a chunk of goo fell right into my mouth!

"Thank you for enjoying Silly-O with us!" yelled the campers, and my heart was at peace.

Bella Mogaka
Nairobi, Kenya
Counselor

Silly Olympics was one of the best events at camp when kids and counselors would go crazy with gross and messy stuff. Campers would move from station to station in a flat grassy area of camp, participating in pie-ing their counselor in the face, shaving cream fights, antiquing their counselor (which involved throwing a wet sponge, followed by flour, on them, thus giving them an antique look), making human ice cream sundaes on anybody and finally a spaghetti slip-and-slide. It kind of reminded me of the Double Dare show that used to be on Nickelodeon.

After we got all dirty, the fire department came and sprayed us with their hose...which is very cold water, by the way. We would jump in the water, sing and play - all the counselors and campers. We're all tired and dirty, we have pudding in our ears, but we tell the campers that we are proud of them and it was a great thing that they did -- not just in Silly Olympics, but of everything they did.

Silly Olympics was one of the best times to see the campers relax and just have fun. It's like we're telling them, here's an authority figure, but you're allowed to throw oatmeal barf at them, you're allowed to strike back, and you're allowed to take control of the situation, when so much other stuff in their lives is just completely taken away from them.

The grins on their faces? From ear to ear!

Annie Dotson
Durham, NC
Counselor

Free Choice: Counselor Wash

Free choice is one of my favorite activities at camp because you never really know what's going to happen. From battleship on the lake to mask-making to recording a music video to tea parties, it's sure to be a memorable time!

One summer, I got to accompany some campers up to the Nature Barn for a "Wash the Animals" free choice. I always enjoy going to the barn because you get to interact with animals, and there are usually smaller groups during free choice allowing an excellent opportunity to make connections. During this particular afternoon, there were only two or three campers plus myself, one other counselor, and Bridget and Joe, who were in charge of the Nature Barn that summer.

Bridget and Joe went over the plan for the activity and then we all got down to business washing a sheep. I don't think sheep normally get baths and this one was a pretty dirty ball of fluff, so we had a lot of scrubbing to do. While the sheep's coat was very thick, we still finished the job in less than 15 minutes. And then we just looked at each other. What next?

I'm not sure if there was another animal Bridget and Joe wanted us to wash, but I suggested that since we already had all the supplies out and since humans are animals too, we wash Bridget and Joe next. And, because it made total sense, we had time to kill, and it was hot, Bridget and Joe somehow agreed. For the next 15 minutes or so, there was just laughing, lots of laughing because, inexplicably, "Wash the Animals" had become "Wash Your Counselors," one of the best free choices ever!

Paige Ryland
Brooklyn, NY
Counselor, Pride Leader

101

I absolutely loved my years at camp. It was a place of deep love, acceptance and friendship, and a place of healing for me. I grew up at camp. It was my second home. I knew that the people surrounding me would always understand my Von Wilebrands Disease, how it affected life, what I had been through, or I was going through at the moment. I could relate to the girls in my cabin, and we could be ourselves.

I was just "Becky" and that, to me, was refreshing.

When my time was up to go as a camper, I was very sad but then I had the opportunity to become a camp counselor. I got to experience everything from the other side. I learned what counselors went through to make camp happen. As a counselor, I was now the one getting covered in oatmeal, colored water, and pudding at Silly Olympics. Each time I was hit with the "barf" my campers got the biggest laugh at my facial expressions.

To see the look on those campers' faces, it was worth it. The happiness and the laughter that Silly O brought to these kids provided me with so much joy. They all worked together as a team and were able to have a blast in doing so. I will never forget the campers that I had and the impact that they had on my life. Because of those campers, I was reminded to always have a smile on my face regardless of the situation.

Rebecca Champagne
Bradenton, FL
Former Camper, Counselor

Everything was going as planned. All the campers had gotten out of bed. All had put on their war paint. We crept by the support staff that were "patrolling" camp for any sneak outs that might be taking place. Alas! The cabin finally made it to the safety of the teepee. It was time to celebrate with fruit sushi. Camila, the camper sitting next to me, picked up her first attempt of fruit sushi between her thumb and index finger. All of the contents of the sushi fell all over her. So, she attempted again. As any 7-year-old would do, Camila picked up her next piece the same way. The contents piled onto the already messy camper.

The serious candle chat was about to start, so the counselor leading the chat that night attempted to quiet down the campers. I whispered to sushi-covered Camila that I would hold my hand out straight in front her mouth, like a plate, and she could place the sushi on there to eat.

As the serious candle chat questions started to roll out of the counselor's mouth, Camila proceeded to eat the fruit sushi out of my hand like a dog would do. I immediately started laughing. She looked up at me with beautiful, big eyes and let out the purest giggle. She began to pant like a dog and make small puppy noises.

For the following 15 minutes, Camila was literally eating out of the palm of my hand. The counselor leading the chat gave me a stern look, but Camila and I were in our own giggle world. She would giggle because she was so messy and acting like a dog. I would giggle at her giggle. The cycle was contagious.

By the end, every person in that teepee was giggling, and I bet no one really knew the reason behind those giggles except sushi-covered Camila. The magic of laughter stems from how contagious it is, and this was the perfect example of that.

Elise Krivit
Cedar Rapids, IA
Counselor

As my chocolate milk guns ran out, I ran back to the arsenal of messy food. I grabbed some chocolate yogurt cups and launched them in the air. One missed the monsters by a long way and exploded on the grass, but the other one landed in the middle of a monster's back whilst another camper was spraying a big bottle of lemonade all over the monster's head! The other campers and I picked up plates of shaving cream and splatted them into the monster's face at the same time!

The three monsters were all on the ground, covered in beans, spaghetti, rice, chocolate milk and yogurt. All us campers ran back to the safety of the cabin, leaving the defeated monsters behind.

For me though, this was an extra-special-super-secret mission. I had never been in a food fight before. I could probably never have one outside of camp either. It's why today was the best day of my life. The reason I'm at camp is because of my allergies. I'm allergic to pretty much everything, especially food. I can't eat soy, gluten, dairy, nuts and even some meats. If I even touch anything I'm allergic to I have a reaction that stops my breathing, and I have to be injected with a special pen full of medicine. At school, I have to eat separately from everyone else so I don't accidentally touch food I can't have. To be in a food fight was something I never thought would happen.

My team leader and camp doctors had determined the messiest foods I could have, and how to prepare them without contaminating them. They had even phoned my mum to triple check. I don't know when they managed to do all this because they're with us all the time playing, singing and dancing. Maybe they just don't sleep!

I don't think I'll ever forget the food fight we had against the monsters in the daring rescue of Pedro, the Orange Team Mascot. Nothing will beat the best food fight of all time!

Harry via Thom O'Neill
Dorset, England
Former Camper

Itsy Bitsy Spider

During Hemophilia camp in the summer of 2013, every time one of the campers bumped themselves, it was a quick trip to the Patch to get some clotting factor. One night, one of the campers, Cameron, was having significant joint pain in his ankle. It was there, upon waiting for the doctor to come in, that Cameron asked us if he was going to die. My first inclination was to say, "No, you'll be fine, just like you have the past few visits." However, I realized I was not in a position to make that promise, and, at that moment, I felt the gravity of how scary it must be to be a young boy with a life-threatening illness, feeling the way he was feeling. Thankfully, the nurse came in before I had to respond, and she quelled any anxieties Cameron had.

After returning to the cabin, at which time it was past lights-out and the rest of the campers were sleeping, we brought Cameron to his bed. He was in the top bunk, and we helped him up the ladder without causing any pain to his foot. He got into the bed and under the covers, and we were about to say goodnight when IT happened. At the same exact moment, all three of us saw a spider dropping slowly from the ceiling right above Cameron's head. He HATES SPIDERS. With no regard for his own safety or his recently medicated ankle, Cameron attempted to DIVE OFF THE BUNK.

And just like that, he was a regular kid with regular fears again! Thankfully, we were standing right there and managed to catch him with half of his body over the side of the bed frame. After doing extensive spider surveillance/removal, we convinced Cameron that it was safe to return and he eventually did. But man oh man, I'll never forget that night.

Jake Levy
Coral Springs, FL
Counselor

My first summer at camp, I worked as a receptionist in the medical facility. The job description included file work, answering phones, data entry…standard stuff. At least that's what my responsibilities were on paper, but in reality it was so much more.

One night the Red Pride invited me out to join Silly Olympics, an epic event that involves goop and food flying everywhere. When I arrived at the cabin, the boys greeted me with jokes. I suppose everyone else in the cabin had already heard them, but I was new and I needed to know these jokes immediately! After the boys went through their inventory, Brody decided that he was going to continue creating new ones. I admit, these jokes may have had some flaws, but seeing the ambition of this little guy was absolutely fantastic and I laughed genuinely at every single punch line. Brody became my buddy for the evening and we cheered our way over to the Silly Olympics. Surrounded by these funny guys, I completely forgot that this session catered to those with cancer. Amazingly, not a single child here acted like they were ill.

My buddy and I arrived at the station where noodles were spread out on a huge tarp. Brody took my hand, and I looked down at him, expecting another joke. Instead he said, "All the bad stuff, it doesn't matter. What matters is what's in here," patting his chest with his other hand. I was awestruck. A 9-year-old had just given me the sagest piece of wisdom, right before diving into a pile of spaghetti.

Later I came back to my desk, enlightened and with a hair full of pudding and noodles. I learned many things that summer, but the greatest being that the bad stuff doesn't matter, because you keep the good in your heart.

Jessica Carroll
Mount Dora, FL
Medical Center Receptionist

I met Xavier in 2008. His mother told me that she had traveled to Guatemala to adopt him. I quickly click with Central American kids, so I was especially excited about our week together. It all started the moment Xavier entered camp, with a bright smile and the urge to get the week started.

Xavier was especially inquisitive about the highly popular Silly Olympics. It was coming up, and he wasn't sure how he would be able to participate. I reassured him that we could help keep his wheelchair nice and clean as the rest of our bodies got m-e-s-s-y, messy. Xavier painted his counselors, himself and everyone he came into contact with. He rolled through the spaghetti and received a fabulous pudding facial.

That week, we played some basketball since he loved it, got tired fast but who cares it was fun, talked non-stop for hours getting to know each other and told each other jokes. We laughed, we sang, we got messy. It wasn't the look on his face, or the smell of pudding, or the feel of water on our skin that I will remember, it was the laughter that Xavier released as the water from the firehose poured over him as he wheeled right through the flow of water.

This kid holds a special place in my heart.

Steve Alexander Silva
San José, Costa Rica
Counselor

During our camp's Respiratory Illnesses week, one of our youngest boys' cabin campers heard that "no-hands spaghetti" happened at the end of the week. Once Nolan heard that there was an event that involved not eating with utensils, he ate every meal of the week without a fork or knife "in preparation." Oatmeal in the morning, sandwiches at lunch and tacos for dinner were all eaten with his hands at his sides and his face in the plate. It took Nolan a little longer to eat than the other campers, but he wasn't afraid to get a face full of sauce, crumbs or meat pieces!

When no-hands spaghetti dinner came around, Nolan was ready. He challenged the other campers to eat like him, saying, "Just eat like I'm eating, it's fun." We had A LOT of picky eaters, but due to his enthusiasm for eating with no hands, the other campers of the cabin joined in. One of the campers ate his salad and spaghetti simultaneously, so his face was covered in red tomato sauce and white ranch dressing. He kept calling out to the other campers and counselors to look at his food covered face, all while wearing an ear to ear grin. Nolan was so happy that his "training" paid off, he cleared his plate and asked for seconds!

At breakfast the next day, Nolan used utensils. I asked him why, and he said he had to get used to eating back at home because eating at home wasn't the same as eating at camp.

Julie Szpira
Denver, CO
Counselor

Camp is an amazing place. Camp allows for community, openness, and self-reflection. Camp enables one to truly be their own person. Even though camp is only a week, it is amazingly transformative. Day one is full of campers being timid but after the campfire, campers become so comfortable with their surroundings that they are soon hyper and yelling the silliest songs with the biggest smiles on their faces. Being in this camp environment, I was able to discover who I am and be accepted for who that was.

When I was sixteen, I remember feeling totally free to be me during the mission impastable dinner. We arrived at dinner just like any other day except the silverware was replaced with random kitchen utensils such as potato mashers, serving spoons, and spatulas. Then we received our spaghetti pasta and tried to devise a plan on how to get our food in our stomachs. This was so fun! Seeing everyone at the table trying different ideas with different kitchenware and getting pasta everywhere made us all laugh.

I had been told from a young age that it was frowned upon to eat your food face-first into the plate, however, I also always had the urge. That night at camp, I was able to complete that dream. I was looking around, trying to see if it would be acceptable at camp to eat without utensils for this meal and sure enough, all around the lounge, people's faces were covered in sauce. I proceeded to put down my utensils and dive into the pasta face-first. It was amazing! That was the best pasta I ever tasted!

Thank you, camp, for allowing me to be me!

Mary Blake
San Jose, CA
Former Camper, Counselor

"I'm so colorful I feel like a rainbow! I would never be allowed to do this at home. This is the most fun I've ever had in my entire life. This is more fun than Disneyland."

One event for me that really sums up camp is "The Silly Olympics" that we put on every week in the summer. Camp magic is visible in every inch and centimeter. First, we would meet up and get all the kids pumped up. We would sing camp songs and each cabin would scream at the top of their lungs with their cheers. Then, the mayhem would ensue and each cabin would engage in the fun. From painting campers and counselors, having bobsleigh races with water, to getting covered in oatmeal, cornstarch and spaghetti, each week there was more and more silliness and new camp games to take part in. I saw kids raise a little hell and each camper be more creative than the next. It was so magical.

What was even more impressive were the looks. The happy glares, the smiles, the nonstop laughing and the sense of knowing that at the end of Silly Olympics, you were a part of something that only a select few people can be a part of. A select few people that are so special. It's like a secret that you want to share with the whole world.

Camp is Magic.
Camp is Special.
Camp is HOME.

Sean Kearns
Galway, Ireland
Entertainment Coordinator

From a young age, I have heard about the magic of camp from my cousin, Meera. She is the spirit of camp in human form. Camp has always been a part of her beautiful soul, and I wanted to experience it for myself. Flights booked, bags packed, I headed to LAX. Before I knew it, the campers had arrived and the fun had begun! From canoeing to zip-lining, there was a plethora of unique activities planned for the campers, and a bonding experience of a lifetime began.

I have many favorite moments, but one of the most memorable had to have been when the campers had their "science experiment" scheduled in the discovery zone. They were making vanilla pudding, and one of the girls had the idea to dump about fifteen drops of blue food coloring in one of the portions. She then asked me, very innocently, to take a big mouthful of the pudding, thinking I wouldn't realize that there were still large droplets of blue food coloring just sitting on top of my spoon. I decided to oblige with a big mouthful since it was in good fun for a camper and pretended I didn't know that there was still unmixed food color on the top.

The laughter that ensued could've shaken the entire building! It was great to be a part of something so simple and silly but brought them so much joy! If you look closely, parts of my tongue are probably STILL blue! That was one of the most memorable and magical experiences at camp for me. Anything for the kids!

Harsha Kasi Vishwanathan
Mississauga, Ontario
Counselor

The Perfect S'more

It was my first time being a camp counselor, and I met a camper that will forever give me the greatest memories. When Grayson arrived, I greeted him and immediately noticed a nervousness. I told him how excited we were that he was here and if he needed anything, to just ask. Grayson was not one to immediately jump into the spotlight but in his own way, he shined. I was with Grayson all week, and he constantly had to be around me. Wherever I went, he had to go and wherever he went, I had to go with him. Despite this, Grayson enjoyed making new friends, visiting the activity areas, and loving the independence that was summer camp without his family.

It was campfire night and we were just starting to make s'mores. I stepped out of earshot of Grayson to set up the next activity while the other counselors continued to help the campers make s'mores. Suddenly, I was startled by his cry of "Oh No! Oh No!..." I immediately ran toward him, my heart pounding as I heard the sentence completed... "Oh No! Oh No! Now I'm going to have to make another one!"

Grayson had dropped his perfectly made s'more in the dirt and had melted chocolate all over him. Thankfully he was not hurt, which was most important to me; Grayson, however, was equally excited to make a new s'more, free from dirt, and he carefully and delightedly ate it by my side!

Josh Pence
Minneapolis, MN
Counselor

Tower Morning with a Twist

It was Spina Bifida week, and we had 11 oldest campers. I was folding laundry on my bed during my night off and thinking about the tower climb the next morning when my co-counselor came running in saying that the bathroom was flooding. I went into the campers' bathroom and there was literally water spraying from the wall where it meets the toilet pipe. I started laughing and went to other cabins to get some more towels. Luckily, everyone was mostly ready for bed. We cleaned up as best we could and started making some phone calls. There wasn't much we could do besides shove towels in front of the door. It took a while to calm everyone back down, and it was fairly late by the time we were all settled. I fell asleep listening to the sound of Juan hitting the pipe with his shovel, trying to find where to shut off the water. At least, I think that is what he was doing!

The next morning I found two gallons of water on the porch with a note on a paper towel saying our water was shut off. Grateful I had set my alarm extra early just in case, we started the next phase of our adventure, which was trying to get all 11 girls ready for the tower. We shuttled some to the bathroom at the dining hall in golf carts while others brushed teeth with the water back at the cabin. I was so impressed with all the positive and cooperative attitudes of everyone in the cabin.

Later, as I watched them work together to conquer the tower, my heart swelled with pride. Each one of the girls grew that day and embraced the challenge head-on. While we debriefed, one of them said, "Well if we can do that, climb the tower after everything that happened, we can do anything." They all started high-fiving and I smiled as I said, "Yes, ladies, you most certainly can."

Hannah Zagar Bibler
Grand Junction, CO
Counselor

One summer at camp, I met a boy, Cooper, during Hemophilia session. It was his first year, and he came with a large behavior report. When he arrived at camp, he was withdrawn, defiant, and had trouble making friends. Cooper refused to participate in many activities, and would not get anywhere near the mess of Silly Olympics. Throughout the week there were times when we could see small signs in Cooper that camp was getting through to him and, despite his facade, I believed that he truly enjoyed camp in his own unique way.

Two years later... Cooper was back. Like previously, he came with warnings about his behavior. Cooper showed up on the first day and was 6 inches taller than the last time I had seen him. He looked like a young man compared to the little boy we had put on the bus 2 years before. He started off the week very similarly to his previous session at camp, withdrawn and refusing to participate with his cabin. As the week went on, though, the positive part of Cooper that had just begun to peek through 2 years before came out even stronger.

In the days leading up to Silly Olympics, Cooper and I talked a lot about whether or not he wanted to join in on the mess this year. He was unsure, but on the day of Silly O, decided to try a few stations. Cooper not only tried something new that day, but he fully participated in Silly O and laughed all the way through.

As we danced in the spray of the fire hose, I watched Cooper and was blown away by this kid who faced so many challenges every day. He had come to camp and grown up in front of me. I have a picture of the two of us from that day, soaking wet and covered in paint, but with big grins across our faces. I'll always come back to Cooper and that moment and know that anything is possible with the magic of camp.

Kelsey Dewey
St. Louis, MO
Counselor

Chapter V

LISTEN FOR THE LAUGHTER, LOOK FOR THE SMILES

We had a camper with Muscular Dystrophy. Every night three strapping young men in their twenties would operate a Hoyer Lift to get him into bed. We were specifically trained how to operate this machine because it can be a bit of a process.

On the first night, we were huffing and puffing trying not to embarrass ourselves, or our camper! After a few minutes we got him into bed and made sure he was comfortable. We felt really accomplished tackling the lift until one of my co-counselors asked, "So, who usually helps you get into bed?" With joy and sly smile, he replied, "My Grandma!"

The three of us paused with bewilderment. Embarrassment swept over me as all I could think about was this little old lady with Hulk Hogan arms that could probably bench press the combined weight of the three of us. We talked for hours how huge her biceps must be. It was fun ending the night with a great laugh and knocking our egos down to size.

Wyatt Thompson
Valencia, CA
Counselor

A "Typical" Camp Morning

Everyone has a morning routine. Usually it involves the basics: splashing water on your face, brushing your teeth or grabbing that much needed cup of coffee. My morning routine, as far back as I can remember, consists of something rather unusual - putting on my prosthetic leg. I lost my leg to cancer at a young age, so every night, I place my leg at the side of the bed, ready to go for the morning.

One morning as a junior counselor at an oncology camp, I woke up and reached for my leg at the side of the bed...but it wasn't there! A wave of confusion washed over me as I tried to figure out why my leg was missing. This is usually something I don't have to think about - usually it's right there. I knew I left it there when I went to bed. What happened to it?!

I started to ask around if anyone had seen my leg. I asked counselors. I asked campers. Nobody knew where my leg went! They all seemed as genuinely concerned with the situation as I was. However, I soon noticed a fellow counselor of mine with a big grin on his face. He said "Come outside." I hopped my way outside and found a large portion of the camp waiting for me. I said, "Where is it?" They all started laughing as I followed their eyes to the location of my missing prosthesis...ON THE ROOF OF THE CABIN!

Pranks are part of the camp culture whether you like them or not. I personally love them. I especially love them when they happen at a place where grabbing someone's leg and placing it on the roof of a building is not only alright but something that brings laughter and joy.

My morning routine has since gone back to normal. Yet, every now and then I wake up and wonder if my leg will be there at the side of my bed. It always is, and so is that special camp memory.

Scott "Super Scott" Liloia
Hadley, NY
Former Camper, Hospital Outreach Coordinator

Camp Running Deer

One of camp's cardinal rules is "no put-downs." More than just prohibiting insults, this rule reminds campers to treat everyone with respect. Or at least give them the benefit of the doubt. But as with most rules, even this one has exceptions.

It doesn't take long for new campers to hear about (and loath) Running Dear. This greedy, malicious, arguably-fictional neighboring summer camp is the antithesis to our camp. Mocking and opposing everything we stand for, the camp has secured a place as the subject for every curse uttered on Ashford Center Road. The "no put-downs" rule does not apply to Camp Running Dear.

My second summer at camp, the roguery of Running Dear was at critical levels. They had pranked countless Units, written insulting announcements to be read to the whole camp, and caused it to rain on days when we were supposed to go to the pool. My cabin, in particular, had had enough and were eager to make plans for revenge. Counter-pranks, new unit cheers that debased the noble name of Running Dear, lookouts who suspected any person they weren't familiar with; the campers were restless.

One night after a hard-days scheming, one camper was having a trouble falling asleep and asked me if he could tell me what was on his mind. He looked very serious in the dim light of the camper room. He looked at the bottom of the bunk above him as he spoke, brow furrowed in contemplation. He said, "I've been thinking. I've never been to Running Dear, have you?" I had not, and told him as much. He went on "I wonder if they're even that bad. We don't really know anything about them. They probably think we're mean too, because they've never met us. I bet it's all just a big misunderstanding."

I can't remember what I said, but who ever knows what to say to a spy?

Ben Beutel-Gunn
New York, NY
Counselor

I have learned so much from my time at camp and not a day goes by where I don't mention camp or see something that reminds me of a camper or camp memory!

One summer I was working with a girls cabin ages 9-12. It was the night of the camp disco party, and there was a great buzz in the cabin with all the campers getting ready for the exciting evening ahead.

I noticed one of our campers wasn't in the common room. Suddenly, I heard a voice coming from the camper room shouting "I NEED HELP." I jumped and ran into the bedroom expecting this to be a medical emergency.

What I found was definitely not what I had been expecting. Fiona was sitting on her bed with an array of bandanas in every color you could imagine.

"Is everything okay?" I asked still worried.

"NO," Fiona replied "I don't know which bandana is going to match my outfit for the disco!"

I looked at her and the two of us burst out laughing, and then made sure we attended to the fashion emergency!

Seeing Fiona make light of some of the circumstances of her illness and just laugh reminds me of how brave and strong these children are and what a privilege it is to get to know them.

Dee Murphy
Dublin, Ireland
Counselor

During camp, we had one little camper, who gave us counselors a run for our money! This young boy, Frankie, was high energy, loved being at camp, and loved Godzilla even more! He could frequently be found playing with his Godzilla toys throughout the session.

At our Purple Unit closing, Frankie told me he needed to use the restroom. I snagged another counselor, and we were ready to go. Frankie was quickly moving in front of us down the hill and did a forward roll on the ground. At camp we're supposed to keep our feet on the ground, but I looked at my co-counselor, shook my head, and smiled. We figured Frankie had so much energy, we'd let the one roll slide. But then Frankie decided it was so funny and decided to do it again, and again, and again, until he had done five in a row. As he rolled, my co-counselor and I chased him down the hill. We caught up, stopped him by his shoulders, before he could continue rolling right at a tree. We stood him up, held his hands, and skipped off to the bathroom, all three of us still laughing!

Kristiann Kassay
Seymour, CT
Counselor

Gary The Fish

I know in my soul that I've had the time of my life making a difference for our campers. It wasn't always that simple. In the beginning, I wasn't sure what would come of my time at camp. Would I be comfortable with people I didn't know? Would I be comfortable with myself? Would I be able to actually participate and lead activities at camp?

All of my apprehensions have since melted away. I have been completely transformed by my experiences as a counselor. Not only did I do one or two things at camp; I did everything at camp.

In 2012, I met a young boy, Luke, and we bonded pretty quickly and easily. As part of my personality at camp, I often wear a ball cap with a fake fish head and tail stitched to it. At lunch on the first full day of camp, Luke was sitting quietly. Then, he looked at my hat. Noticing this, I smile. "What's up, dude?"

Luke smiled back. "You know, I think your fish needs a name."

Recognizing an opportunity to connect more uniquely with Luke, I asked, "Okay, well, what do you want to name him?"

Face straight as can be, Luke replied matter-of-factly, "Gary."

Throughout the week, Luke and "Gary" spent a few minutes each day chatting, their unique friendship one of Luke's special camp gifts.

Camp gave me the chance to be a part of the family and to be myself in the process. What makes me different outside of camp became virtually invisible within this fun, magical place, and that was huge for me. I needed a place to truly belong, and I found it. Not only on the camp grounds, but in the overall life-changing experience of helping kids be kids, of giving them a chance to live in the moment, and giving their souls a place to call home.

2 years later, "Gary The Fish" waits patiently atop my head at each camp session in hopes that Luke might come talk to him again.

Zak Grimm
Fredericktown, OH
Counselor

"I'm going to miss you, dude."

That's what Colton said to me right before he got on his bus home. Leaving camp, his other home. It's a moment that I will never forget. He knew the camp backward and forwards. Everyone knew his name, he knew everyone's name and they were all his friends. He climbed a 42-foot tower that week and went down a zip line. He swam, he fished, and he laughed and played games.

Colton is blind. But that didn't stop him. It still doesn't.

Colton united our cabin.

It was his laugh. His view on life. The happiness he displayed was contagious.

That night, after all the campers went home, I went for a walk. After one lap I continued and went past my cabin. I wasn't ready to go to bed yet. It was a quiet night. The stars in the sky were shining, there was a calm breeze.

As I went past Blue 13, I could hear it. That laugh. It came from our cabin. His laugh that brought our group of campers and counselors together. That laugh, that smile.

I stopped. It was brief. Just a few seconds. But it was then I realized the power of camp. No matter where life takes you when you leave the gates, the love of camp will always be with you. It's an amazing feeling when you hear the voices and see the smiling faces from years ago.

It's a feeling that has never left me.

You are loved.

Wes Young
Fort Worth, TX
Counselor

It was Kidney Disease and Transplant week at camp. Comedian and camp friend George Lopez was greeting campers and counselors alike at the Shamu pool. The camp was abuzz with talk of his presence. I was lucky enough to be paired with counselor Evan in a cabin full of rowdy young boys. One of our campers, Henry, was quite excited to meet the famous actor. The first and only thing Henry said to George Lopez upon meeting him was, "George... If I could cast you in a movie, you would ride on the back of a T-rex that shoots lasers out of its eyes, all the while guarding the border of East Germany." Nobody knew what to say, not even George. Everyone was speechless. It was tremendous.

Wait for it... One day Henry will be a famous movie producer in Hollywood, and we'll remember when he created a T-rex shooting lasers out of its eyes, protecting East Germany from whatever came its way.

Justin Bonanno
Pittsburgh, PA
Counselor

To describe camp is nearly impossible as it is such a special place for so many different types of people; doctors, nurses, pharmacists, counselors, volunteers and especially the campers. It is a place a kid can escape the reality of their disease and feel safe and loved. In summer of 2010, I was a counselor. Everyday something amazing happened as children experienced unforgettable moments of escape from their illness and, instead, have purely joyful moments.

One of my favorite moments is a constant reminder to me to never take life too seriously. Sometimes you just have to lose yourself in the moment and laugh. The week was for campers who had Sickle Cell, a congenital illness that involves times of intense pain. It was morning activity time before breakfast, and I had four campers with me as we ventured out to the lake. They decided to take out the john boat, since it was the only option for us to not have to split up. The five of us piled into the boat and another counselor pushed us off of the shore. We were truly enjoying the summer sun out on the lake, laughing and talking about fun girly things. Suddenly, one girl realized we were just floating in the middle of the lake, having not paid attention to how far we had "paddled" out. None of us were truly good at paddling in a particular direction, so looking back at shore it dawned on us that we had to paddle, not just to paddle, but to make it to a certain destination. Instead of panicking, the four girls started waving at those on the shore and giggling uncontrollably about our situation. In that moment those girls were able to just be pre-teenagers in the middle of the lake with each other. After their outburst of joy, we made it safely back to the shore for breakfast and realized that paddling in a certain direction is not as hard as it seems as long as we work together.

Anna Kay Daggs
Columbia, SC
Counselor

Mama Bear

During my second summer, I faced an unique challenge: I was placed in a youngest boys' cabin. What seven year old boy wants to listen to a girl? I was extremely nervous because I was afraid I'd fail. I couldn't have been more wrong. The counselors in that cabin welcomed me with open arms, and assured me everything would be alright. We became the counselors of the Red 5 Bears.

Within a day of the campers arriving, I had become "Mama Bear," and my cubs would always hold a special place in my heart. In particular, one seven year old boy changed my life forever. Hunter was unique, funny, and embraced what it meant to be able to be yourself at camp. Halfway through the week I asked Hunter what his favorite part of camp was, a question I ask all my campers. His response wasn't what I expected. There was a short silence then Hunter just started to laugh; a deep, wholehearted belly laugh.

I didn't understand so I asked why he was laughing. Hunter told me that at camp, I was the weird one, not him. Back home he had to keep his shirt on in the pool so people didn't make fun of the scar on his chest. But it wasn't like that at camp, where everyone had scars. They could all compare and share stories, and feel normal. I was the weird one because I didn't have a heart surgery scar.

It took everything in me to not start crying. It was in that moment that I decided I would devote my life to making sure camp wasn't the only place these children could feel comfortable and "normal." It was because of this camper and his answer to my question that I decided to embrace what I now know is my life's passion. It was because of Hunter that I found my career path working with wonderful children like him.

Emalie Styles
Fort Lauderdale, FL
Counselor

Monopoly with a Twist

Once upon a time, I was checking in on campers and pals during Kids' Night In on a family retreat weekend. There were beautiful sounds of porch parties all along Cabin Row, but the most laughter was coming from Yellow 12. As I walked up its sidewalk, I could tell something magical was happening on that porch. Instead of participating in the oldest camper activity for the night, these campers had chosen to go back to their cabin to play with their pals. The players: two brothers, around 13 years old, and their male pal, and one 16-year-old female camper and her female pal. The game: Monopoly.

This was like no Monopoly I had ever witnessed before! In a whirlwind of energy and enthusiasm, the players were making up their own rules. For instance, if a player did not like a move by another player, the former player could sue the latter player. At that point, any of the other players could claim the role of judge, hear both sides of the case, and decide the verdict and the sentence. Verdicts were met loudly with friendly arguments, cheers, and laughter, and the game moved on, with various players adding additional rules as they saw fit along the way. Their creativity was in full force! While I wanted to stay on that porch all night to watch this game, I eventually moved on to visit other cabins.

I have kept this story in my back pocket for years, sharing it here and there as a reaffirmation of camp in so many ways. The joy can be shared among people who were strangers the day before. How a camper can make an imprint on a counselor. How counselors and pals can allow campers to make choices. Oh, the magic that can happen when kids are given choices!

Kirstin Cauraugh Youmans
Mount Dora, FL
Assistant Camp Director

I volunteered with the Hospital Outreach Program during PT school. At this same time, I was teaching myself how to play the ukulele! One day at UCLA, I decided to bring my ukulele along to go around to the kids receiving transfusions and sing them songs. I went from room to room playing simple kids songs, and got a really positive reaction from the kids and their families. Most of them would sing along. Then I entered the final room.

The child receiving the transfusion did not look at me when I entered, didn't acknowledge my "hello," and scowled when I offered to play a song. Chloe was in pain, tired, and just not in the mood. Her little sister, on the other hand, was ecstatic to sing along with a ukulele, so I started playing "Old MacDonald," figuring I'd make it through a few verses for the sister, and then leave as not to overwhelm the child getting a transfusion.

One verse in "...and a moo moo here," and I noticed a slight smile, and Chloe was looking in my direction. Second verse "...and an oink oink there," and I noticed a smile. Third verse "...here a baaa, there a baaa," and Chloe was singing along! Time for the next verse. "Horse!" she exclaimed giggling. We, sisters, parents and me, sang until we exhausted every farm animal imaginable, and didn't stop until my novice hands literally could strum no more. Chloe thanked me as I left, and I smiled and thanked her and her family for opening their doors to me. Truly an unforgettable experience for us of all.

Amy Peachy Neyer
Redondo Beach, CA
Hospital Outreach Volunteer

Poncho Fashion Show

When I think of my favorite camp memories, it is the endless moments that occur outside the schedule, often unplanned, often after lights out. At one point in the summer, we had a surplus of plastic rain ponchos. Every drawer and every cabinet was overflowing with them. Kelly, a fellow counselor, suggested a poncho fashion show. Would that even work? We had a cabin full of inner–city 15-year-olds with Sickle Cell, who occasionally refused to participate in camp activities. We gave each girl a poncho, and explained they had been invited to a fashion show, which would be held the last night of camp. The commitment and passion to showcase their creations was astonishing!

On the night of the show, paparazzi lined the sidewalk, which had transformed into a runway. Ushers handed out popcorn, and the headlight of the golf cart created the perfect spotlight. One by one, the budding fashion designers-turned-models proudly strutted down the runway wearing their handmade masterpieces. To quote a camp friend, "The excitement, enthusiasm and energy that are illustrated by these young children throughout camp are similar to witnessing a mini miracle." It was magical.

Meera Ramamoorthy, MD
Cincinnati, OH
Counselor

Pure Joy

It was the summer of 2012 in the Yellow pride where memories were created that will last a lifetime. I was in a cabin with eight of the most wonderful seven-year-old girls, who were just as excited as they were nervous to be on 232 acres of hope for the very first time. We decided to pull a counselor swap one evening, where the male counselors would have the opportunity to spend time with our campers and we would have the same with theirs. After tucking our girls in for the night, we promptly exited their side of the cabin to allow the late night activities to begin. The male counselors came inside our cabin and brought cookies, candy, makeup and nail polish; all of the essentials to have a makeover party with our campers. The girls could not contain their excitement! Each one took a turn painting the male counselors' nails to make them as pretty as possible.

My co-counselors and I returned to the cabin and yelled loudly that we wanted to make sure our girls were sleeping because we had a fun day planned for the next day, and it was very important for them to rest. As we said this, we heard giggling and panic erupt inside of the cabin as the male counselors were still inside. We slammed the door open and looked everywhere. We took turns asking each other if we smelled nail polish or if we saw a candy wrapper on the floor, to which, of course, we replied that we did not. The male counselors were hiding under a blanket in the corner, when my co and I said that we should check the bathroom. As soon as the door closed gently behind us, we heard scrambling as the male counselors bolted without a second to spare. We walked out of the bathroom and said that we thought everything looked fine and we were glad that our girls were sleeping soundly. As soon as we closed the door, our girls erupted into inconsolable laughter, and pure joy filled the air.

Alysha Stoner
Rockledge, FL
Counselor

One of our counselors, Carolyn, came all the way from Ireland. She was sassy and funny and taught the girls Irish sayings, and what certain American words were called in Ireland, like "jumper" for sweater, and "boot" for trunk. Part of camp is about sharing different cultures with one another, and it was great to listen to 7 year-old inner-city African-American girls practice Irish sayings, like "Top of the Morning to Ye!" as they got dressed in the morning.

We needed all the counselors we had to handle all the attitude we received on an hourly basis. Ruby, especially, was already earning a reputation around camp. Her stout little frame carried a lot of personality, her wide brown eyes with huge cheeks always had a clever grin spread across them, and her hair was often a little wild and untamed, just like she was.

The start of the week was a learning curve for all of us; monitoring attitudes when they were a bit inappropriate, but trying to reinforce all positive behaviors. By the middle of the week, Ruby had captured everyone's attention and hearts. Her enthusiasm, loudness and willingness to try anything caused staff around camp to simply smile and laugh when they saw her coming. You never knew what was going to come out of her mouth, but you always anticipated it would cause you to laugh.

Ruby had established that she would be a very memorable camper to many, but the most memorable incident for all her counselors, I think, came on the departure day. We were all bustling around the cabin, supervising the girls in cleaning and gathering their belongings up to pack. It was a sad day, but we tried to make the most of it through singing and dancing around.

Ruby was looking for her underwear that she claimed had gone missing. In response to this, Carolyn, began singing her way around the cabin, "Knickers, where have my knickers gone?" All of a sudden, Ruby stepped into the hallway very authoritatively with a hand on her hip. She cocked her head up the way she often did when she was questioning us, her little brow furrowed, and said very confidently, "You can't call me that!" and pursed her lips defiantly at Carolyn.

We were all in different rooms, but all stopped in our tracks, confused as to what had just happened. All at once, we figured it out. Ruby had misunderstood Carolyn's song, and thought she said a different word than "knickers." This was NOT one of the Irish words Carolyn had gone over with them. Whoops.

We immediately began to laugh and Carolyn quickly said, "Oh no, Ruby! I was calling for your underwear to come out!" and she emphasized slowly the word "*underwear*." "Knickers in Ireland means underwear" she explained, "and I know it must have sounded like something else. I would never call you that, but I am glad you knew that it was a bad word, and let me know." Throughout Carolyn's explanation, Ruby's furrow stayed fixed with her hand on the hip, but she was listening. We all stood surrounding her, anxiously awaiting her response.

"Ohhhhhh!" she finally giggled and shook her little body around, like she was letting out a big breathe. "Carolyn, you gotta speak your Irish clearer!" With that, everyone burst into laughter and returned to the bustle of packing. Ruby uncovered her missing underwear, and shouted, "Here are my knickers!" triumphantly.

We were all relieved that Ruby understood Carolyn's explanation, and realized the severity it could have caused, all because of a difference in culture. We were also glad, though, that a little girl like Ruby, who was experiencing camp and all of us for the very first time, had the moxie to stand up for herself when she thought something was wrong. I thought to myself, "She is one strong girl."

We finished our packing and headed down the path to the dining hall for one last meal together; the girls encircling us singing their camp songs and us laughing the whole way, knowing this first week would stay with us for a long time.

Michaela Page
Pittsburgh, PA
Counselor

The summer of 2013 was my first time as a Pride Leader. Rather than hanging out with one cabin of boys, I got to play with and supervise four cabins of boys and girls. During one of the first sessions, one of the girls' cabins told me that I had lost a bet, and my punishment was having my nails painted by them. I don't remember making a bet, let alone agreeing to allow them to practice their beauty skills on my hands, but they were a tough crowd to argue with, so I relented. I sat on their porch, and was surrounded by 10 aspiring artists who were too young to even paint their own nails. I bore witness to true creative greatness, with my hands ending up looking like a Jackson Pollock canvas. They decided that my new nickname would be "Sparklefingers" and then let me escape off into the night.

The rest of the week, I was known as Sparklefingers to an incalculable number of children, including other Prides. When the week ended, I was sad to see the kids go, but happy that my nickname would be put to rest. I was so wrong.

At the start of the next session and most sessions after that, a camper would, at one point or another, run up to me and call me Sparklefingers. Inevitably, it would spread, and I would hear that name called out constantly. Despite my best investigating, I couldn't figure out how this could possibly be happening to me.

Towards the end of the summer, it was finally revealed to me that the girls who had originally painted my nails left notes for each camper that would later stay in their cabin. The idea of the notes was to let each new camper know how much I liked having my nails painted and being called feminine nicknames. Thanks, girls!

Aaron Litz
Orlando, FL
Pride Leader

Star Hike

I had the delight to be a cabin counselor for ten teenage boys. I'm an older gentleman, and a bit unique in this camp full of 20 to 30-year-old counselors. But I teach college science, and soon the boys realized that I "knew stuff" and saw me as a "cool old guy." We were in the mountains. The air was crisp, and the sky was clear. It was perfect in every way.

One of the counselors found out that I taught astronomy and asked me to lead a "Star Hike." I enjoy teaching about the cosmos, especially when the students begin to understand the immensity of it, and how small we are in comparison. Late one evening, our cabin trekked out to an open field for a view of the sky. There was little moon; the sky clear and full of stars. I suggested that we lay on our backs to look upward. Boys this age don't mind the dirt, and before long we were all comfortable and glimpsing the heavens.

I started my usual presentation, pointing out the basic constellations, planets, and the Milky Way edge of Galaxy. I think I may have bored them to tears as some started to snooze a bit. So, I thought I'd play a little trick. During the quiet lull, I pointed out the planet Mars. The Red Planet. It was low on the horizon…so bright it seemed so close.

The group went completely quiet. I continued my diatribe, explaining how Mars is so close, and how we will visit it soon, first with robotics, then humans, etc. The group was even more silent… And one brave boy said…"Bones…Bones, I think that's the light on top of a radio tower". I exclaimed, "No! That's Mars, and how dare you question my vast knowledge of astronomy!?"

And these boys…these wonderful, brilliant boys, showed respect for me and let me continue to believe that a radio tower caution light was indeed the planet Mars. And then I started to giggle…and they started to giggle! Isn't summer camp wonderful?

Trey "Bones" Pitruzzello
Riverside, CA
Counselor

It was the last night of the first session at camp and the counselors planned a "sneak out" to have our final cabin chat. We REALLY hyped up the importance of being extremely quiet, stealthy, sneaky, and NOT GETTING CAUGHT! Despite most of our boys being returning campers, they all bought into it and were excited (some nervous!) to sneak out. It was decided upon to sneak into the costume room, the perfect spot!

Prior to the sneak out, we had arranged with the leadership team so that they would be "making their rounds" around camp to "make sure campers weren't out of their beds." After a few "close calls" and lots of giggling boys, we made it to our final cabin chat destination. If someone were to come in, we all agreed to hide among the costumes hung all around the room. At one point, our volunteer coordinator made her way into the room, "looking for sunglasses," and we all dove into costumes, waiting for her to leave. Eventually, she left and we regrouped in the middle of the room to continue cabin chat.

A few of the boys were intense! They were watching the door and whispering so softly that we couldn't hear their answers for cabin chat....when suddenly...the back door started opening. THIS WAS NOT PLANNED! As all ten campers, as well as six counselors jumped, dove, and slid into the costumes, we heard several strange sounds as we rushed to our cover. We soon realized one of our counselors had left to use the restroom and returned through the back door. As we regrouped in hysterical laughter, I noticed a stench in the room. Turns out half the boys (and a counselor!) had passed gas from being startled! I will never forget the "cloud of fart" that formed in that room and how genuine of a moment it was.

Hana Lim
Seattle, WA
Counselor

"OMG you're the girl working with the HUGE family, you must be exhausted!" I heard this over and over on what I like to call, "The weekend that got me hooked." It was November 2008, my 1st camp session!

We didn't learn any of the cheers as we sat on the bleachers. As it is, we were having trouble learning each other's names. The name tags were buried under the sweatshirts, and there was no way I was going to be un-cool and ask the kids to expose their name tags. I memorized their names off the list before bed that night.

"Mercyyyyyy!" I heard my name being shouted on cabin row as I was tackled down with hugs at 7am the next morning. How the heck did that happen? They haven't even had breakfast!

Then, MY CAMPER ATTACKED HIS BROTHER WITH HIS CANE. That was not safe, respectful or loving! "Do you remember the rules at camp?" I gently asked.

They explained, "We try really hard not to fight all year long so we can come to camp. Mom says we can only come again if we behave well. We shouldn't fight because Mr. Spivey's fire wont be big anymore. If we don't fight anymore, do you promise to stay our counselor?"

I was playing with 7 camp veterans. A family of adopted children that reminded me that this world has kind, loving people that exceed whatever arbitrary standards for "good" we set. I cried when we said see-ya-later.

I wasn't sure camp was a piece of cake anymore.

I can't stop coming back to play with these kids. The feeling I get when I hear them shout my name down cabin row before breakfast, as they tackle me with hugs; it's special and only something that can be explained as the magic that grows at camp.

Mercedes Garcia
Miami, FL
Counselor

The Bachelor Party

A few weeks before I got married in the summer of 2011, I had the opportunity to go to my favorite place on Earth, camp. My curious campers, of course, wanted to know everything about me, and quickly learned about my upcoming wedding. As they were 10-12 year old boys, their collective responses of, "Oh...Cool...Hey, who's your favorite superhero: Spiderman or Batman?" pretty much was where I assumed the conversation would end. Boy, was I wrong.

A few nights later one of my campers complained that he was sick; not just sick, but REALLY sick. So, I took him to the Patch so that he could get all fixed up before bed. After what seemed like an eternity, he came out of the exam room with a "prescription" for a granola bar and glass of milk. As we walked the short distance to the, oddly pitch-dark, Dining Hall, we chatted about how delicious our little snack would be and how excited we were for the next day of camp. We walked through the door and...SURPRISE!!! shouted a cabin full of boys - boys ready to have a bachelor party...at camp.

The bachelor party was better than anything I could have imagined. We had the special cinnamon ice cream, Dorcas let us wear her boas, and I even got to ride in the Birthday Chair! It was one of the most touching things that has ever happened to me. Those campers, who I assumed heard my good news and then continued being middle schoolers, instead schemed to throw me a party. I often think of how incredible the kids are who make camp the amazing place it is. For children who struggle with illness, to be so selflessly caring, kind, and loving is a testament to the type of place that camp is.

The next day when the Book of Firsts was read, I smiled with appreciation, because "The boys of Y9...went to a Bachelor Party...for the very first time!"

Nick Gesualdi
Boston, MA
Counselor

The Power of Family Camp

Family weekends at camp are incredibly special - a time for families to create happy memories together amidst illness and support one another. Impromptu performances, sudden acts of bravery or simple moments of hilarity are common around camp, and the campers are praised for such moments.

One weekend, a mom and her two kids came to camp for the first time but dad had to miss it. The family didn't really know what to expect before they arrived.

Throughout the weekend Mom was in awe of her daughter's new found spirit and confidence at camp. The little girl danced, made friends and even shared a few jokes at stage night: What do monsters have for breakfast? (A: scream cheese); What did the almond say to the pistachio at the gym? (A: almond better shape than you!). At one point, Mom called her husband, and told him, "I can't wait to introduce you to our daughter. You should be here because I'm seeing our daughter as she is supposed to be."

They left family camp singing and dancing all the way to the car, waved off by all the volunteers and the other families who they'd made friends with and seen coping with exactly the same problems they were having to cope with. And, soon after the weekend, Mom met with her daughter's teachers and administration to reassess her IEP.

Carys Horgan
Englewood, CO
Assistant Camp Director

The Tale of the Farts

A common phenomenon in the life of boys' cabins at camp is flatulence, the body's expulsion of gastrointestinal gases. Over the years, many a young man has had a fun time at camp simply by, as we like to say in Maine: "fahtin." The fun ranges from the reading of Walter the Farting Dog to the actual act of dispensing the gases.

This story is not necessarily about flatulent acts, but about cabin expectations. People often ask what the funniest thing I ever saw at camp was, and without a doubt, this round of cabin expectations takes the cake. We had five youngest, rambunctious Sickle Cell campers, who quite honestly, became my favorite group of campers ever. They were funny but respectful; a wonderful group to end the summer with. As we went through our cabin expectation routine, we arrived at two parts where the children pick words to symbolize particular phenomenas: wetting the bed and "fahtin." How funny could this process possibly be?

While wetting the bed usually comes back as something to the effect of "checking the weather" and "fahtin" as something to like "safety," this group of campers had one amongst them, Jaxson, who had a mind of his own.

We asked what the boys wanted to say in advance of letting one rip, and Jaxson said just as serious as he possibly could: "fixing to elf" or what became known in the way that we all chose to say it: "FINNA ELF." What does that even mean? Elf is not a verb. Your first reaction in the moment is usually to say "What?" but that is not what our reaction as a staff was. Between the five of us, we had, shall we say, seen it all. Our reaction in the moment was literally ROFL. Quite honestly, it might be the funniest thing I have ever experienced in my life. It became the running joke of camp for the entire week.

Matt Dube
Old Town, ME
Counselor

Too Smart

It was an all-camp extravaganza. We had six stations, and the twelve cabins were paired up to make six teams. Each team had twenty campers along with counselors. While the themes varied, these events always shared the similar goals of problem-solving and team-building along with ample portions of fun and fulfillment. Ultimately the kids, aided and encouraged by the staff, would collect clues or put puzzle pieces together around camp to achieve a common goal.

My station was in the gym. When our first group arrived, we set out their task. While these girls were trying to make a line with everyone touching, the other five teams were given complementary challenges throughout the camp. As facilitators we gave hints but did not reveal solutions. We had to hope the kids would solve the problem in time to make room for the next team.

We were still learning how to lead the activity. The girls figured out how to meet their particular challenge, but were still carrying out the solution when a loud banging at the doors indicated that the next team had finished at their first station and were ready for us. Leaving my co-counselors in charge of the pay-off and summation, I volunteered to go outside and stall team number two.

I announced to the boys outside that the team first had to add up the total age of everyone in the group. There was a silence followed by shouts of, "I'm nine." I'm ten." even "I'm twenty-three." I was satisfied I had come up with the perfect time-eating stall until one usually very quiet boy stepped out of the crowd and said, "Listen to me. If you're eight years old, stand over there. All the nines come to me, and the tens go there. Everybody multiply. Then we'll add." Without any further instruction, even the counselors knew what to do. Camp is the most surprising and rewarding place. Just ask any kid.

Mark Maxwell-Smith
Studio City, CA
Counselor

139

Wallace and Rocky

I was so nervous to start the first week of camp. I wanted so badly for the campers to have fun. Luckily, the youngest group of campers were up first in Red Pride. Orientation was enough to get even the most timid person revved up and yelling cheers. We took a last minute trip to Walmart the night before camper arrival to grab some props and as many red items as we could find. First week's theme was Bed Rock, and one of my pride members and I both happened to buy the same red stuffed dinosaur.

I was told the youngest campers would believe just about anything, but I had no idea just how true that statement was. We set the stage: Wallace was the last dinosaur on the planet, and we needed their help to find him a friend. They more they showed him love and the louder they cheered, the closer they would come to finding another dinosaur. They carried Wallace around all week, taking turns carting him around in the little red wagon and bringing him to all events, including Silly Olympics.

At the end of the week, everyone gathered around, and we pulled out a large paper maiche egg. Every single camper became silent, sitting at the edge of their seat waiting for what was going to "hatch." Sure enough, Wallace found a similar looking friend, Rocky. I've never seen eyes that wide and such squeals of delight and excitement in my life.

That's the magic of camp. Something so seemingly little, woven into a story that each and every one of them could believe in. I may have thought I could get them to believe anything that first week, but by the end of the summer, those kids could make me believe in anything.

Hayley Harris, DO
Austin, Texas
Counselor

Chapter VI

I'M A CAMPER FOR LIFE

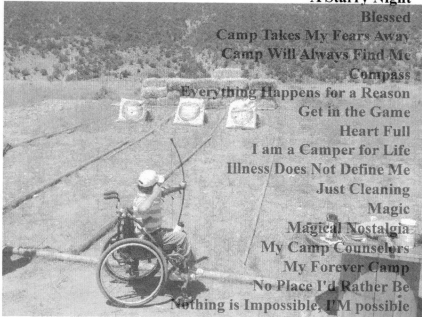

A Boost of Confidence
A Starry Night
Blessed
Camp Takes My Fears Away
Camp Will Always Find Me
Compass
Everything Happens for a Reason
Get in the Game
Heart Full
I am a Camper for Life
Illness Does Not Define Me
Just Cleaning
Magic
Magical Nostalgia
My Camp Counselors
My Forever Camp
No Place I'd Rather Be
Nothing is Impossible, I'M possible
On the Same Page
Safe, Respected and Loved
The Last Night of Camp
What Camp Really Is
Where Everyone Understands

I heard about Camp from my hospital after I received a kidney transplant. They told me it was this magical place where kids like me could have FUN for a week with no parents. My mom thought it was totally safe because my doctor would be there so it was like a weight was lifted off her shoulder every summer. I have a crazy personality, but when I was home or in school, I was too nervous to be myself and show who I really am. It is intimidating to be wild and crazy when you are worried what other people think of you, and before camp I never really had a place where I could just be myself! When I went to camp it seemed so easy to make friends because everyone was just like me and I wasn't being judged. It was my getaway because nobody at school or home really ever understood what I went through between hospital stays, taking so many pills, seeing doctors, and various procedures.

I did more in a week of camp than I had even done in my life, without my daily care getting in the way. I danced, I sang Miley Cyrus at the top of my lungs, and I even rode a horse! Camp was exactly what I needed – everyone here loves you for who you are, and they're wild and crazy too! When I'm at camp, I show a side of myself that a lot of people at home don't see. I'm talkative, more confident, and outgoing with my cabin. I also loved all of the activities at camp – you can do almost anything.

Every year when I came home from camp, I had more confidence in myself and who I am. At the end of the summer, I went back to school ready to show people more of who I really am and how crazy and fun I can be! I know that I have changed so much because of my summers at camp.

Nicole Keplinger
New Smyrna Beach, FL
Former Camper

A Starry Night

My fellow campers and counselors have made a huge impact on my life, and I know I wouldn't be who I am today without them. The fondest memory I have was shared between myself, my sister, and Kimmy, our family pal. It was my last family weekend since I was turning 16 that summer. During lunch, Kimmy casually asked my sister and I what we were doing later on that evening. We told her that we didn't have any plans, and maybe would walk around with our mom to look for animals.

Later that night, when it was very dark out, Kimmy came knocking on our cabin door. She took me and Aimee, my sister, out by the lake, where she had a campfire and marshmallows waiting for us. We talked, laughed, roasted marshmallows, and then we went out on a paddleboat. The best part of the night was looking up and seeing thousands of stars in the sky. This night was just so incredibly special. She knew it was our last time at camp and made sure it was extra memorable. I felt so safe, respected and loved. I hope one day I can give a camper and their family an experience like the one Kimmy gave mine.

Crystal Guralnick
Coral Springs, FL
Former Camper, Counselor

"Your best thoughts come to you while you're on the toilet, because all the crap gets out of you, and you start thinking REAL."
-Camper

It'a hard to put into words how much I have learned and changed, and those who have ever been to camp can testify to that. I worked with kids with serious medical conditions, and was trusted by their parents to take care of them for a whole week.

A WHOLE WEEK.

As someone who was very sick as a kid and knowing how much my parents worried about me, I felt extremely privileged to spend that much time with these kids and made the absolute most of it. We watched them conquer their fears on the ropes course, experienced their first time catching a fish, ate spaghetti with no hands, and watched their eyes light up as they performed at stage night. We witnessed shy kids transform into the camp clowns, and the bond that formed between the oldest and youngest campers.

To say it was magic would be an understatement.

I worked with an amazing staff who helped each other through difficult times and watched as they grew into even more astounding individuals. I honestly believe that I made some of the best friends I will ever have. They helped me understand that it's actually okay to be myself, still accepted me at midnight as I broke down on the Arts and Crafts floor in a fit of crying/laughter/incoherent sentences, and left me love notes when I was in Quarantine.

What it all boils down to is that I am blessed. Even though life with Crohn's Disease is little rocky at times, knowing I've got some loving supportive people behind me makes a difference.

Dylan Lowe
Cedar City, UT
Former Camper, Counselor

Camp Takes My Fears Away

I went to Camp for three years as a camper. It had such a strong and positive impact on my life to turn a difficult situation into something positive. I became a Junior Counselor once I was too old to be a regular camper. This program is put together to teach past campers how to be counselors and, most of all, leaders.

As a camper, I was one of the timid children, never wanting to cause trouble, or have all the attention on myself. As a Junior Counselor, I was taught how to delegate jobs in groups and that being a leader really meant serving others. On one of the last days that we were at camp, I was asked if I wanted to lead one of the morning songs. My first reaction was, "No way," but as I thought about it and with a little help from my mentor, I decided I would lead my favorite song, "Aroostasha." Another Junior Counselor would also be performing it on the dining hall stage with me.

Both of us practiced all afternoon and evening until we were confident. I woke up the next morning, nervous, but remembered the non-judgmental atmosphere the camp had. I was probably shaking as I got up onto the stage, but I knew perfectly what I was supposed to do. I spoke loudly and lead all the kids in my favorite song. The other Junior Counselor and I decided it was so much fun, to my surprise, so the last morning we led the morning aerobics!

Bernie Gorman
Debary, FL
Former Camper, Counselor

Camp Will Always Find Me

"It's said you can leave camp, but camp never really leaves you."

I heard this quote during my first year at camp, and I soon realized how true it was as soon as I left camp. I was in high school participating on my Cross Country team at an invitation across the state. I remembered one of my best friends from camp lived in that town, so I contacted her to let her know I was visiting. By the time I left for the race, my friend had not replied back.

Much to my surprise, right when I finished my 5k race, my best friend from camp was standing there eagerly waiting for me. As soon as we made eye contact, I gave her the biggest hug in the world. The feeling of exhaustion from the race did not matter anymore because I was surrounded again by the one person who could understand a part of my identity that not many people could relate to. Right there in the middle of a Cross Country meet, I was overwhelmed with the magic of camp which made me very emotional. I was reconnected with my favorite place on earth again; all the camp songs, cabin chats and silly inside jokes I had with other campers. Tears rolled down my face because I never imaged that I would see someone so special to me outside of camp.

In that moment I truly believed that even though my camp experience might only been five days long, the special bonds and countless memories I make there last a lifetime. No matter where I go, camp will be a part of me. The little piece of goodness from camp will find a way into my everyday life and fill me up. For me, in the most unexpected of places, I found that little piece of camp again at a Cross Country meet.

Megan Brown
Silverdale, WA
Former Camper, Counselor

The first time I went to camp, I was seven years old. Still on treatment, I was scared out of my mind to be away from home. But, as my family and I walked into the Patch, we were greeted as if I'd been going there a long time. The doctors and nurses reassured us, and I felt safe. At the time I had no hair, my scars were really visual and I didn't like for people to see them. After just one day there, I wasn't afraid to show my scars. Better yet, I was PROUD of them. I felt like I truly belonged, and this crazy bunch of people became my family. I went as a camper for 11 years.

Last year it was my first time as a counselor, and I felt even more blessed to experience camp as a part of the magic-making team. Like being woken up to the sounds of the pitter-patter of little feet and laughter in the next room... like talking to a child so excited they can hardly put words together... like having a child run up and hug you for no reason... like singing a camp song with a little one in your lap... like a camper telling you this is her favorite time of the year... like a camper asking you to promise to come back... like wiping tears off their faces when they leave... like stepping away and wiping off your own.

Camp is a magical place, that knows just what you need. Whether it's knowledge, understanding, a fun time, friendship, or even closure, camp always knows how to fill you up to the very top with everything you are searching for.

Camp is my compass; it has given me incomparable direction and led me to discover kindred spirits in friendships that will last a lifetime.

Brionna Reed
Ocala, FL
Former Camper, Counselor

I believe everything happens for a reason. Summer of 2004, my first summer as a camper, I finally found the reason for the liver transplant I had when I was two…Camp. My transplant saved my life, but I felt lost until I came to camp. It became a way of life. The lessons and people I have met there inspire me everyday to be the person I have become and want to be. Whenever I'm having a hard time, I think of those friends and counselors, their love and passion for others and life and their strength to face their own personal challenges each day. I am happy and grateful to say that I will always be reminded of their love and spirit.

One of my favorite camp stories was when I was a camper, and we had our first sneak out. Our counselors had us sneak out to the pool and on the way we "became trees" to not be seen by anyone walking along the road. Once we got to the closed pool, we had to change in the boy's locker room so we weren't seen by anyone cleaning the girl's locker room. When we were all ready and about to go swimming, we heard someone walk in and talk to the lifeguard who also knew we were there. The person talking to the lifeguard told her, "Make sure no campers are swimming at night and if we find out they are, you will be fired."

After hearing the conversation, all the campers were nervous. I remember being afraid yet excited, and I initially refused to go swimming in the pool or leave the pool house. I finally went outside into the pool, but was completely paranoid someone would come back and find us all out there.

Looking back on this story now, having been a counselor myself and planning out my own "sneak outs," it really makes me smile thinking about how many "extra" things our counselors did for us to have a memorable experience.

Allie Biess
Jacksonville, FL
Former Camper, Counselor

Have you ever experienced a drastic change in opinion? Well, this is what happened to me because of camp.

A few years after treatment for leukemia, I was experiencing difficulties socializing with people my age. I had spent so much time with doctors, nurses and other adults. My mom heard about this camp for seriously-ill children, but I refused to go. I don't know exactly what I was scared of; maybe fear of socializing or fear of a new and unknown experience. I only knew I had no intention to go.

When time came for camp, I had been convinced to, at least, try the experience. I soon realized how wrong my worries were. It was completely different from what I had imagined and turned out to be the best experience of my entire life. Every aspect of the program helped us grow and succeed, despite any weaknesses. And when the session was over, I felt a little sad and impatient to return to camp. The following year of camp was even more incredible, but sadly my last summer as a camper. I promised myself that, one day, I would return…as a counselor.

In 2013, I was selected to become a LIT, a special program for former campers to learn skills to become the new counselors of tomorrow. I instantly accepted. It changed me and my approach with others. If the experience as a camper helped me to open myself again, the one as a LIT allowed me to put aside the limits we set for ourselves in letting our emotions out. So amazing!

But all of this would never have happened if I didn't choose to give that mysterious camp a try. So, to everyone reading this: don't limit yourself only because you don't know how it will be. Just get in the game! Don't worry if the result is not as expected. What's important is you keep an open mind and try your best. Buona fortuna!

Umberto Mascheroni
Como, Italy
Former Camper, Counselor

I was born with Hypoplastic Left Heart Syndrome which means the left side of my heart didn't develop. Because of my heart condition, I was able to go to camp. It's the best camp on earth. I thought about it every day of the year. I thought about it when I was in the hospital receiving a heart transplant. I thought about the horses, pool and arts and crafts. I thought about Silly Olympics because I loved getting messy and having my face painted.

Camp is the best way to spend your summer – I promise! You meet your best friends, and you get to spend time with counselors that really care about you. I have never been somewhere where everyone loves you so unconditionally, and once you realize how rare that is, you don't want to leave camp!

The biggest lesson I learned at camp was personal independence. In addition to learning to manage my health, I learned I was ultimately responsible for the quality of my life. I hope to go back to camp next summer and volunteer because I love kids and want to welcome them to their home.

Jori Hall
Hahira, GA
Former Camper

I am a Camper for Life

I was nervous because it was my first day as a counselor. As a former camper of six years, this was a big deal for me. When I was 11 years old and diagnosed with ovarian cancer, camp gave me everything and more. After chemotherapy, I never felt like I had friends at school that I could talk to without them staring at my bald head or playing twenty questions about my diagnosis. It started to make me feel isolated. In 2007, I experienced my first session at camp. For the first time since my diagnosis, I didn't feel like the girl with cancer, but as myself again. Going to camp was the one week of the year I would count down the days in excitement. Now, as a counselor, my goal was to give my campers what my counselors gave me. I wanted to be that person where a camper could say "because of you, I never gave up."

For opening campfire, campers take a stick out of a bucket that a past camper has written a wish on. We share some of the wishes, and when each cabin is dismissed for lights out, they throw the past campers' wishes into the campfire. At the end of the session, they then write their wishes for future campers to do the same. When the past campers' wish sticks were passed out, one of my girls tapped me on the shoulder and asked what her stick said. It said, "to find amazing companionships." When I explained to her companionship meant friendships, she looks up at me with the biggest smile and told me, "I've already made ten, plus all my counselors."

Without camp, I would have never found confidence in myself, my desire to become a child life specialist, and, most of all, the amazing friendships I never thought could exist. I could work at camp forever, and still not be able to say how thankful I am for them changing my life. I do not think I could even imagine a lifetime without camp, because without camp, I would not be who I am today.

Cassandra Milham
Franklin, OH
Former Camper, Counselor

Illness Does Not Define Me

At the age of twelve, I became really sick and was diagnosed with Ulcerative Colitis. While I was in the hospital, I met a girl who had Crohn's Disease. We both were discharged, and I thought that I would never see her again. The next summer of 2006, I went to a Crohn's and Colitis picnic. At the picnic a girl told me that she had gone to an "awesome camp for kids who are just like us." My dad and I walked back to the car and I told him, "I have to go. I want to meet other kids who are just like me!". Next thing I knew, I was getting on the bus to go to camp, crying, because I had never been away from my parents since getting diagnosed. Lo and behold, the same girl I had met in the hospital sat down next to me.

We flew from Arizona to camp! I was amazed when we drove into the camp gates. The counselors were jumping up and down, screaming and yelling "WELCOME." I was so happy. The week at camp changed my life. They understood what it was like to constantly be in the hospital and feel alone in having a disease where a toilet becomes your best friend. Camp inspired me to have a positive outlook on life. I learned to believe that my illness was a part of me, but does not define me. I continued to go to camp year after year. I cried every time we drove out the gates at the end of the week, and counted down the days until I could go back the following year.

Camp has helped shaped me into the person I am today. I am humbled to have been able to experience the camp magic, as well as help bring it to the children who now attend as campers. As I graduate from nursing school in the Spring, I can't wait for the day to be able to go back and work at camp as a camp nurse. I never thought I would come to grasp with having a chronic illness, but because of camp, I am happy that I get to call the toilet my best friend.

Theresa Maloney
Omaha, NE
Former Camper, Counselor

I started attending camp at 9 years old when I was diagnosed with Class 2 Lupus Nephritis. I remember one year in particular when my counselors planned for us to "sneak out" of the cabin after lights out. I was in a wheelchair due to my arthritis, and I remember our counselors tell us that if anyone saw us, we had to pretend to be trees and no one would see us. We made it to the end of our sidewalk when one of the head counselors appeared in the street. In terror, we all froze like trees pretending it was normal for trees to be in the middle of the street. She finally left and we continued on our mission. The plan was to make cookies in the kitchen, and we were not going to be stopped.

Later, when the cookies were almost completely done, we were cleaning up. Our counselor on watch showed up a little too late with the camp director who didn't look happy. She said, "What are you girls doing out of bed?" Without skipping a beat, one of the girls holding a broom said, "We were just cleaning!"

Camp has been my family and my greatest support group. They have taught me that there is always someone who understands what your going through when it feels like no one else does. I've come to the realization that life comes and goes. It's not something to take for granted because you don't know how much time you have left. All of the campers I've met have grown up a lot quicker than the kids I graduated from school with. Camp was the only place we could just be kids and not worry about what other people thought. We didn't have to worry about people judging us for our swollen faces or lack of hair. Everyone just understood. We were a family.

Tessa Shoemaker
Lake Wales, FL
Former Camper

Camp means everything to me. It means home. It means love. It means magic. It is the place where I found the Irene I was, the Irene I am and the Irene I want to be. It is a little piece of heaven. I still remember every single name of every single person I met. I still remember every single smile and every single act of kindness from all the campers and the staff I spent that session with. My life was changed and since the very first time I stepped on camp, I fell in love with it. I had so much fun encouraging others, doing all the activities and trying to improve my skills that it was so clear to me: "I will come back as a counselor."

And the magic of camp made my dreams come true: I became a volunteer interpreter, and I tried to give a bit of what I received, even though I know there's not enough time on earth to give back everything I was given. Being a camper was great but being a counselor is amazing. I can see myself in every kid I have the honor to share camp with, and I become a piece of the big, fun puzzle of their memories forever. I feel blessed to experience this opportunity. I feel blessed to see the big beautiful smiles they have during camp and I feel blessed to hear, "I want to come back and become a counselor as you did." This is the magic of camp.

Irene García Burguillo
Madrid, Spain
Former Camper, Counselor

Magical Nostalgia

Magical: the one word that perfectly sums up camp in a nutshell. My home away from home. The most magical place on Earth. Where fairies roam, little girls can be princesses every day, and boys can be inducted into knighthood. Campers live the dream every moment of being in this surreal bubble where no harm will come to them. For just one week, they can forget about their illness. For just one week, they learn that they may not be as different as they thought. For just one moment, they can be a normal kid.

Nostalgia: that is the feeling I get every moment I embark on a new journey on Brantley Branch Road. The destination is always the same: happiness, friendship, kindness, and love. The steps we take to get there do not take the same form, however. There are new faces, different backgrounds, different stories to tell. Yet, there will always be plenty of laughter, hugs, and familial bonds.

Camp is... the most magical place on earth. Camp is where you are loved for you, and where your illness does not define the person you are. Camp is forgetting about your sickness and troubles and realizing you are not alone in the world. Camp is cheering at the top of your lungs, dancing and laughing all day and night, and helping the campers have the best week of their lives. Camp is putting a smile on a camper's face who may not have smiled in a long time. Camp is intentional. Camp is treasuring the sweetness in life and spreading the smiles. Camp is family, love, kindness, hope, and my home away from home.

Leia Schwartz
Miami, FL
Former Camper, Counselor

If I had to list the most significant influences in my life, my camp counselors fall into the top five. For one week every summer, they made me feel as if I was the center of the universe. They searched for me in a sea of kids and asked if I wanted to play UNO, always letting me win. They let me have the best line in the skit that made the whole audience laugh. They showed me what being a leader means: responsibility, respect, love, friendship, courage, and honesty. They talked to me. They asked about my life, about school and my hobbies and health, about family and hurts and healing. They drew me out of the shell that otherwise would have become my home. And at the end of the day, they came to my bunk, gave me a hug and thanked me for being me. I desperately needed that. I very much needed to know that I mattered, that I counted. They made sure of it.

It is with these people that I was able to absorb the nature and beauty from all around. I could get away from all of the complications of the world, and take time to breathe. Cliques and barriers that would normally exist were nowhere to be found, and our conversations were always enthralling. I felt safe and loved, and when I am with those who care for me so much, I comfortably open up parts of myself that I normally feared to show to the rest of the world. They have given me all that I could ever need.

Catalina Bustamante
Temple Terrace, FL
Former Camper

My Forever Camp

When I first arrived at with my family, I thought it would be a rustic campsite with tents, lanterns, cooking by the fire, etc. After checking in, we were taken to our sleeping quarters: a huge log cabin! It was so beautiful with a handicapped accessible entrance, a big screened-in front porch with rocking chairs and cupboards filled with various games. The cabin had hardwood floors and beds with handmade afghans and teddy bears on each. My wheelchair could spin in circles, without hitting anything! My counselor was there when I arrived at the cabin. She was so pretty, kind, fun loving, intelligent, who I trusted and loved immediately!

The medical staff and counselors volunteered for the entire weekend, so a camper like me, along with my family, could have a chance to encounter an experience I will never forget. Days away from chronic illness and pain, to live free, be loved and cared for. Laughing until you cry, making friends for a lifetime, experiencing stories shared in group settings with the medical experts and helping parents learn more about our condition. With my counselor and sister, we did woodshop, painting, fishing, archery, swimming, performing on stage, playing in the gymnasium, horseback riding, and the Saturday night dance, to just be a kid.

How do I begin to say thank you to all of the people who allowed me the privilege to share the camp experience, at no cost? The experience of camp changed my life and will forever hold a special place in the deepest part of my heart.

Jaclyn S. DeCarlo
Palm Harbor, FL
Former Camper

In 2010, I was no longer attending as a regular camper, but instead as a leadership camper, otherwise known as a LC. This was going to be a new experience for me because I would also be attending a different session than the one I attended as a camper in a new role. There were many thoughts going through my head about what to expect and if I was going to like it or not. All of those thoughts were quickly put to rest as soon as we drove through the front gate. As the week started I didn't know any of my fellow cabin mates, and by the time we left on departure day we were all best friends. The counselors went above and beyond to make the week so special, which they did by serving us breakfast in bed, sleeping under the stars on the dining hall porch, and giving us the opportunity to grow and develop our leadership skills.

A prominent memory of this week is when we were coming back into the cabin after nighttime activities, and I decided to growl at one of the counselors who was holding the door. It scared her and she accidentally cursed in front of us. We, on the other hand, thought it was the best thing ever and having just learned about incident reports earlier in the day, we jokingly threatened that we would report her. For the rest of the night, myself and one other LC hid in cubbies around the cabin, jumping out at her whenever she passed, all in good fun. It is one of my best memories from camp and whenever I think of it a huge smile comes across my face. The counselors made camp so special that year and motivated me even more to continue to grow each year until I eventually could become a summer staff member.

Katie Griffith
Overland Park, KS
Former Camper, Counselor

Nothing is Impossible, I'M possible

My last time as a camper, I was most looking forward to the Tower: a 42 ft. high rock wall. When it was my turn to go, I climbed more than halfway before things got... difficult. I didn't believe I could finish. My arms were shaking and my hands were so sweaty, I could barely hang on. I looked up at the counselor and one of my friends who were already on top of the platform, and I told them that I couldn't do it. The counselor told me that I could, I was so close to reaching the top. Again, I told her that I couldn't do it. From below, one of my counselors yelled up at me to remember that, "Nothing is impossible, I'M possible!" and to think about all the hugs I would get when I finished. She gave me enough courage to climb a little higher and, as I did so, everyone cheered louder. But, again, I got scared. I looked back up at the counselor and my friend and I told them that I couldn't hang on. So the counselor told me to just let go. She said that I wouldn't fall, that I'd be okay. Carefully and slowly I let go and just hung there. As soon as I realized I wouldn't fall, I started climbing until I reached the top. And when I looked down and saw everyone cheering I felt so good about myself.

The next challenge was the zip line. Thankfully, it only took 10 seconds of courage to just jump. There was no going back. It felt like I was flying. I was actually feeling a mix of excitement and fear. Once I finally was back down on the ground, everyone formed a big hug circle around me!

Life is like that Tower. You cannot look down or look back, you have to just keep moving up and pushing yourself or you'll never get anywhere. And you always need friends to help and encourage you. But my camp friends are more than that, we're all a family and we don't give up on one another. They certainly never gave up on me.

Katie Borschel
Monticello, FL
Former Camper

It's hard to describe what camp is like because it's so magical, and words can't do the experience justice. Camp is a place that reminds us that it's never too late to become who we thought that we might have been before we got sick. Outside of camp, we're told that we're different and asked why we can't just go back to the way things were before our treatment. We're still struggling to find our new normal whether that's six months or six years later. We aren't the same people as we were before illness, which is very difficult for many people to understand. Our illnesses aren't just a dot on our lives' timelines because they continue to affect us psychosocially and cognitively long after treatment ends.

The friends that we make at camp understand what that feels like. We are provided with the opportunity to open up about how treatment has affected our everyday lives without judgment. It was the first place outside of the hospital where I met people my age dealing with the same obstacles, fears, and experiences. They too had experienced effects of treatment. There, relearning how to walk, talk, and rest from fatigue is the norm. We're all on the same page.

Alex McCarter
Enterprise, AL
Former Camper

Safe, Respected and Loved

I had been to twelve family weekends, but never summer camp because of my complex medical condition. After discussing it with the camp doctor, they let me try a week.

I was unpacking in my cabin with my counselors and mom on arrival day. As my mom was leaving, I started crying my eyes out. It was the first time I had ever spent the night away from my mom. My counselors and cabin mates, who I barely knew, started hugging and reassuring me. They all created this beautiful hug over me. I knew I would be safe, respected and loved.

Throughout the week, I really bonded with one of my counselors. We would sit together at every meal, talk forever, and laugh. That counselor was special to me because I could tell she cared about me. I felt like I had known her my whole life. It was like having the big sister I never had. A Camp Big Sister! I knew she was the kind of person I would want to be like as I got older.

When I was reunited with my mom, I told her that she was my favorite counselor I ever had. Later that day when I was home and unpacking, I found a note in my suitcase from that counselor, telling my how much I meant to her and how I affected her life. I broke down in tears because I had also written her a similar note and left it on the porch of our cabin.

Camp is so special to me because it's the one place in the world where I can be 100% myself. It's a place where people don't judge me for my illness. The counselors and other campers love me unconditionally. I can just be a kid. Not a kid in the hospital. Not the kid who has a condition, but a normal kid.

Nina Marino
Clearwater, FL
Former Camper

The Last Night of Camp

It was my first year at camp after being diagnosed with Liver Cancer. On the last night of the session, we went to a special place in the woods called Sue Lila Hollow where you can leave a stone with a loved one's name who has passed away. I loved to wander along and see all of the names of the campers that came before us. The stones were not a memorial, but a testimony to the part of them that they left at camp. There were blankets set up for us to sit on and string lights on the trees. It looked magical.

Each counselor spent time talking to us about how we are here for a purpose and how much we had inspired them. Then came a specific counselor named Kayla. She shared with us how she had leukemia several years prior, which I didn't know until that night. She told us that we are strong, and we can do anything we put our minds to! At that time, I was in the trenches of chemotherapy and radiation. My mortality and morbidity were constantly on my mind. That evening gave me hope for the future THAT I would have a future. Needless to say there wasn't a dry eye to be seen!

That evening still gives me chills when I think about it. This is my favorite and most inspiring moment at camp out of the years I was a camper. I hope to become a counselor there in the future and impact campers like my counselors did.

Nicole Keller
Bentonville, AR
Former Camper

There is nothing better in the world than camp. Camp is a million things, but overall, camp is spirited. That is a huge understatement. Camp is filled with more smiles, laughs and cheers than most people even dream of. There is no judgment, no insecurities, no negativity.

People in the real world often look upon kids with chronic illnesses with pity or disgust or oddly enough, envy. Children in one breath are sighing how unfortunate we are and in the next breath saying we are more fortunate than them because we get to experience camp. But, in all honesty, the stories I tell of camp are not true adventures. Yes, the generic outline of archery and canoeing and woodshop are all true, but I always leave out the parts about the genuine elation that I felt in that moment. You may be wondering why, and truthfully, I have no idea.

I think it may have to do with the fact that so much has been taken from me because of illness. Things like school, extra-curricular activities, even friends. I feel that if I were to keep my genuine feelings a secret, for just a second I can turn to life and say, "You can't take that from me".

For a true example of this spirit, this positivity, I don't have to think very hard to find one. The cabins at camp are aligned in two rows down a long street. The camp came up with the very original name of "cabin row." Much happens on cabin row. Much.

My cabin, the Yellow 10 Dream Team, had all tried and fell in love with the cereal "Honey Smacks" at breakfast one day. When we finished a full box of them, we stuck the box on a portable flagpole and paraded it down cabin row chanting "Hon-ey Smacks, Hon-ey Smacks." The feeling I had in that moment was indescribable. Hilarious. The best part was, by the end of the camp session, the whole camp was chanting "Hon-ey Smacks."

Lindsey Valenti
Tampa, FL
Former Camper

Before I came to camp I felt like the weird sick kid. I would always received strange looks when I was in a wheelchair or had my nasogastric tube. But then I went to camp and there were hundreds of kids just like me being themselves and not worrying about people. It was incredible. Throughout my first week at camp I began to change. There was something special going on. We, the campers, began sharing about ourselves and began to form close personal bonds, bonds that can never be made with people who haven't been through the traumatic experiences we all had experienced.

These kids knew what hospitals were all about and the exhaustion one feels after traveling to and from different hospitals for treatments.

They knew what being sick meant, not just flu sick, but sick for weeks and months. So sick that each day seems like it is becoming just another brick on a road that appears never-ending to a faraway gray future.

These people understood sadness, yet they all gave off such a light that even though we were all relating our conditions, it was impossible to be melancholy for too long. The great thing about our cabin is that we lifted each other up.

By the end of our week, I became attached to everyone, from the campers to our understanding counselors. Here was a group of people my age that could empathize as best as anyone could about what had happened to me. For the first time I could share with people, beyond my family, who could really understand. It was the experience of a lifetime.

Sami Steers
Wesley Chapel, FL
Former Camper

Chapter VII

YOU'VE GOT A FRIEND

A Beary Special Boy

The last night of camp is always heart wrenching for me, especially when a little boy from a difficult home situation comes up to me with tears in his eyes saying he doesn't want to go home. This has happened more times than I would like to recall. This week was no different.

We had a little boy in our cabin named Jayden. He was too cute, with little cornrows in his hair and the softest voice I have ever heard. Camp always gives each camper a handmade afghan and stuffed bear to take home with them. Jayden was so surprised at this. When I found 5 extra bears, I gave them to him. He promptly named each one with a "J" name...James, Johnson, Jonathan, George (with a J) and Johnny.

Each night he would line them up in his bed and console them. He never left the cabin without telling them he would be right back and not to worry. I did the same thing as a little boy, so I started to chat with all the bears. Jayden asked me if they talked to me. I said, "Sure" and he beamed like we belonged to the same club.

On camper departure day, I NEVER walk them to the bus, but today, Jayden grabbed my hand so we walked to the bus with me trying to contain myself all the way. When he stepped up on the first step, he stopped and looked at me. Then he proceeded to give me a string off of his tumbleweed around his neck as a way to say thank you. I had to bite the inside of my cheek to not show any emotion. How can one heart be so filled with joy at any given moment, then be totally ripped apart by the actions of one little boy with cornrows in his hair? Such is the price one pays to play with the greatest kids on earth! BEST CAMP ON EARTH!

Mista Bill Vessier
Orlando, FL
Counselor

I was sitting in the dining hall one day getting ready for lunch when I felt a tap on my shoulder. Someone was trying to get my attention. That someone was Ethan, a camper I had met a few months ago at a family weekend. Ethan and I had hung out for a little bit and even performed a couple of skits together. Needless to say, it was the beginning of a beautiful friendship.

This day, Ethan wanted to give me something. Ethan pulled a piece of wood from his pocket with a piece of yarn attached to it. I smiled, it looked like a name tag, and sure enough, I was right. As he handed over my name tag, he started to tell a story.

Ethan told me how my new name tag had been cut from a bigger piece that was originally in the shape of a heart. He wanted me to know that the wooden heart represented his own heart, and that there were other counselors and fellow campers receiving "pieces of his heart." He wanted me to have my piece to remember our friendship and memories we shared together through camp. It was his hope that one day, pieces of his heart would come back together and be reunited.

I was speechless. I managed to say a thank you, give Ethan a hug and a high five before he went on to make someone else's day brighter. I still carry that name tag around. It carries with it a beautiful story of a thoughtful, kind heart who continued to give selflessly. I am reminded everyday that small acts of kindness make a huge difference.

Linh Nguyen, RN
Jacksonville, FL
Counselor

I have a chronic, incurable illness that I've been dealing with for over 16 years now. Since I have such a rare illness, I actually didn't think I'd be chosen for camp.

My first favorite memory is sitting in the circle with fellow campers and counselors. I immediately felt safe, accepted and loved. Those are feelings I wasn't used to feeling at all. I was used to being alone with my illness and emotions.

As the campers and counselors introduced themselves and told parts of their stories, I cried. A counselor named Patty held my hand and as I cried harder she took me into her arms and held me for most of the evening. I was in a safe place with other young people who had faced great struggle and death. I didn't realize until that moment, just how much I needed that safe space to cry and be comforted in. I sat among counselors who wanted so much for us to have a normal, happy week, that they gave of their own time, year after year, many for 10+ years.

Camp helped me find ways to love, cherish and appreciate even on the hardest days. In that week, the campers and counselors helped me relearn to trust good people. I'll always be grateful for my time at camp.

Gillian Trumbull
Chicago, IL
Former Camper

The summer of 2008, I finished my freshman year of college and decided to work at a camp for children with Muscular Dystrophy. That was where I met Jack. He was a wise-cracking 13 year old boy who had a heart of gold. He was such a jokester and began talking so much smack about all the camp games that we were going to play within 30 minutes of him arriving at camp. I immediately came up with the nickname "All-Star" for him, and everybody in camp called him that. In fact, some people, by the end of camp, had forgotten his real name because he was All-Star to them.

Jack and I had an amazing time connecting. We shared our stories with each other and grew from our combined experiences. At the point, I was still contemplating my major for college. My time at camp with him was extremely influential in my decision to work hard, to become a physician and to help as many kids as I can through the medical field. I've always believed in a holistic approach to practicing medicine, where patients are unique and the symptoms affecting the soul and mind are as important as those affecting the body. Camp is a place that supports this philosophy. It focuses on possibilities over fears. It offers an atmosphere of "team" to caring for kids. That's the real difference."

My friendship with Jack continues to teach me. A physician is obligated to continue to check on their patients until their job is done. I've been checking on Jack as a friend for the past 7 years, and he is doing great! Being friends with this amazing guy even benefitted my bedside manners all these years later. I did not realize just how rewarding camp would be.

Evan Layton
Bradenton, FL
Counselor

Due to the fact that they shared the same name, we all referred to them simply as "The Shelbys." The Shelby's had just walked by in a group of smiling faces and waved to me as if their arms were going to fall off. I quickly generated a smile and waved back, but my heart sank as they disappeared from view. It was almost the end of the summer. I was tired, dirty, and just plain feeling low. I was in my favorite place in the world. I should have been happy. I knew that. But having that knowledge didn't seem to change anything. I tried giving myself a mental shake. I knew I needed to snap out of it and remember that I was there for all of the kids.

In the meantime, though, I saw nothing wrong in leaving the office. I did some wandering and was about to give up, when I spotted someone familiar standing on the trail. It was one of the Shelbys. She was with her counselor and looked terrified. As I drew closer, I could hear her rapid, shallow breaths and see her tear-stained face. She couldn't breathe, and my heart skipped a beat.

Quickly, I drew my arm around her and encouraged her to take slower, deeper breaths. A medical staff member arrived and began to assess her. I held her hand the entire time. It was determined that she was simply hyperventilating. She was given a paper bag and told to breath into it. Eventually, her breathing leveled and we both began to relax.

The doctor commented that it seemed like we were awfully close and that she was lucky I had been there. "I know," she responded, "she's like my big sister. She'll always be there for me."

After Shelby settled into the dining hall with her friends, I knew my week was going to be great. I hadn't lost the chance to be with my favorite campers. And I had a unique opportunity to impact even more kids now that she had helped me remember what was important.

Elizabeth Barnes
Cincinnati, OH
Counselor

An Eye for An Eye

After three years at camp, there is still one story that stands out to me and resonates the true meaning of camp. In the summer of 2012, it was clean-up time after a delicious lunch. As I walked over to the counter to grab the vinegar-water spray we use to wipe down the tables, I saw a younger camper pointing a spray bottle at her eyes. I frantically started running over and yelling "NO NO NO," but before I could make it over she had sprayed herself.

I immediately crouched down and asked her if she was okay. With teary eyes she looked at me and nodded. I then asked why she did this? She pointed at her friend behind me, who I had not yet noticed. This selfless camper then proceeded to tell me that she had accidentally sprayed her friend in the eyes with the vinegar-water; as an apology she had turned the bottle and sprayed herself.

As I walked these little girls back to their counselor and told her what had happened I thought about the meaning behind this action. All campers including these two little girls have a very special interpretation of camp—to them camp does not just mean archery or swimming; instead it means acceptance, of one another and of ourselves. The love and kindness campers show one another is incomparable to anywhere else. These children inherently understand one another and what the other has been through; whether they are comparing heart surgery scars at the pool or discussing chemotherapy medications that they hate. I think this is the magic of camp: an unspoken tolerance and unconditional love that drives our campers to form lasting friendships and even spray themselves with vinegar-water, just to feel what their cabin mate is feeling. I saw these two campers this past summer and both were thick as thieves bonded by their experiences at camp, and in life.

Emily Farmer
Oakton, VA
Counselor, Unit Leader

An Unforgettable Bond

In my three years as a camp counselor, I always strived to create an atmosphere that would allow my campers to build friendships that would be remembered long after the tie-dye faded on their new t-shirts and many years after their time at camp. I wanted my campers to connect with each other and feel a sense of acceptance that is not always possible in the world outside of camp.

It was the first session of the summer, and the five campers in my den instantly clicked. The chemistry that was present between these five girls was something that all camp counselors dream about and hope for in their den. They wanted to do everything together. It was a week full of laughter, inside jokes, and memories that I still carry with me today.

The last night of camp arrived, and the girls were sitting in a circle on the den floor playing a card game. One of the girls then stated, "I have Sickle Cell." One by one the girls started to reply that they also had Sickle Cell. These five girls had already formed a strong relationship with each other, but upon discovering that each girl in the den was like them and went through the same daily struggles, their bond deepened.

Camp was a place for these girls to meet others with a similar story. It was a place that allowed them for a week to be accepted, forget about their illness, and to create memories and friendships that they still carry to this day. It was rewarding to see the "aha" moment happen for them and for them to instantly feel a sense of belonging that they aren't alone in their journey.

Erin Harris
Campbellsville, KY
Counselor

Barry's bald head and ashen pallor of his skin were evidence of his struggle against cancer. Instead of spending the summer romping, exploring and discovering, Barry was in the battle of his life, literally for his life. The camp staff had coordinated with Barry's doctors to provide a week of respite in between chemo, if Barry did his part to stay as healthy as possible. This included drinking a milky-white liquid that resembled dissolved chalk. I was in the infirmary while this brave boy made attempts at swallowing the vile-tasting liquid.

Barry nursed his drink, his tongue occasionally dipping in for a quick visit. I tried my tricks from "How much can you swallow while I stand on one foot?" to red licorice up my nose and the cry of "Nosebleed!" Nothing helped. The liquid remained unmoved, as unmoved as Barry's wilting spirits. Then the cavalry arrived.

One boy, not astride a palomino, but rather riding a chair, wheeled himself over. Dante could not help but see what was going on. After introducing himself, he stated, "I've been where you've been. I had to drink that stuff too. It works. Look how much bigger I am than you. I know how it tastes, but I also KNOW you can drink it so you can grow older and bigger."

Barry inhaled, let it out and sucked in the nutrition booster. He then walked to the lobby to brag to the nurse about his achievement and hop on the scale to see if he had gained any weight.

I turned to Dante and asked his age. I said I was decades older, larger, and louder. Yet, it was he who had been so powerful to give this younger boy the strength to move past the fear. Dante looked at me and said, "Any time you need me, Pun, just let me know."

For years, Barry has returned to camp, healthy and happy. Dante comes with me, in my heart, forever ten, forever a source of strength.

Pun Forphun
Studio City, CA
Counselor

A magical moment of my summer at camp happened during the Hemophilia session! There was such brotherly love and solidarity between the boys who made camp their home! Working with the youngest boys this week was amazing not just for themselves but because we got to pair up with the "Big Brothers of Green 2" who became family and mentors to our little guys. They were 15 and 16 year old boys who showed incredible leadership. They helped us make a flag and offered to teach us to play chess. When one of our little guys was unable to make it to ropes course with our cabin, all we had to do was ask the older boys, and he was warmly welcomed into their cabin for the morning!

I saw magic happen when I walked into the oldest boys' camper room. Our youngest camper, Easton, was sitting on the top bunk looking down and chatting to all the big boys with a wrist full of friendship bracelets and a giant smile on his face! Easton sat at breakfast the next morning with his "Big Brothers." When asked later that day what he enjoyed most, without a second of hesitation, Easton said, "Hanging out with my big brothers of Green 2!

Camp really brings out the best in people. Those boys will grow to be incredible leaders because they have been surrounded by inspiring role models at camp, and the cycle will continue to the next generation of campers. They truly are Blood Brothers!

Amy Boyd Lyons
Dublin, Ireland
Counselor

When people think of magic moments happening at camp, arts and crafts isn't usually the first place that they think of. In the summer of 2014, I was lucky enough to have the opportunity to work in arts and crafts. While I saw magic happen in little ways everyday, one moment in particular stands out to me.

This particular morning we had our oldest campers with us. Each of the campers was working on creating a gift for a youngest camper who they had been paired with as buddies. This was one opportunity throughout the day where the campers had the chance to socialize as a larger group and not just with their cabins, so many of them gravitated towards their friends, but not Carter.

Carter was a special camper. While he had friends at camp and was well liked by his cabin, he also seemed to always be looking out for other campers who might be struggling. While working on their projects, I noticed one of the girls sitting alone and struggling to complete her piece of art for her buddy. I started to make my way over to her in order to give her a little extra support but before I could get to her, Carter was already there. Just like a counselor might do, Carter jumped in and asked her if he could help her. He spent the majority of the morning helping her to complete her project. Carter easily could have hung out with his friends or let a counselor handle the situation but he chose to embrace the spirit of camp and support someone else in the camp family.

Camp is a magical place where putting others' needs and happiness at the same level of importance as your own is second nature. It's a beautiful to see kids care for each other in ways that most adults don't even know how to do. At camp, we are lucky enough to see that every single day.

Gabby Chesney
Durham, NH
Counselor

Dribbling

It was my first summer, my first week, my first day at this unique camp. I didn't know what to expect and had no idea what I would gain from this unfamiliar experience. Volunteering was a new thing for me, something I had never taken the chance to do.

On the first morning of camp, I was sent to the gym for "Morning Manatee" with a few of my campers expecting to help them expend a little energy before breakfast. After a few minutes of playing with my campers, I noticed in the corner a little 8-year-old girl attempting to dribble a basketball. Samantha was the most adorable little thing with little sprouts of hair growing back from the Cancer treatment she had previously. I ventured over to help her out but eventually just sat next to her and counted how many consecutive dribbles she could do. Starting at a record of 4, Samantha kept surpassing her previous record with more excitement each and every time. When she finally got to 20 it was like we had won the super bowl; the smile on her face was unforgettable.

Eventually the day went on until lunch time where we had the web of kindness. The web of kindness is an opportunity to publicly thank people for anything they might have done. Last in line was the little girl I had played basketball with. Samantha was handed the microphone and spoke into it these words that I will never forget, "I want to thank Ean for being my friend." I was at a loss of words, completely shocked. This little girl that I had hardly done anything for or even known more then 24 hours had thanked me for being her friend. It was there and then that I realized what a magical place I had come to. My life was changed by Samantha as she helped me to realize what true happiness feel like.

Ean Phillips
Gainesville, FL
Counselor

How do you even begin to tell a story about camp... A magical place that defines beauty, strength, bravery, and enough laughter to make your belly ache. Even as years pass, camp memories are just as vivid as the afternoon rainbows that cast across the summer skies of Florida.

When I first arrived at camp as a summer counselor, I came with the anticipation that I was here for the kids and to ensure they had the best time of their lives. I had no idea of the type of impact these kids and this place would have on my life. I knew camp was fun. I knew camp was exciting. I knew camp was silly. What I didn't know, was that camp truly is a living, breathing creature. It inhales the excitement of bags being packed and unpacked and re-packed deep in its lungs and exhales something so pure and so wonderful that no words can truly, ever describe.

Recently, I had the pleasure of hosting a fellow camp counselor at my house for a night. Mind you, I had not seen her since my counselor days over 7 years ago. My husband asked me, "How do you know this girl? You haven't seen her in years... Do you know her well enough for her to stay here?" Without hesitation, I smiled at him and firmly responded, "Yes, she's a camp friend."

As simple as my response was, it was all that was needed to be said. No matter how many years had gone by or how far the distance, the bond of being at camp is undeniable and completely unexplainable. What we share as counselors with these amazing kids is inspiring and brings a nostalgic smile to my face when I think back to those sunny days on cabin row. My heart will forever beat at Camp.

Charlotte Dang Kemp
Lake Mary, FL
Counselor

I always hope that my campers have fun at camp. I do everything I can to make sure they have the time of their lives and leave doing everything they want to do – even if it's jumping off of the diving board 100 times, making 57 bracelets in the arts and crafts cabin or never napping during rest time. Because for one week, they get to be normal and I want them to have it all and live it up to the fullest.

And while everyone appears to be having fun and there are lots of smiles and happiness and joy, you sometimes never know exactly how much camp means to these kids. Until the last day of camp a couple of years ago – that's when I knew.

Everybody was leaving, everybody was saying goodbye. Camp was over, the buses were loading, we were doing one last once-over of the cabin to be sure that no stray necklace or flip-flop was left behind. I heard a little voice from several yards behind me saying, "Miss Lauren, Miss Lauren!" And I turned around, and it was one of my campers, running as fast as she could toward me and sobbing hysterically. "I'm just going to miss you so much! I just had so much fun at camp! I'm going to miss you so much!"

And of course, I started crying right alongside my six-year-old friend. She was crying because she didn't want to leave. She had so much fun that she wasn't ready to go home. And while I never like to see kids crying, it hit me right then and there exactly what camp does and means for these kids.

For a week, we give them fun, friends, understanding and normalcy. We make them feel special. They don't get funny looks because they have cancer. Their bald heads, wheelchairs, scars, chemo pills – it's all just part of being a kid. And in that week – everybody is happy and everyone's life changes for the better, especially mine.

Lauren Moskowitz
Charlotte, NC
Counselor

Mason had to be catheterized at a certain time every night, and was insistent that it be at that time. His routine lasted about an hour and a half, and involved either a nurse or counselor pumping water into his catheter via a syringe. Most people would expect these evening procedures to be sensitive or even awkward. However, it was during those times that I got to know Mason so well.

He was a big fan of country music and an even bigger fan of NASCAR. We would sit there talking about Jimmie Johnson, or sing our hearts out to Scotty McCreery. We enjoyed our time together that week at camp, from arts and crafts, bowling, and racing on the NASCAR simulator. But of all the memories, it's the ones sitting with him, that I'll remember most. In a moment of vulnerability, Mason rose above and didn't let it affect the REAL Mason, who I thankfully got to know.

Camp expresses a respect and acceptance of many different levels of ability and talent, and fosters a climate in which each person can explore his own gifts, which sometimes had gone unnoticed. Out of all the campers, Mason is the one I'll remember the best.

Kevin Clark
Charleston, SC
Counselor

"Living the dream," Cade shouted in his raspy, exhausted 9-year-old voice, still wearing his Alpha Dog tags as he lay in his hospital bed, still fighting for his life. It was the first time Cade had spoken in a week and it was, without question, the most powerful three words I had ever heard, bringing us both back to the week we shared, months earlier, at camp.

A week themed as Camp University, Cade and his fellow seven 9-year-old cabin mates, all battling cancer, were pledging the Alpha Dogs to be brothers for life. It was Cade's first time at camp and because of brain surgery a week prior, he couldn't participate in every activity, unless he was wearing a shower cap. Cade was not a fan of having to be the only kid at camp to wear a shower cap, and fortunately, neither were his brothers. Forever seared into my memory were the actions of Cade's cabin mates, who vowed to be their brother's keeper by refusing to allow Cade to wear a shower cap alone. Amazingly, every time Cade put on a shower cap, all of camp followed.

Thousands of shower caps later, as the week ended, we initiated our boys as brothers for life, giving them their well-deserved Alpha Dog tags, hoping it would serve as a reminder that as an Alpha Dog, you are your brother's keeper and are always living the dream.

As our visit came to an end, Cade spoke through the pain once again. "Aho, Aho, Aho" he bellowed, picking up his paralyzed right arm to do our handshake one last time, proving to his mom he was an Alpha dog, proving to the world the power of brotherhood.

Cade's story and spirit lives on through the men of Phi Tau, who learned of his wish to one-day join a fraternity and decided to make him an honorary brother. If you ask any Phi Tau brother "how they're doing," I can guarantee you they're "Living the dream."

Evan English Ernst
Tallahassee, FL
Counselor

Camp food. I speculate that most campers, counselors, volunteers, and visitors probably won't write home or spend too much time remembering what they ate at camp, but hopefully they will remember who they ate with. For me, many of my most vivid memories from camp revolve around specific encounters or conversations with co-counselors and campers over late night snacks. The best part is, we weren't eating fancy international cuisine or items from a Michelin-rated restaurant menu; we were eating cereal, and we were eating it often.

After hours, the dining hall — which would, earlier in the day, be filled with wild laughter, high spirits, and hungry children — became a quiet, relaxing, and peaceful location for decompression and deep conversations with a camper that wasn't sleeping well, a co-counselor budding for medical school, or a friend just up late. This seemingly boring meal plan became synonymous with the richest experiences and conversations.

We became a pretty tight group of friends over these impromptu gatherings. At least once, the cereal showed up on nights when counselors were away from the central camp experience, and it was on those short adventures that the group grew tightest. The bond behind a box of Marshmallow Mateys became surprisingly strong.

Now, soon to be a decade after my camp counselor experience, as I sit and eat my cereal, I still think of the conversations I had with those unforgettable people. They are now my best friends and most exciting out-of-town visits.

To all the campers and counselors who didn't get to enjoy a "charmingly lucky" cereal experience that summer because the stock ran out early, please know that it wasn't eaten in haste.

Andrew P. Hill
Boston, MA
Counselor

I was only six weeks old when I first arrived at Camp with some boy named Mike D who kept calling me Irish...I would later learn this was my name. We both took a 10 hour trip from North Carolina, and by the looks and reactions of those there to greet us, I'd say they didn't know I was coming. Especially the one they called Dorcas, the Camp Director, who would call me fat and say my ears were crooked! This particular night I learned what love and home meant.

I didn't realize I would soon start training for a job. I was to be the next Camp Dog, a position that was currently held by a Golden Retriever named Guinness. I loved him! I could run between his legs, I could reach just high enough to lick his face, and I was the perfect height to sniff his...well, you know. Guinness led an activity at camp called the Dog Walk. It was so cool to watch him proudly walk down cabin row, followed by a group of children taking turns holding his leash. Soon that would be me!

My time had come. It was Saturday morning of a Family Weekend...basically the minor league of dog walking before the big time of summer camp. I couldn't even stand still. There was so much to look at, so many kids, and they all smelled amazing! We left the dining hall porch and made our way towards cabin row. With the camper who was assigned to walk me in tow, I ran ahead of everyone as fast as I could. First day on the job, and I must've been doing amazing! I could hear all the screams from the people behind yelling "IRISH!!!!" It was awesome! I knew I could make it around the circle faster if only I didn't have to drag this kid behind me. Every 50 feet there was a new smell, usually on the edge of the road, but occasionally I would head towards the woods to get a good whiff. Have you ever pulled a 60lb child over wet grass into a tree line? Let me just tell you, it's a real drag...pun intended!

Eventually, Dog Walks became part of my routine, and I was pretty good at it. There were those occasional moments a rabbit or deer would run by, or the time someone tied my leash to a camper's wheelchair while other kids were playing with a tennis ball in the distance...I mean...Hello? I'm a dog!

Outside of my dog walk duties...HA! I said doodies; I left a lot of those around camp too. Anyways, my days were filled with every dog's dream. I would roam leash free over the 280 acres. I would visit the nature barn and torment the baby pigs, watch the chickens freak out, then stroll to the horse barn and visit my big friends. I would catch some kids eating their lunch outside of the cafeteria and score a hot dog. On really hot days, my boy would "accidentally" leave the pool door open for me to take a quick dip. Camp installed a putt-putt course for the campers, with a waterfall that poured into a small pool just for me. I would lay in there for hours on a hot day.

I was the Camp Dog for 9 years. I don't know how many times I walked around that circle. I don't know how many campers held my leash, but I know I made a lot of friends. I know I made a difference to home-sick campers, or to the child who had the severe seizure on our walk, and I waited patiently by his side until he felt better. There was also the little girl who had trouble focusing on other activities, but really wanted to give me a bath. Year after year, the campers came back and they remembered my name, scratched my ears and rubbed my belly...proof that I was good at being The Camp Dog.

Now I'm 14, that's like 92 in dog years. I live in NC, but think of Camp all the time. When the kids down the road are laughing and playing in the sprinklers, my tail wags more than usual. There's an old pick-up truck that looks just like the one at camp. I bark like crazy every time I see it. Most of all, I think of all the brave campers. Most dogs at my age are probably scared of the end, but I know my dog walking days aren't over. There are a lot of campers that never made it back for another summer, and they're waiting to take me on another great walk, with lots of new smells, and hopefully a squirrel. My job is far from over. I am The Camp Dog.

Irish, The Camp Dog
Charlotte, NC
Typed by Mike Daly, Assistant Camp Director

One of my best memories at camp was the sleepover night. Our counselors had put all the mattresses in the center of the room under a parachute. We were getting ready to make butterscotch pancakes in the cabin. I was new to camp and still getting used to the fact that you could be sick and still be yourself. I was feeling sick but didn't want to miss out on pancakes in the cabin. This wasn't my first time that week I'd run off to a bathroom, and my new friend knew I was having stomach issues while I was hiding it from everyone else. For me it was the norm, but I knew it wasn't for everyone else.

My friend found me and exclaimed "pancakes!" and my stomach just lost it. My friend was amazing! She stayed with me and got help when it wouldn't stop. The nurse even came to the cabin with my meds to make it stop rather than making me miss the party. I was able to wait for my medicine to kick in and go back out where pancakes and laughter were awaiting me!

Why is this my favorite memory you might ask. Well, my friend was cool with the fact that I was feeling sick, entertained me and was kind about it while people outside camp would never understand. I LOVED all the activities at camp. I loved my counselors and the songs and the entire atmosphere. But the best part was being able to just be me, no judgment, to let my illness do what it does and still have a great time.

Lisa Simmons
Davie, FL
Former Camper

Tristan was a special camper that grabbed your heart from the start. He needed a lot of one-on-one attention from counselors, as he had Autism and a unique way of communicating, which included making sounds and using "words" from his own personal language. This made interaction with other campers very difficult for him. Tristan was usually found fleeing from indoor activities to run around outdoors. As his counselor, I happily followed along, finding these times to be the best times I was able to interact with Tristan and truly connect with him. These wonderful times constituted a large part of our day, since he was happier away from the more structured camp activities.

Near the middle of the week, during one of these unstructured times outside while the other campers went to arts and crafts, another camper, Gavin, and his counselor approached us. Like Tristan, Gavin often spent time outside and interacted only with his counselors. Tristan looked at Gavin, let out a playful screech, and took a huge jump. To our surprise, Gavin observed Tristan, then proceeded to repeat the same motions. Next, Tristan took two hops and made three silly noises, and Gavin again repeated him. We watched in awe for a hour as these two new friends, who found it so hard to relate to other campers, made circles around the courtyard, taking turns copying each other's noises and actions with little smiles on their faces. It was a time to appreciate the true beautiful nature of these children.

This is where the miracles are in camp. Sometimes it's in the smaller moments when a child interacts with another or finds someone who finally "gets" their world. This was why I came here, and this was why I believe in all that is camp. It provides friendships and love to all children, especially those who might struggle to find connections in other places.

Courtney Goldsbury
Carmel, IN
Counselor

We were walking back from the dinning hall after lunch and on our way to rest hour. I casually was talking about places that I like to Mackenzie, a 9 year old camper. I had mentioned that I love the beach. I then asked Mackenzie where her favorite place was. She said camp. Mackenzie said that her favorite place is camp because every time you come, you leave with a smile on your face and a new best friend. She has a lot of responsibility at home and hearing her say that she leaves with a smile and a best friend filled my heart with joy because I saw in her face how much she meant that sentiment. It surprised me that a girl who is so young could teach me a reason for camp.

In case you are wondering, Mackenzie left that week with a new best friend. They were hugging for about 30 minutes in the dinning hall and telling each other how happy they were to have met while the music was playing in the background before they were picked up to go home. It is amazing how close these campers can become in just 5 days and the love that they will spread when they go home especially since these girls were so young. Camp is… friendship and happiness and smiles for miles.

Alice Pauly
Gainesville, FL
Counselor

Take a Chance on Friendship

Sebastian was one of my very special campers who came to Skeletal Dysplasia week. His need for full-time care prevented him from staying overnight at camp, so his father rented a hotel room for the week nearby and dropped him off every morning and picked him up every night. The counselors and I wanted to make sure that even though he couldn't stay for the nights, that Sebastian felt like he was part of our cabin.

Well, our work was made easy because the other boys in the cabin started making up their own ways to make sure that Sebastian was an important part of their group. It all started with a shyer camper who befriended Sebastian, which set off a chain reaction and made it the cool thing to make up nicknames for Sebastian or cheer his name anytime they saw him. It was incredible to see how such young kids can come together, unprompted, and demonstrate what it means to make your environment an inclusive one.

At the end of the week during our Unit closing, Sebastian was sitting with me in the back of the big group gathering on the lawn. When the counselors who were leading the closing mentioned that camp is a place where you can make friends for a lifetime, my entire cabin came back to where we were sitting and made a circle around Sebastian and took turns giving him a hug.

The maturity and brotherhood that I witnessed between those boys made it one of the most special weeks of the summer. It was full of moments where I realized that even when we're the ones leading the songs and teaching them new skills, children will always teach us what can't be taught: the kindness that comes from budding friendships.

Molly Rohan
Chicago, IL
Counselor

187

Music gives a soul to the universe, wings to the mind, flight to the imagination and life to everything.

When I was eight years old, I went to a camp for children with Cancer for the first time. I was dancing to the music after breakfast one morning when the Chicken Dance came on. During the part of the song when you're supposed to swing a partner, I looked around and realized I didn't know anyone around me. There was a boy next to me who was probably 14, which at the time seemed incredibly old and grown up to me. Even though he was surrounded by his friends, he noticed that I didn't have a partner, so he took my arm and swung me around as a huge smile appeared on my face.

Camp always strives to make everyone feel safe, respected, and loved; that is exactly how I felt in that moment. He died a couple of years later, but I will never forget the gift of joy he gave me that morning when he looked away from his friends and instead towards a little girl without a partner during the Chicken Dance. Without meaning to, he touched my life. A little bit of him will live on inside of me forever.

Ally Mechling
Jacksonville, FL
Former Camper, Counselor

The Robot

It was the summer of 2006. My pride had really stressed going to the dance together, as a pride, so we all mingled while waking to the dining hall. I happened to strike up a conversation with this little firecracker, Aaliyah. I had laughed all week at how Aaliyah had more than 100 little plastic berets in her hair (trust me, we counted). We started talking about the berets, but within 15 seconds, we were talking about something completely different. Somewhere along the trail, Aaliyah told me how amazing she could do the robot, so I challenged her to a dance-off.

Two hours later, we had figured out how to do the robot to every song, regardless of genre or tempo. It was a moment that really stuck with me, but what really moved me was the following summer. Aaliyah walked in on arrival day, ran up to me, gave me a big hug, and called me "Mitchell." She called me the wrong name for the next three summers, but it didn't matter. I think I even preferred it that way.

Marshall Toy
Paducah, KY
Counselor

It was the summer of 2005 in the sweltering summer heat when my first camper, Landon, arrived. I'd generally been a quiet, introverted person the majority of my life but I took a leap by signing up for the entire summer as a cabin counselor. As Landon and his parents made their way into the cabin, I realized it was his first time at camp too. His parents made small talk with me about the activities we were planning to do, the other boys in his cabin, and what the food was like. Landon was quiet the entire time and had a worried look on his face. They helped him unpack and then decided it was time to leave. As soon as they left, he started to tear up, and I could tell this was going to be a hard week for him. It reminded me of my first time at camp. I cried when my parents left but then made friends with the campers and counselors and had an awesome time.

I took out some cards I had brought and asked if he wanted to play a card game. Landon wiped away a few of his tears and shook his head yes. We sat on the porch and played a variety of card games. At first it was me just talking and telling him all the cool things at camp he could do. Soon, Landon started to talk more and before you knew it, he was laughing and joking with me.

Throughout the week, if I could sense he was hitting a rough patch, I would pull out the deck of cards and start up a game with him. By the end of the week, Landon wasn't ready to leave camp when his parents came to pick him up – having made a lot of friends and having experienced a lot of fun! We had helped each other out unknowingly – Landon helped me become more outgoing, and I helped him when he felt homesick.

Drew Galligan, MD
Gainesville, FL
Counselor

Chapter VIII

HOPE GROWS HERE

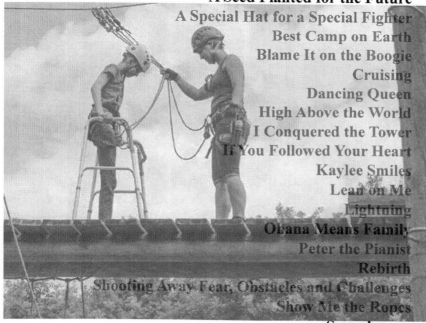

30 Seconds of Hope, Struggle, and Triumph

It was our first full day of the camp session and the afternoon rotation consisted of pool time. I witnessed an incredible display of support and brotherhood. One of my campers, Harrison, who has no function in his legs because he is paraplegic, passed his swim test. The swim test at camp required swimming from one end of the pool to the other and then treading water for 30 seconds.

Harrison swam across the pool without hesitation. It was not until he had to tread water where he experienced the most difficulty. He tried 8 times to pass the treading water portion of the test. Since he was only able to use his arms, he grew more and more tired with each attempt. He did not want to give up, though. All the counselors knew he could do it, but he needed to believe he could. He set goals of 10 seconds, 14 seconds, 19 seconds, and 26 seconds. He met each one but fluctuated times until he finally reached 28 seconds. It was on his final attempt that he finally passed! 30 seconds of hope, struggle, and triumph!

In between the 4th and 5th attempt, a couple of Harrison's cabin mates came over with some water to cheer Harrison on. They were not prompted. They were not asked. They just did it. They knew he was struggling, and they came to support and encourage Harrison on. For teenagers to have the awareness to do the little things like bring water and encourage someone they had only met less than 24 hours ago was an incredibly powerful display of camaraderie to watch.

James Rujimora
Miami Lakes, FL
Former Camper, Counselor

A Seed Planted for the Future

One of the favorite parts about camp was being at a place where my whole job existed to better someone else's day. Our purpose was to make campers feel safe, respected, and loved. That almost always required sacrifice on our part, and as an individual who likes to be needed, I thrived on that.

We were approaching Sickle Cell week, and the inspirational message left on our beds was about cheesecake and the unique challenges that this population presented. I was pretty confident I could handle it easily. I was wrong. Two nights later, I was hiding in the laundry room sobbing hysterically. I had one camper that presented negative behaviors the more I reached out to her. Audrey also seemed to target me specifically. After a particularly challenging day, I was at my breaking point. Camp and I weren't enough to breach her walls, and I didn't know what to do. A fellow counselor reminded me of something else we had been told: people show their worst behaviors to someone with whom they feel safe and loved, because they know no matter what they do, love will not be withdrawn.

During the dance, Audrey did not feel well and asked me to take her to the Patch. As we sat there, she allowed herself to be vulnerable in front of me and even asked me to hold her hand. I was so encouraged, but the rest of the week consisted of the same negative behaviors. It was only when we were together without an audience, that Audrey allowed herself to accept any sort of kindness from me. For her, that was significant and I trust she learned more and more of her value each summer she returned to camp. At that point, hers was not necessarily a heartwarming story. However, the result was a seed planted in the heart of a girl who finally accepted there was a camp where she could be safe, respected, and loved.

Hannah Zagar Bibler
Grand Junction, CO
Counselor

A Special Hat for a Special Fighter

I went to camp after a diagnosis of a rare bone cancer. Camp was my favorite place; it gave me a childhood, hope and friends who understood. My wheelchair, bald head and scars were not laughed at. As I aged out of camp, many tears were shed, but a ray of hope and light appeared when I was accepted into the LIT program. That week happened to be my old camper session, and I met an amazing young lady who ended up changing my life.

Stella, despite one leg, was spunky, fun and loved life. Although shy at first, Stella quickly became the light in our cabin. We were told that her cancer had recently relapsed and she may talk about it or be emotional. I understood, being a cancer kid myself.

At stage night, we were enjoying the acts when all of a sudden Stella began to sob. Since I was sitting right next to her, I tried to talk to her, and we stepped outside the theater. She then began to pull out her hair with a lot of emotion to include sadness, anger and frustration. Exclaiming that she had just begun to get her hair back and it finally looked "cute again." Stella talked about bullies and I said, "You are beautiful. You are a fighter. You have beaten cancer and will beat it again. These bullies cannot say that they are a fighter!" Stella then pulled out more hair, and it came out in clumps, so I gave her my hat. We laughed, cried and hugged and went in to finish stage day!

By the last day of camp, Stella was nearly bald again. She had been wearing my hat since that stage day, so I wrote her a message under the brim, gave her a big hug and said, "Keep Fighting, you can beat the 'C' word. See ya later!" That camper is my "why" and reminded me why camp is so special to me, for I was once in her shoes. Camp has my heart forever.

Cassandra Honour
St. Augustine, FL
Former Camper, Counselor

Best Camp on Earth

A couple of summers ago, we were was sitting in the dining hall when I saw one of our youngest campers reading a fellow counselor's shirt from a Sickle Cell fundraiser walk. We told him, "Kayden, they're trying really hard to find a cure for Sickle Cell", and he responded, complete with the biggest eyes I have ever seen, "Why would they want to do that? I hope they don't find a cure! Then I won't be able to come here anymore! This place is FUN!"

If you're wondering how a special needs camp is different from a "normal" camp, it isn't...much. The main differences I observed were; a very high counselor to camper ratio, more medical staff, and sometimes accommodations of an activity. The rest was exactly what you'd expect, kids having old-fashion fun. Laughing, being loud, trying new things in the presence of others trying new things, which tends to make "trying new things" easier! Girls whispering to each other, boys running around, squirting each other with water guns! Some kids stick right by their counselor's side and others assert their new found freedom amongst friends! It is a spectacular sight to behold. I am forever changed for having spent time with these kids!

Sheri Brown, RN
Ocoee, FL
Camp Nurse

Blame It on the Boogie

It was a sunny day in Ireland, the hottest day of the year actually. Some absent-minded clouds were still trying to find their way, sweeping down the last remainder of spring. It looked as if someone had intentionally put together every childhood dream.

Our group came out of the dining hall towards the first challenge of the day: high ropes. A red carpet full of disguised caras was awaiting them outside. Some swear to have seen a Spanish camper, dressed up as Superman, building a castle of plastic cups.

Long queues stretched around New Heights, where all campers listened attentively to the explanation. Helmet. Harness. Sailors' knots. Some *fun* cream of course. Everyone was willing to try.

After applauses, joy, excitement and battle cries, I suddenly realized that a wheelchair was left alone in a corner, but it was empty. He wasn't there. I looked around and tried to find my boy.

Up above our heads, Luis was climbing.

Luis was tightly holding the activity leader's waist, smiling, little tears of joy coming from both eyes. A big and spontaneous roar came from down under, where a dozen children from all over the world cheered him on. All I could think about was his mother, to whom I had talked to a few days ago, and how extremely thrilled she would be. Luis had been diagnosed with cancer eight years ago, when he was only 7, and the right half of his body had been paralyzed since then. That was the first time he had left his hometown.

Late at night, the chatting dies down as the music sounds. Caras and children sit around the cottage and share the most touching, hilarious and magical moments of the day at camp. Old guitar chords resound in the bedroom while ice cream still smears over campers' faces. It's time to sleep, the adventure continues tomorrow.

Blanca Vázquez Barco
Madrid, Spain
Counselor

Cruising

I have been a camp nurse for the past 2 years. During Spina Bifida week, I had a camper in the Patch getting a procedure. After Adam was done with his procedure I asked him if he wanted a golf cart ride back to his cabin since it was almost lights out. He looked at me very excited with wide eyes and the biggest smile on his face. He then hung his head down. With a cracked voice and tears in his eyes Adam very calmly said, "I have never been in a golf cart before, but I don't know if I can get up in it." Because of his illness, Adam had no feeling in his legs and used a wheelchair.

At that moment I vowed to myself that no matter how many people it took, we were going to get Adam in that golf cart. I pulled the golf cart to the back of the Patch and positioned his wheelchair next to the seat. It only took his counselor and I but we were able to get him in, safely and comfortably. I purposely took the long way back to his cabin. The smile and look of pure joy on his face as we cruised down cabin row accompanied by a calm summer evening breeze was priceless, and I'll never forget it. Adam taught me to never take anything for-granted and always enjoy the little things.

Debbie Kipp, RN
Kissimmee, FL
Camp Nurse

Dancing Queen

My first family weekend volunteering, I was blessed to be paired with a friendly family of six. It was their first family weekend too, so we all didn't know what to expect, but we were all excited for the time ahead of us. My camper, Gabriella, had recently been diagnosed with cancer, and, with a large tumor on her pelvis, she had difficulty walking. Throughout the weekend, we all took turns pushing her in the wheelchair and doing things she was strong enough and able to do.

On the last night, there was the dance that they hold every family weekend. Gabriella was so excited! She put on her best dress, and came to the dance, ready to dance the night away. We began dancing with her in the wheelchair. I held her hands and helped her spin around.

A few minutes later, Gabriella asked me if she could try to stand up and dance. I was so excited and helped her up. After she was able to stand and dance around, the joy on her face was unexplainable. She wanted everyone to see her standing and dancing! Gabriella called over her nurse, and all the volunteers she had met that weekend, just to show everyone how proud she was of herself that she had gained the strength to stand up and dance for that little bit of time. That to me showed me how valuable a single trip to camp is to these campers and their families.

Brennan Batten
Tampa, FL
Counselor

Way back in the summer of 2007, I was working on the High Ropes Course at camp. I had worked High Ropes back in Australia and was able to navigate my way through, but never really had to do much to help people succeed. I also never felt like I was making a difference when those kids would finish a course.

One boy, Hudson, was really enthusiastic for the course and for our day to get started. He listened intently and was even enthusiastic to help out his fellow campers.

When his turn arrived to climb he started climbing the cargo net and got halfway up. Hudson was already fatigued and struggled to climb up. Seeing how much he really wanted to do this, I helped him get up to the platform and begin the course elements.

With Hudson already exhausted, navigating our way through the course was going to be difficult, and I thought to make it easier I would clip on with him and help him through the course.

After 30 minutes of making our way through the course with constant encouragement and hand holding, we sent Hudson down the zipline to the cheers of his cabin mates. I quickly climbed down off the course to meet him at the bottom and to congratulate him and give him a massive High 5.

I went to the bottom of the zipline where Hudson had just been taken off, and I was met with the biggest smiling face and the biggest bear hug. He told me it was the best thing he had ever done and up there, he felt bigger than the world.

Afterwards I was told by the nursing team who were on hand for the day that Hudson had been in a medical-induced coma for the past three months and had only been taken out of it a week before camp so he could attend.

Trav Jack
Melbourne, Australia
High Ropes Instructor

We were at the tower, and it was a typical hot and humid June day. Chase, who had been diagnosed with a form of brain cancer less than a year earlier, was about to climb the rock wall. I was a little concerned that he may not make it to the top due to his left side weakness, which had occurred as a result of a stroke two months earlier. He couldn't stand or walk far, so I knew this would challenge his physical strength. However, he, like so many other amazing kids at camp, was resilient and determined, and made it to the top of the tower at the encouragement of his cabin mates.

After all of the campers had conquered the tower, we had them sit around in a group and one of the counselors, Kris, started debriefing the experience. He asked the campers what it took in terms of inner strength to make it up the tower, what it felt like to hear their cabin mates cheering for them, and other similar questions. At the end, Kris asked everyone to put their hands in and at the count of three, to yell "I conquered the tower!" I looked over at Chase as the boys shouted the chant. As he yelled, his eyes filled with tears, and he had this look on his face like he had never been more proud of himself.

At that moment, I couldn't think of a time I had been more proud of anyone. This 16-year-old boy, whose life had drastically changed over the last year, accomplished something that he was unsure whether he could still do. To see his emotion and pride from conquering the tower and willing his body to try something that it seemed impossible to do, was one of the best reminders of what camp is all about. I hope his ability to beat the odds at the tower encouraged him to beat the odds against cancer, too. I will always feel fortunate that I got to meet Chase and that I saw him conquer the tower on that hot and humid day.

Ashley Kimberling
Baltimore, MD
Oldest Camper Program Coordinator

If You Followed Your Heart

"If you followed your heart, where would it lead you?"

This was the question posed to us during summer staff orientation. I am eternally grateful that my heart led me to camp, in the summer of 2007. Spending nine weeks playing, laughing, and celebrating life with the most amazing children changed my life.

It is so hard to choose one story that summarizes the inexplicable experience of my time at camp. I spent that summer as the music specialist, but was also paired with a cabin. One memory that sticks out to me is spending time with the oldest campers during Asthma week. A perk of being an "oldest camper" is that your cabin gets to climb The Tower one of the mornings. I loved Tower days because it was an opportunity to see the cabin grow closer as they helped each other conquer the 42 foot tower. I remember climbing the tower during staff orientation, so each time I watched one of our girls climb, I knew the challenges they were conquering with each rung.

One of my favorite tasks was making a playlist for Tower Day. I asked each camper to name a favorite song, and I compiled a list of songs to play as they climbed. It was a chance to see a glimpse of each camper's personality in the song that they chose. As each camper had their turn at the tower, they seemed to receive an extra little boost of motivation from hearing their song as they climbed closer to the top.

Seeing the campers zipline was always a cause for celebration of this great accomplishment. I remember one particular camper talking about how she felt "free" as she rode the zipline from the platform at the top of the tower down. For that short moment she was free from her illness, free from criticism, free from limitations. And that's an experience that can only happen at camp.

Jenny Denk
West Des Moines, IA
Music Specialist, Counselor

Kaylee Smiles

I was camp photographer during the 2012 summer camp season. As a member of the yellow pride, I interacted often with yellow pride camper, Kaylee. Kaylee may have been the shyest camper I had ever met. I was told explicitly that she was scared to be photographed close-up because she was so shy and uncomfortable at camp for the first time. She spent the week sitting in the back with a counselor or two, participating as often as she dared, and remaining quiet to all but a select few people on camp. Her transformation was subtle, but incredible.

Over the course of the week, Kaylee became more and more at home with her new friends and counselors. She smiled infrequently, but every so often she would peek out and give us a grin. Finally, on dance night I approached her and her counselor, Alysha, in the course of my evening taking photos. Amazingly, Kaylee not only agreed to be photographed, but she beamed the fullest smile I had seen her give yet.

The campers and many of the counselors did not know the significance of that photo when I used it as the final photo of the slideshow at the end of the week, but I was approached by the counselors closest to her and thanked for proving to the rest of us what they already knew: that Kaylee blossomed, despite her shyness and certainly adapted to have a good week, one that all of us could be proud of.

Andy Gattis
Jacksonville, FL
Former Camper, Counselor

Lean on me when you're not strong
And I'll be your friend, I'll help you carry on
For it won't be long
'Til I'm gonna need somebody to lean on

As an entire unit, we were all in the Arts and Crafts room having our Unit Closing. We had finished giving camper shout-outs and had just started on our wish sticks for the Closing Campfire. I gave Carson, my camper with Cerebral Palsy, the option to try and write the wish himself or together. He said, "No, that's okay, you can write it for me."

Then he said, "My wish is to be closer to God."

I remember the rush of chills I felt as I wrote his wish on the stick. In that moment, I indeed felt closer to God. And this inspiriting moment lasted as we rolled up the hill to the campfire and met up with another counselor that Carson had the summer before. Carson began to weep as the three of us sang and swayed together to "Lean on Me." We didn't want that moment to end. That moment has no end for me because Carson lifted me and changed my life eternally.

Drew Taylor
Randleman, NC
Program Counselor

He went by the name of "Lightning McQueen." It was his first week at camp, and we had heard from his mother's letter that he was so excited to join the camp family and make new friends. At 9 years old, he had a gift. He could create an instantaneous bond with anyone he came in contact with. We sat outside on our rumpuses and played with two hot wheel cars and our imagination. It was all we needed. It was beautiful as he examined the cars and asked questions about the colors, shapes, and not to mention, speed.

Spinning around in circles on the porch while closing my eyes was indescribable, only to take a little trip out of my world and into his reality. The first time I gave him my hand, he felt my rings and bracelets. The whole week, our cabin got to see how camp is experienced in a different way. We received tips from our supervisors on how to lead a person who cannot see and common behaviors when they are in a new area of mapping it out.

Another boy in the cabin, Isaiah, who had very high energy, asked if he could walk with Lightning on cabin row to Beauty Shop where nails would be painted, hair would be sprayed, and faces would be painted. We were fine with it because then Lightning could have some direction of knowing where to go. As Lightning walked with his stick in one hand and the hand of another camper, it occurred to me that not only was he walking with another camper who he knew just by his voice and touch of his hand, but Lighting was actually directing Isaiah. Isaiah's attention was easily distracted but Lighting made sure kindly that Isaiah was safe from any harm, stick, or bump in the road. To see such genuine care for someone else at his age was truly a heartwarming experience. I learned a valuable lesson to never assume the ability of anyone. You will be humbly proven wrong.

Anna Marita Kuhns
Jacksonville, FL
Oldest Camper Coordinator

In the movie Lilo & Stitch, they say, "Ohana means family, family means no one gets left behind – or forgotten." I introduced it to my cabin of oldest girls. They took off with it. I had never seen a group of girls love each other so much in such little time. They were all part of my ohana, but one girl became so deeply invested in my heart that I think about her every day.

Norah had metastatic bone cancer, resulting in a brutal surgery that took out half of her thigh. She could walk, but it was unbearably painful, so we tried to keep her comfortable in her chair, which she hated. She was seven years younger than me, but someone I wanted to grow up to be. In a world where apathy is "cool," Norah stuck out like a sore thumb; she had many passions and was not ashamed to be honest about how she loved "Walking Dead" and "Supernatural." She was spunky. She was maxed out on pain medicine, and the pain was beginning to defeat her as she felt incapable of doing anything.

It was ropes course day, and I wanted to see her victoriously stand on top of the challenge course. Norah had climbed the "easiest" route before, so I asked her if she wanted to climb the challenge route. She looked at me with disbelief. She did not think she was capable of that and was almost appalled that I even suggested it. We exchanged a mischievous smile; Norah was going to climb up the hardest side. When she needed that extra "umph," I pulled her up with all my might, but she never gave up. To her, it wasn't an option. After lots of grunting and sweating, Norah made it to the top. A girl who could barely walk, was maxed on pain killer, and had cancer with a questionable prognosis, conquered the world for a day. And that's something that never leaves you. It's never left me. She continues to make me want to be a better person and that makes my heart smile.

Megan Riley
Lexington, KY
Counselor

Peter the Pianist

Peter had the looks of a model. His intense blue eyes sparkled beneath tousled golden hair. It was Saturday morning on Special Diagnosis Family Camp Weekend, and Peter was exploring some toys while his mom conferred with one of the doctors. Done setting up for my magic show, I went over to visit with this boy whom I had only met the previous night.

He was examining an electronic keyboard, and I asked if he wanted me to plug it in. He eagerly said "yes." While I wondered where the "On" switch was located, Peter found it immediately. I randomly pressed another button: background rhythm began to play, and the translucent keys lit up in a particular pattern.

Without instruction or hesitation, Peter followed the lights and was playing along with the song generated by the keyboard. Had I not spoken with this boy and discovered his developmental and cognitive challenges, I would have thought he was an accomplished pianist. He must have done this before, perhaps at home.

His mom came around the corner. The look on her face told me that this was the first time Peter had ever done something like this. I asked Peter if he would like to play a song at Saturday evening's stage night. To his mom's amazement and delight, he eagerly accepted the invitation.

He played the song that evening, receiving thunderous applause and cheers. Peter's face beamed brightly in the shower of love and approval. Through teary eyes, mom attempted to record him on video. On Sunday morning, she declared she was going to show Peter's school the video as proof that he should have his I.E.P (Individual Education Program) changed to reflect enhanced abilities the school had thus far refused to recognize.

The next summer, when Peter came to camp, his mom announced proudly that he was now mainstreamed in school.

Mark Maxwell-Smith
Studio City, CA
Counselor

Rebirth

I'm the sister of a wonderful 17 year old girl, who loves climbing and riding horses, and of a brother, a dreamer sibling. We arrived at camp three years ago, and I remember we were told, "Leave your baggage over there!" It sounded like they were telling us to leave all our problems behind and don't worry about anything! With big smiles and sparkling eyes, they promised us that magic was waiting for us.

It was an unforgettable week! For the first time, someone was to take care of us. We realized that we are on the right track and that was a gift, the first in our lives. I knew I was finally in a place that shared the values I had always believed. My brother could meet other siblings. Our parents could speak with other parents in a happy atmosphere, unlike the cold hospital corridors. My sister finally could fly! It was a rebirth for the whole family.

My sister was happy to see us happy and all do the same things together! No worries, no anxieties. She also felt a bit proud to have brought us there. While we were returning home in tears, she jokingly told us, "Thank me and behave yourselves if you want to go back!" She fell in love with the pool. In that water was magic. All the children quieted down, relaxed and seemed to sleep on the water. To ride horses made her ecstatic because she liked the speed! She feared the climbing wall at first but showed us how to be brave. As she was climbing, I saw her become smaller and smaller! Then she rang the bell, came back down...and wanted to go back up!

We gave our heart to the camp, and it did the same to us with a recharge of happiness, enthusiasm and pure joy. Camp changed our lives. Forever.

Engy Smoqi
Prato, Italy
Sibling Camper, Counselor

Shooting Away Fear, Obstacles and Challenges

In the summer of 2013, I was assigned to the oldest girls cabin for heart transplant camp. Many faced challenges with medication compliance and had endured long stays in the hospital due to poor self-management. In addition, many faced challenges in their home lives including homelessness, unemployment, poverty, alcoholism and drug use among family members, trouble at school and with law enforcement, depression and anxiety. The counselors and girls decided that it would be a week of transformation and overcoming obstacles. Many hours were spent over the week discussing how to cope with the various situations the girls faced at home.

On the final night of camp, each girl used a paper plate as a "canvas" to write down the challenges she had problem-solved and strategized solutions for all week. When the girls had written their challenges and obstacles, they added their fears they had overcome.

The cabin quietly made their way to the archery course. The targets and the lanes were lit up with glow sticks. The girls taped glow bracelets around the edge of their plates. The counselors mounted the paper plates to the target at the end of the lane, one at a time. Each girl waited for the "all clear" to be given and then took her turn with a bow and arrow, "shooting away fear, obstacles and challenges." The air was filled with only the quiet "swish" sound as the arrow left the bow, followed by "thwok." Each time an arrow hit the target the group cheered, hugged, laughed and danced. Then silence would fall again as the next paper plate was taken out to the target.

Each camper brought their paper plate back from the archery range with them, and their personal "mastery" over the problems was the topic of a very tearful and sweet cabin chat around a campfire, as the full moon hung in the horizon, and all was right with the world.

Tav Huffman, RN
Portland, OR
Camp Nurse

It was a cool morning during my third summer at camp, and I was standing with a group of campers at the ropes course. A camper who I had known since my first year eagerly tugged on my arm wanting me to accompany her on the course. Two years earlier, I could barely get Zoey to put on a harness, so I knew even asking me was a feat in itself. The previous year we managed to get across the tight rope together. This year, despite her anxiety, we ended up completing seven elements! Even though Zoey was exhausted, I recognized the same feeling of pride and accomplishment I had felt the first time I conquered the course. She kept exclaiming, "I did it, did you see that? I really did it, that was so awesome!"

I knew Zoey could do it. All she needed was someone who would believe in her, encourage her and support her, to realize that she was capable of anything she set her mind to. Her continuous determination on the course was awe-inspiring, and I also learned a lot from her that day. Zoey showed me that it is okay to be scared and to ask for help, and even though blindly trusting someone takes a lot of courage, it can also open up so many doors in life. When I am having a hard time, I think back to those moments on the course where she never gave up, and it gives me the strength to continue forward.

Every day at camp, campers achieve something they never thought they could do, and I feel privileged to have been able to share those experiences with so many kids. Camp is the most authentic, heart warming and fun place in world. Nothing can compare! The growth that happens in both campers and counselors during one week at camp will last for a lifetime.

Trylla Tuttle
Seattle, WA
Counselor

Superheroes

It was my first time attending camp as a counselor for the youngest boys during Liver Transplant week. The turtle was being passed around during cabin chat as the boys answered the question, "Who is your favorite super hero?"

The answers were given by child after child..."Spider Man," "Batman," "The Hulk"... And then the turtle went to the last camper. His answer was, "My favorite super hero is the family whose son died, and they chose to give his organs to other kids so they could live. If it wasn't for them, I wouldn't be here."

Not all superheroes wear capes. Some swoop in when you least expect it and save you from the miscreant evildoers with their abilities. Our campers are like most iconic superheroes, who at first special glance are typical citizens – underdogs even – but secretly use their super powers to spread hope. Hope slays despair and shines a bright light in the darkest room.

I am grateful to have been a witness and beneficiary of their super powers.

Erin Hood
Covington, KY
Counselor

Because of Hemophilia, Alexander was in the Patch a lot receiving Factor, and I was usually the counselor that accompanied him. We talked about what our lives were like outside of Camp, and most of his was spent in hospitals doing the same thing he was doing in the Patch, getting the infusion he needs.

That session, the Patch teaches campers who are willing to stick themselves with a needle how to self-infuse the factor so they don't have to be relegated to going to a hospital or parent to infuse them. During the class, they practice on fake veins to get an idea of what it looks like to have themselves put a needle in skin, see the "blood" go in the tube, and the entire process of infusion.

After they were done with the fake veins, they wanted to really test it out. Alexander had passed the fake vein portion with flying colors, so I volunteered my veins for him to practice on. The portion where he would try it on himself was tomorrow, so we kept practicing until he felt comfortable.

With a very sore arm, Alexander and I walked back to the cabin, and on the way back, Alexander said to me, "Thank you for freeing me." He made me realize that, here at Camp, we don't just give campers a week of freedom and fun. We teach them how to be free for the rest of their lives.

Joe Couture
Howey in the Hills, FL
Counselor

It was another typical dinner, eating spaghetti with my face and hearing nothing but cheers and laughter. That evening, I stayed behind to walk with one of my campers who would typically take a little longer to get from point A to point B, usually with the assistance of crutches or a wheelchair.

As we walked past the nurses, on our way to the theater, Lincoln looked up at me and asked me to please get a wheelchair because he was tired and too slow. I could see the frustration, so I asked another counselor to retrieve one for him but encouraged him to keep walking along in the meantime. I asked if he had ever walked by himself to the theater. Lincoln said, "No, I am too slow." My eyes about filled up with tears. I asked if he would like to. I didn't care if it took all night to walk there. As long as he wanted to, I would go with him. Lincoln smiled at me and said, "Yes." He was like Thomas the Train saying, "I think I can, I think I can."

Moments later, I held his hand with another counselor as we slowly and safely took step-by-step. Lincoln looked up at us with a smile brighter than the moon above and eyes filled with tears of joy. He took his first steps by himself at camp, something he was allowed but too nervous to do. Everything stopped in my life for those brief moments as I looked ahead and looked back at Lincoln and at that moment realized why camp was so special, how camp empowers the campers, and why camp truly is the best place on earth.

Beau Loendorf
Carmel, IN
Counselor

During Kidney Disease and Transplant session, I was blessed with a cabin of five 11-year-old girls who made the week truly amazing. Three of the girls had received kidney transplants and two of the girls were still on dialysis awaiting transplants.

One day, our cabin went to the horse barn to ride horses. The theme for camp that week was time travel, and the horse barn had been converted into a "time machine." As we entered the time machine, the barn staff asked where in time we would like to go and one of my campers responded, "To the future, when I receive my kidney transplant." This was heartbreaking to hear, and I wished so badly that we had a real time machine so that we could make this happen for her!

Well, perhaps that time machine was real, because before the session was over, I said a cheerful yet tearful goodbye to one of my campers as she made her way to the hospital to receive her transplant! It was a wonderful surprise to us all to receive the call in the middle of the night, and one of the most amazing events I have ever been part of. I guess I take my kidneys for granted, but when you are surrounded by kids who may not even have a kidney, you really gain some perspective on things. I get excited when I get new shoes, but imagine receiving a new kidney, especially after waiting years for it. There is no way that I can convey to you the excitement of this moment, but trust me when I say it was magic!

During our nightly cabin chat that evening, our other camper who was awaiting a transplant shared that she had been giving up hope of ever receiving a transplant, but after knowing her camp friend was receiving hers, her hope was restored! To know you're not alone, to share in the journey, to bring about hope-that is the magic of camp!

Rosalyn Skelton
Lake Hughes, CA
Counselor, Camper Recruiter

During my first week as a counselor, I was terrified. Even with training, I did not know what to expect or how to react if a camper became ill. Then I met Brooklyn, a sassy nine-year old girl, who complained that her shaved head revealing a large scar from a recent brain surgery made her "less fashionable." She had Refractory Epilepsy, but it was her free-spirited energy and fervor for life that I remember most. She shared with me her ambition to become a model "once her hair grew back," and which boys she thought were cute. She even coerced me into performing her choreographed dance moves for stage day with her.

The first time she had a seizure, she grabbed my hand and I watched as her animated face faded. I held her in my lap and will always cherish her absolute trust in me during that moment. When the seizure subsided, she looked up at me with an ear-to-ear grin and said, "Where did all the boys go?!"

Mel Lee Robinson, DO
Columbus, OH
Counselor

Victory Laps in the Pool

When I think of camp, so many stories come to mind, but there is always one story that sticks out; the day I spent at the waterpark walking around the lazy river with a camper.

This may seem pretty ordinary, but at camp I find there is little that is ordinary. Peyton has Cerebral Palsy, needs help with almost all of her ADLs (activities of daily life), and uses a power wheelchair to get around. So, as I was saying, we spent this entire afternoon *walking* around the pool. I would hold Peyton underneath her arms and let go. She would take about 2-3 steps in the water all by herself and then fall underneath. I, or the other counselor we were with, would help pick Peyton back up and we'd start the journey around the lazy river all over again. We did this again and again and again for 45 full minutes, and I can truly say it was some of the best 45 minutes I've ever spent at camp. Watching Peyton's face light up with pure joy and excitement every time she took those few steps on her own made my entire summer – really it made my whole year. She could feel in control of her body while in the pool. Anytime I would get down or have a bad day, I would think about that day in the pool.

Camp is such an amazing place – it's a place where there is no such thing as impossible and every "can't" can be turned into a can. It's a place where dreams turn into reality, and every child is looked at just as they should be – as a child. There is a feeling of possibility, love and magic in the air at camp, and I feel so lucky to have been a part of something as special and powerful as my summers as a camp counselor.

Lindsey Czark
Randleman, NC
Counselor

It is the last night of camp at all-camp closing. We had decorated the gym and set up a huge screen for the kids to watch the slide show on. "Put a little camp in your heart" was the summer theme. At every closing for the summer, our campers wrote a wish down and tied it to our wishing tree. By the end of the summer, our tree was full of wishes!

One of my campers, Lucy, was sitting at the back of the gym with another counselor. Her wish, for me to be her mom, was heart felt and truly tugged at my heart strings. She wanted to stay at camp and live there, with me, forever. She was visibly upset and knowing tears are contagious at camp, it wasn't long before Lucy and the other girls had turned on the waterworks.

It was decided a quick bathroom break was needed to distract and compose ourselves. As we snuck off to the bathroom, I remembered there were some pool water toys kept in a tub under the sink. As we splashed our faces to freshen up, a water challenge began to take place. Of course, we were soaked by the end of our 5 minute break, but it definitely brought smiles to the faces of our campers!

Erin "Bella" Bell
Mornington Peninsula, Australia
Assistant Activities Director

Chapter IX

BELIEVE IN THE JOURNEY

A Transformational Week

Eli really needed camp. Since being diagnosed with cancer, his life has changed drastically. He went from being a very active 13 year-old, deeply involved in sports, to being deprived of all those activities he loved because of his unfortunate illness. Eli first heard about camp while he was in the hospital getting treatment. As soon as his nurse started talking about all the fun activities that went on at camp, his head popped up from his bed and he asked to be signed up. The medical staff made sure Eli could come to camp and rescheduled his chemotherapy for a different week.

At the start of session, it was evident what an incredible young man Eli was. Even though he displayed a shy exterior, his inner joy was so noticeable. All throughout the week Eli participated in all the activities, from swimming to canines, playing ball with his cabin mates, and going camping at Outpost.

The day came for the teen campers to go to the high ropes course. We had spent all week discussing a strategy for Eli so he could feel safe up on the course. The morning of, Eli decided not to participate in the course. I told him I would go up with him, and after some consideration, he put the harness and helmet on. We walked over to the "taco net" and got ready to climb up. Eli was concerned that his legs wouldn't hold to get him to the top, so I went up right behind him, spreading out the net so he felt supported. We went together, step by step, up the net. He felt so encouraged as his fellow campers cheered for him. After a lot of hard work, he scaled to the top of the net. Eli was then able to successfully complete two of the elements on the high ropes course. I felt so much joy in my own heart to be part of this amazing transformation Eli experienced.

As we were leaving the high ropes course, he said "I'm comin' for you next year."

Collin Hanson
Noblesville, IN
Counselor

218

Accepted

It was the summer of 2007. Colette had been diagnosed with Lupus a few months earlier, at the age of 16. She had a "punk rock" look, along with a nose ring and bright streaks of blonde throughout her black hair. She had spent the past few months of her life rebelling against all that she was told to do, which included being forced to come to camp. She was very closed off to counselors and campers, barely willing to engage in conversation with any of us. She was angry. Angry at the symptoms she was experiencing and angry at the ways her disease had changed her life. The other campers in our cabin did not let this faze them. They showered Colette with love at every opportunity, something she had not expected to find at camp.

It is remarkable the transformation Colette made each day. She slowly let the spirit of camp take over her heart. She had finally found friends that could relate to having a "disease" and the huge impact it had on her life. As the girls sat in a circle on their last night, the conversation went far deeper than I had expected. They shared stories of pain and triumph, and eventually Colette took center stage. "I thought you guys would not accept me. I thought you would judge me, like others do. But you didn't, and I can't believe it." It instantly hit me how a young woman, who had started the week out full of anger and closed off from everyone around her, was now letting her feelings spill out. Her walls had come down, and she let herself be vulnerable to those around her. She felt loved. So, so loved.

On her day of departure, Colette signed the wall like so many campers had done before. However, I think few have captured the essence of camp as well as she did in a single sentence. "It makes me feel accepted." Camp is a magical place. A place that can bring joy and love to people when they need it the most.

Megan Foster
Wichita, KS
Counselor

I recently switched jobs. I had been working at an elementary school where I never felt like I fit in. The staff was competitive with one another, the school leadership was uninspired, and it was hard to track down a dependable mentor. Upon unpacking in my new classroom, I started to feel some "new kid" anxiety. Will it be the same as before? Will teaching feel good again? And then something wonderful happened. A colleague stopped by to say hello and hang out. After lots of laughter and talking about our summers he said, "I want you to know this is hard. It is an amazing place but it's hard. And no one will judge you for crying in the bathroom. Hell, no one will judge you for crying in the hallway."

Over the course of the next few days, I found a community of teachers, mentors, and leadership who were inspired. Energized. Passionate about their craft. For the first time since camp, I had found a community whose mission was to better this world through the love and care of children. As I traveled from meeting to meeting, I found myself thinking about dancing in the dining hall, hard cabin conversations, laughing until it hurt, power napping while peeing, arts and crafts till all hours of the night and one good friend who grabbed my hand when she knew I was struggling to make an experience wonderful for the campers as if to say, "This is hard, it will be hard, but no one is judging. You are changing lives, and your life is changing as we speak."

I am so grateful to camp for so many different reasons. Thank you for helping me to come alive and to know what it feels like when it happens again and again.

Blair Welsh
Brooklyn, NY
Counselor

Through an amazing partnership with a local horse ranch, campers of all medical diagnoses are able to get on a horse, just as any healthy child would. The staff does an amazing job of programming through "Challenge by Choice" and adapting programs to give campers an experience that they are comfortable with.

Sadie was NOT comfortable with the idea of getting on the horse, because she was scared of falling off. My attempt to reassure her was complicated by the fact that Sadie had developmental delays, was deaf in one ear, and had a cochlear implant in the other. Her sign language interpreter worked with me to let her know that she could try whatever she was comfortable with, from putting on a helmet to riding a horse.

I helped her through putting on a helmet, meeting her horse, and getting on the horse. I walked beside her has she rode. I asked her if she was okay probably around 50 times in 10 minutes. About halfway through the walk, I asked her once again if she was okay. Her response made my day. Sadie put her hands in the air, and shouted, "I'm so happy" with the biggest grin on her face.

For me, that moment displayed the power of camp. A child went from being scared and unsure to being safe, challenged, empowered, accomplished, and happy in a matter of minutes.

Julie Szpira
Denver, CO
Counselor

Denial to Acceptance

Klarisza arrived at her first camp in 2010, a session for teens living with Diabetes. She was grumpy and uneasy. Clearly, she didn't want to be there at all. After a few minutes she shared that it'd been six months since her diagnosis, and it was her grandmother's idea to go to camp. Klarisza was 16, loved sports, especially handball, and perceived diabetes as something incredibly unfair happening to her, a disaster that ruined her life. Klarisza remained quiet; but as she took part in the activities, she started to make friends with some of the girls.

As the days passed and the evening chats became more intimate, Klarisza and the campers shared more and more reflective thoughts. On the third night, Klarisza labelled diabetes as a "condition she has." It was a massive difference compared to how she previously described it: "this stupid disease I have." The last cabin chat was particularly emotional. All the girls, including Klarisza, were weeping. Klarisza said she was "happy" she had diabetes because if she hadn't, she'd be a different person, and wouldn't have met all these amazing people. She had the time of her life, "thanks" to her condition.

I was thinking about this perception-shift, and how much it showed the magic of camp, long after we all returned home. A few weeks later I saw a blog, by Klarisza, encouraged by her grandmother to write about her time at camp. She described the week as a life-changing experience, which helped her accept who she is and focus on what she is good at.

Camp has given me great memories and amazing friends, and it has also helped me discover what I wanted to do with my career, and now I'm working for a charity, in learning and development. At each camp session, I have seen at least one story like this, all of them special in their own way.

Zsuzsanna Ujhelyi
Budapest, Hungary
Counselor

The Web of Kindness. The frame is like a giant hula hoop, approximately seven feet in diameter. During summer sessions, the camp family weaves the Web in two simultaneous ways: verbally and literally. Campers and counselors are invited to go to the front of the dining hall to thank someone or share other kind words as a couple of people weave yarn onto the hoop.

One summer, as Rob and I prepared to weave the yarn on the Web of Kindness during a closing banquet, two oldest campers approached us with serious faces. Tys and Armin, asked if they could weave that night. Now, during closing banquets, the weaving of the Web could take from one to two beautiful, brave, moving hours, a long time to remain patiently standing and weaving.

Tys and Armin had that patience, though. We told them we would love to have their help. Rob and I would do the first shift, and then they could take over for us. They agreed and found seats close to the front of the dining hall, and the weaving of the Web began.

After a while, Tys and Armin quietly approached us again. They were ready to take over, but they had a question first. Tys asked, "So you wrap the yarn around twice each time?"

With that question, I knew they had been watching exactly what we had been doing so they could weave exactly like we were. For a couple of reasons, we did always wrap the yarn around the hoop twice, and that is something I usually taught people when they helped with weaving. Tys and Armin? They didn't need to be taught, because they had been observing so carefully. With their great respect for camp, they wanted to lead this special custom by weaving down to the last detail. My heart was full of pride: pride in Tys and Armin and pride in the intentional camping that lead us to that moment.

Kirstin Cauraugh Youmans
Mount Dora, FL
Assistant Camp Director

It was my first time volunteering for Special Diagnosis week. I knew, as with all sessions, their conditions made their life drastically different from mine. I'd volunteered at camp before, but still I was intimidated by the thought that disparate life experiences would keep me from relating to the campers and make me a bad counselor.

Christopher had Cerebral Palsy and fell right into the area that was new and uncomfortable for me. I was determined to work hard and overcome any discomfort, rational or not, to give all of the campers a memorable experience. But I didn't find it hard at all. It was one of the best and most joyful weeks at camp I'd ever had.

On the last day of camp at the Closing Campfire, I realized that it had been such a great week because Christopher had genuinely loved every activity and moment of camp, and spread that positive energy to others. It wasn't in spite of his condition or circumstances. Christopher was just fully present in every moment, enjoying as much as he could, no matter how mundane they might be.

And that's how a camper taught me how to live my life moment to moment, acknowledging how things are, could have been, and might be; but only worrying about what was happening right now.

Ian Lee
Los Angeles, CA
Counselor

Natalie was 14 years old. This was her second summer coming to the Cancer session. As soon as Natalie entered my cabin, I knew she was going to be a leader, and a positive one at that. She was.

During one night we all sat in a circle talking, and Natalie shared her story about what camp had done for her. She said the previous year before coming to camp she had lost all her hair due to the chemotherapy. She became extremely self-conscious about it and wouldn't leave her house without her wig. The kids at school would tease her because of it, but since the previous summer she came to camp, Natalie had found new joy and acceptance in being different and embraced every bit of it. Natalie no longer wore her wig because she said she "didn't want to hide who she was."

The next afternoon, we were paired with the youngest campers at the pool. I saw Natalie interacting with one of the younger girls who didn't want to get into the pool because she was embarrassed about her surgery scars. I heard her tell the younger camper that she was once the same way but now she's proud of it. It means that she's brave. And before I knew it, both of them were doing cannon balls off the deep end.

That summer, I saw Natalie radiate a sparkle she had about herself to not only the campers but also a lot of the counselors. She had a poise and strength about her that I will never forget.

Stephanie Gilman
Miami, FL
Counselor

It's a story I was lucky enough to witness chapter by chapter. There was a young boy at camp, full of energy but also deeply affected by his condition. Nicholas couldn't always find the appropriate way to channel his energy, but with time, by getting to know his surroundings, by talking to camp and counselors he felt more and more at ease and settled in quickly. Nicholas had a great session and left with all the lovely memories only a place like camp can provide.

Nicholas returned 2 years later, almost a grown up, taking part in a camp leadership program. One time we were catching up and he looked at a few of us still working there and said, "Those chats during my summers as a camper changed me as a person and, ever since, I have wanted to come back as a counselor myself." And there he was, right underway!

And, of course, it wasn't us changing him; it was all Nicholas being the wonderful, one-of-a-kind person he is. Camp, the place that brought us all together, made it possible for him to blossom during his time there and after he went home.

A year later Nicholas completed the camp leadership program, and I was lucky enough to be there for the closing ceremony where they all had to deliver a public speech about one of their mates. He was standing there, a tall, confident young man, nailing it perfectly! You could tell he was delighted with himself! I always knew but that night it was especially clear: people like him change the world every day and I cannot wait to hear what he will be up to in 10 or 15 years!

Mónika Hernek
Budapest, Hungary
Counselor

The fourteen-year-old camper in my cabin was a bit younger than the other boys, but there was a hardness which made him seem older. When Kevin was thirteen, he was caught in the crossfire of a gang shooting, leaving him paralyzed from the waist down. To be entering his teenage years and have so much taken away from him suddenly left him understandably angry. It was now his second year at camp, and Kevin already appreciated what camp allowed him to be; a teenaged boy who loved music, basketball, funny pranks, and being around others who understood, whether their medical needs were acquired or congenital.

With each year he returned, his spirit seemed brighter. I have had the privilege of watching Kevin grow up into a wonderful young man; graduating high school, learning to drive, turning 21, and more.

The summer Kevin came to camp in his car, having learned to drive through an adaptive device, he was so excited. It was an incredible moment, and I felt such a surge of pride knowing just how far he had come. The 22-year-old young man sitting before me had taken his experiences and circumstances and learned both to challenge himself and help others along the way. He is an incredible person.

Megan Martello
Santa Barbara, CA
Counselor

This young rock star was a 12 year-old first time camper in the summer of 2003. Along with the ropes course, Julian was particularly interested in an old beat-up acoustic guitar that his cabin had laying around. Julian hadn't ever played before, but the thought of learning even one chord seemed pretty cool to him.

One day, Julian asked if he could try to play the guitar at the end of rest time, which the counselors said "no problem." Once the time came for him to try out the guitar, he picked it up and played the WORST sounding, most ear-piercing, chalkboard-scratching sound that anyone had ever heard. Yet, regardless of this howl, the counselors cheered Julian on and nodded their heads to his strumming. They made him feel perfectly comfortable and confident in his guitar playing abilities even though he knew just as well as them what he was playing was skin crawling.

Each day after that Julian would practice during rest time, and even learned a few chords by the end of the week. This in itself was a success, and from the day he left camp, he decided to take lessons each week throughout the year. As the year went on Julian actually became a very capable guitar player.

When it came time for camp the following year, Julian was front and center on stage night and ripped a guitar solo for the whole camp to hear. The camp went wild in disbelief that he had morphed into a confident rock and roll guitar player in one short year. The counselors that had helped encourage him on his first chord were in the audience and saw how that moment of encouragement quite possibly helped lead to this.

Now and then, it's fun to think of Julian touring in some band and ripping guitar solos to an envious crowd cheering on this rock star.

Zac Gannett
Vancouver, British Columbia
Counselor

Eight year old Mila climbed the rope ladder cautiously and very slowly. She wasn't in a hurry to make it to the top. This was partly due to the fact that she left her coke bottle lenses on the bench, but mostly because she was terrified.

At two feet off the ground, the ladder began to sway, and Mila started to cry.

At five feet, she froze and clung to the quivering ladder. Campers and counselors shouted encouraging words, but she remained glued to the ladder. After a moment, her crying stopped. "I don't want to get down!" Mila shouted. "I can do it!" Gradually, her grip on the ladder loosened, and she started taking slow and small steps up the ladder.

At eight feet, the crying resumed (happy crying). A counselor at the top looked down the ladder, clapped, and celebrated her determination.

At fifteen feet, Mila made it passed the ladder and onto the climbing staples. The counselor at the top recalled that she had never seen such a happy kid look so gritty and brave.

At twenty feet, Mila started to get tired. I don't think anyone noticed when the counselor up top gave the rope a little pull as her energy diminished.

At twenty five feet, she reached for the platform. She climbed up and onto the boards and her tears turned into laughter and excitement. Mila jumped to her feet and shouted "Everyone! Everyone! Hey! Look!" Everyone looked. "This is so exciting! Everyone! I did it!"

The crowd of onlookers hollered and gave her the biggest cheers imaginable! Mila was undoubtedly the most excited and proud camper I have ever seen climb to the top of our ropes course.

Bryan Wage
Santa Monica, CA
Assistant Camp Director

There was a palpable hum of energy in the air as staff prepared for camper arrival; construction paper name tags were carefully taped above each bed, bandanas and t-shirts passed out to each cabin group, and counselors laughed and talked with excited anticipation. We were in Botswana, and camp was about to begin.

The next morning, children from villages all across southern Botswana began their journey to camp. A little six-year-old boy in a brown tracksuit was the first camper to arrive; he had traveled on a dusty, bumpy bus for four hours from his rural village. His name was Kefentse, and despite his counselors' best attempts to make him feel at home, his nervousness kept him reserved. Throughout the week he participated in all camp activities but rarely smiled or laughed with the other boys in his cabin. When he left at the end of the week, I worried that we hadn't given him that "magical" camp experience.

A few days later, I stood at the front door of the clinic with a clipboard in hand; ready to check in the next group of children for their session at camp. As I started registering families, I looked up to see little Kefentse walking up the front steps with his mother. Instead of his brown tracksuit, he was wearing his lime green camp t-shirt and his blue camp bandana. He had a routine appointment at the Clinic that happened to coincide with our check-in. While his mother waited to see the physician, Kefentse walked up to some of the boys nervously waiting in line for camp. Without introduction or inquiry, he began speaking to the boys and a counselor graciously translated for me:

Don't worry. I was nervous like you but camp is a good place. It is bright because the people are happy and make you feel happy too. When you leave you will be sadder than you are now because you will have had such happy time. It is the best place in the world.

Melissa Adamson
Berkeley, CA
Counselor, Hospital Outreach Coordinator

Then, it was my turn. Tim, a fellow counselor, passed me the microphone, and as I raised it to my lips I could already feel a lump forming in my throat. Preparing to raise my voice to its maximum volume (which really isn't very loud), I took a deep breath, and with heartfelt gusto shouted my sweet little brother's name after a dramatic, "And last, but certainly not least..."

My eyes darted around the large circle of campers and counselors that had formed around the center of the dining hall, looking for him. Sure enough, he emerged from a group of buddies who had—somewhere between dancing after every meal, zip-lining down the ropes course, fishing, singing, and everything else that comes along with camp--turned into who he still refers to as his "blood brothers."

I walked over to him and placed the colorfully decorated stick that I had been holding in his hand. This stick, or "Big Stick Award" was just one of the many that had been handed out that day to those brave Hemophiliac boys who had succeeded in learning how to self-infuse that week. Socially and medically, learning how to self-infuse was a giant step towards independence and a true right-of-passage. I couldn't help but cry thinking about how much more freedom he would be able to have. He could attend sleep-overs and go on trips without my parents, etc. It amazed me how much courage he had, then only ten years old, to stick himself with a needle multiple times until he finally "got it."

It was moving to be able to present this award to Miles both as his camp counselor, and as his sister. I was able to acknowledge how far he had come in life as well as how far he had come in that one week of camp. I will forever cherish the moment that I gave Miles his "Big Stick Award" during my first summer working at camp.

Allie Cole
Santa Barbara, CA
Counselor

My husband and I were headed to camp for the first time. We poured over the orientation manual, and quizzed each other endlessly on rules and procedures. We had waited a long time for this opportunity and didn't want to mess up!

All the children that week had heart conditions, and had undergone procedures, from valve replacements to transplants. Layla was a beautiful seven-year-old camper with a complex congenital condition and had already had several open-heart and spinal surgeries.

Our cabin consisted of ten girls, and by bedtime they had begun to form a fun, happy vibe. I noticed, however, that Layla seemed politely reserved with everyone. As the girls were getting into their PJs, Layla excused herself to change in private.

At the pool the next day, Layla emerged in a short-sleeved wet suit that covered her from her neck down to her knees. The pool was crowded with campers of all ages, from seven to sixteen, playing, swimming, laughing and being tossed from the "kid-a-pult." Layla looked shocked and then grinned. Almost all of the other kids had scars on their bodies. From that moment on, Layla gradually began to transform. That night she began interacting with the other girls. On day three, she tossed her shirt in the air and yelled, "Whoot! Whoot!," before bed. On day four, she "misplaced" her bathing suit and asked to wear one of the extras.

On departure day as Layla spotted her family, she shouted, "Mom, we have to go bikini shopping! All of my friends here have scars just like mine!" At that point, her mother burst into tears, hugged me and said, "This place has given my daughter the greatest gift she's ever received and we thank all of you."

Layla has returned for many years and always brings her bikini.

Karen Fox Bolles
Ormond Beach, FL
Counselor

Make Me Smile

You, you always make me smile, when I could only frown
I wish I could see you now
Ooh, I'm just a step behind, you're always on my mind.
We'll meet again somehow.

About midway through my first summer as the camp music specialist, I was feeling a bit insecure about my job performance. I had learned the camp songs and even written a couple of my own. I was the DJ at dances, and had expanded the music program with some fresh and innovative ideas. I had not, in my opinion, gotten a grasp on the counselor aspect of my position. I was still awkward while trying to apply the skills I had learned at orientation, and I did not feel as though I had made any of those magical camper connections my peers were sharing with me during down time.

One of the things I introduced was a music free choice. After a refreshing post-lunch nap time, campers could choose to come back to the dining hall and write a song with me. One week, there was an oldest camper named Michelle who liked to sing and write poetic lyrics. She was very excited about writing a song together. We talked about music and then got to work. The song itself was written very quickly, as if we were just plucking ideas like apples from a tree. The result was a song called "Make Me Smile", which would eventually find its way into the camp songbook, to be enjoyed at campfires, lunches, and closing ceremonies for summers to come.

The legacy of that song is not the point of the story. The real subject is the connection I made with this special girl, which gave me confidence to finish the summer and return for three more. It was also a connection that led to a wonderful friendship that Michelle and I share to this day.

Dale Youmans
Mount Dora, FL
Music Specialist, Counselor

Nathan's Ziploc Bags

Nathan was sweet, shy, slightly socially awkward and extremely homesick. He was 16 and had never been away from home, not even for a night. At rest hour, we would sit on the porch and talk. He would say he wanted to go home every time we met, but then he would decide to stay for just a little bit longer after discussing the upcoming activities. This continued for a few days. Part of his anxiety about staying stemmed from not knowing what clothes to wear the next day. His mom had packed ziploc bags and in each bag was a complete outfit packed very nice and neat. Still, he was anxious to know what were the right clothes to wear each day. His counselor asked me if we should remove the clothes out of the ziploc bags. I told him we can give Nathan that option but that would be his decision. Nathan said no, he wanted to keep it the way it was, and we left it at that.

As the week progressed, he started to loosen up. He still wanted to chat each day but things were getting better. Success came the last full day of camp. I went into the cabin to help the boys pack and what I saw made my heart smile. Nathan's clothes were all intermingled, and there was not a ziploc bag in sight. Later, I learned that he had picked out his own clothes that day, not by grabbing a ziploc bag, but by choosing the items he wanted to wear. I was so proud.

That week at camp, Nathan made a friend, tried new things, gained some independence and most importantly, built up his confidence. That's what camp does. Camp builds kids up. Camp helps them grow. Camp helps them shine.

A month later, I received a hand-written thank you card from Nathan. I still have it today because I never want to forget. His mom wrote that camp was the best thing that had happened to her son. Camp was the best thing that ever happened to me as well!

Emily Tracy Toy
Paducah, KY
Former Camper, Unit Leader

Proof that Anything is Possible

Stars filled the night sky as campers enjoyed their first night by the campfire along Lake Vanare. I was one of the counselors for the oldest boys. They were extremely high energy, eager to maximize their time at camp, and, for some, this was their last week ever as a camper. Robert was in my cabin for the third year, and it had been a privilege watching him blossom into the young man he has become today. However, upon his arrival, I noticed Robert did not have the usual contagious energy he radiates while at camp.

Following campfire, I pulled him aside and asked him how his year was. He explained to me how he had struggled with bullying and had felt heartbroken to cope with the reality of life. From that moment forward, I was going to make certain that Robert saw his greatness again.

He embraced the role as a leader for our cabin. For the last 5 years, Robert had wanted to stand up on stage and sing for everyone in the audience, but nerves and lack of confidence have prevented him from doing so. However, this year was different. Robert would sing, not just to entertain the camp, but because standing on that stage stands for so much more. It's PROOF that anything is possible, and adversity is not meant to tear you down, but to bring you back to your feet stronger than before.

Once on stage, Robert's hand began to shake as he held the microphone. Sweat dripped down his cheek, and his face was frozen with fear. The rest of our cabin stood to their feet and walked over to the stage. They all hugged Robert and with their arms linked, stood behind him smiling out at the audience. Robert's eyes flooded with tears, as his voice projected through the dining hall. At that moment, we were all witness to the effects of empowerment. That was Robert's last night at camp, and it will echo in all of our hearts forever.

Evan Xanthos
San Diego, CA
Counselor

235

This past summer I had the most remarkable experience working with four 16-year-old campers with Spina Bifida. For the first few days it seemed like they couldn't have cared less about being at camp. They had been to camp for years, so most of our activities seemed repetitive. As a counselor I started feeling a bit down, thinking there was nothing I could do to make these guys have a good week.

The last night of camp, we went to camp closing and our Unit Leaders began throwing wish sticks into the fire. I looked over to Camden, one of our campers, and saw that he was sitting in his wheelchair with tears streaming down his face. I was shocked; maybe this week did have an impact on him.

After camp closing, we told our campers that we had a surprise planned. We blindfolded them and led them to the tree house for shakers. Shakers are an activity we do at camp with the oldest campers. The campers remain blindfolded, and we give them each a shaker. Then, the counselors read specific statements and, if that statement applies to the camper, they shake their shaker. So we started. "Shake if your favorite color is blue." *shake shake.* "Shake if you do not let your illness define you." *shake shake.* "Shake if camp has changed your life" *shake shake.* This continued for ten minutes and, by the end, all you could hear were sniffles and shakes.

We took them back to the cabin and had open candle where campers could say anything on their mind. Camden spoke quietly at first, but he told us how camp had changed his life, how camp had given him a positive outlook on life, and how the friends he made at camp would be his lifelong friends. By the end of the night we were all soaked with tears. Never again would I doubt that this place has an impact on every single camper that walks through the gates.

Carly Blatt
Lutherville, MD
Counselor

We called them Summits. A late night meeting where the group would sit around a single candle and converse about topics as small as pebbles or as large as mountains. With thirteen-year-old boys, a Summit can be an interesting blend of thoughts including deep emotions about finding yourself or even opinions to the peril, "Do girls have cooties?" However, what set this Summit apart was these boys around the candle had one serious thing in common: HIV.

Summit always started silent, serious, and thirsty for discussion. The group would first be asked a question by one of the counselors and, if they chose, they would express their answer. We asked, "How has your illness changed your life?" The boys shared, bonded, and found that they had more in common than an immunodeficiency disease. As the tears were wiped away and Summit was seemingly ending, one boy asked a question that no one will ever forget.

"But are any of you happy you have HIV? Because I am."

For what seemed like an eternity no one spoke. How can someone be happy living with a disease that might someday take their life? The 13 year old continued, "I'm constantly terrified that I have HIV. But, if I didn't have HIV, I wouldn't work as hard as I do now. I wouldn't have met my heroes, the people in my support groups. I wouldn't be as strong as I am now, and I know I wouldn't be as brave. If I didn't have HIV...I wouldn't be me."

The group immediately came into agreement. Instead of running from HIV, they would face it. Instead of HIV being a weakness, they would make it a strength. Instead of being ashamed, they would be proud. It was that moment that they took something horrible and made it beautiful. It was that moment that this group of individuals would no longer be called boys. They would be called men.

Stephen Lansing
Lovell, ME
Counselor

In the fall of 2009, I spent $50 on a full fur, head-to-toe, chicken costume for a Halloween themed weekend at camp. Little did I know the impact this chicken suit would have on a particularly shy camper.

The chicken suit and I made many appearances at family weekend dances. As several years passed, the suit was nearing its retirement. The fur feathers were getting dingy, and it smelled odd. We made fewer appearances at camp, but one weekend I hadn't planned for the theme, so I brought the suit. That's where I met my camper pal, Charles.

At 12 years-old, Charles was super polite and always helpful but painfully shy around the other campers. As much as we tried to engage him in group activities, he would blend into the background unnoticed. That all changed when he agreed to wear the chicken suit to the dance.

In all honestly, I was joking when I offered Charles the chicken suit. I didn't think he would say yes, and I didn't know what I was going to wear if he was the chicken. But when he said he wanted to wear it, who was I to deny him the suit. And I've never seen a finer looking chicken! The smile on his face was priceless!

Charles, his family and I entered the dance through the front door and all eyes were on us. Even at camp, it's hard NOT to make a grand entrance in a chicken suit. I was a little nervous how he was going to react to the attention, but Charles was the star of the show! Younger campers wanted to meet him, and fellow volunteers lined up to get their picture taken with him. He loved every minute of it! Charles was a changed kid. I was thrilled that my suit could make such a difference in my camper's experience. From that point on, I've never questioned how such a small thing can cause such a huge impact.

Cory Lynne Mulligan
Orlando, FL
Counselor

The Evolution of the Smile

My family and I have been attending family camp for the past 3 years. As parents, we always want what's best for our kids. We hope that they can have fun and enjoy life regardless of their medical condition. We want them to be happy and proud of who they are. Camp is unique in that everyone and their individuality is celebrated. Everyone is welcomed to be just who they are. We have experienced joy and growth, as individuals and as a family. I have seen my children grow, laugh and smile.

This past weekend, I was able to give back by volunteering as the camp photographer. To be on the other side of the camp was a wonderful experience. There were over 12 new families. Since I had already had an opportunity to experience the wonders of camp, I was able to see the excitement change in the families.

On arrival night, each family kept pretty close to their own family and sidekick, with anxious smiles. Everyone was basically still trying to figure out "what was going on." The next day, all the families began interacting with each other, taking time to learn about each family, and strengthen their own family. By the end of the night, the parents' smiles had changed. They were relaxed smiles, full of laughter and normalcy. It was a wonderful privilege to photograph this weight lifted off of the parents to remind them how to smile, how to laugh, and how to live.

Riann Taylor
Columbus, OH
Camper Parent

The Second Week

I was still flooded with the feeling of what I like to call, "nervited," or in other words, nervousness and excitement. Camp provided me with challenges that I had never faced before. Never had I taken care of children with severe disabilities or illnesses for a week, but I wanted greatly to give it my all, no matter how daunting the tasks may have seemed.

During the second week, I met a camper who made a tremendous impact on my life. Alyssa, who had a form of cancer, could not walk, see, eat, or speak clearly. However, she was highly intelligent, kind, and very beautiful. I remember her first day at camp when she was so anxious of what to expect. I remember watching Alyssa on the second day get comfortable with her surroundings, and the thrill I experienced as I discovered her love for music. As I reflect on the third day of camp, I am reminded of the moments splashing in the pool, and of her playing mini-golf and getting a hole-in-one while listening to the sound of the ball roll into the hole. My heart filled with overflowing warmth as she wrapped me in her arms in the tightest and most loving bear hug I had ever had.

The fourth day was unforgettable for everyone in the theater as Alyssa sang "The Climb" by Miley Cyrus on stage. Her victory against fear sent tears down my cheeks. Considering everything this young girl had been through and be so brave provided me, as well as everyone else in the audience, with a sense of radiant joy.

By the end of the week, my heart ached to see Alyssa go. Even though I often could not understand her words, I grew a strong love for her and thought of her as if she were my sister. While giving me one final hug, Alyssa asked, "Will I ever see you again?" With tears streaming down my cheeks, I said, "Yes, I sure hope so!"

Savannah Maynor
Asheville, NC
Counselor

Three Days to Change A Life

A families' first time at camp can be quite daunting. They are greeted by enthusiastic counselors who know what camp is all about. For them, they don't know what's ahead of them. The Smyth family were nervous and shy on arrival. Lily was annoyed she was taken from school early; Oliver had spent the majority of his life surrounded by family and doctors and was nervous about having others look after him; and Mum and Dad thought that camp was all about the kids. They did not realize what was about to happen.

Three days later, the Smyth family had transformed. Lily, who was shy and withdrawn before camp, had spent hours with counselors playing games and having fun. In the words of her Dad, "Two months ago, she would have been curled up under my arm. Now look at her with complete strangers, having the time of her life." Oliver equally enjoyed himself, especially dancing in the dining hall after meals.

But the biggest impact of all was on Mum and Dad. For the first time in as long as they could remember, they got the chance to dress up and spend time together at the banquet without having to worry about the kids. When you have a seriously-ill child, this is often difficult to do. Camp gave them this opportunity. It was no longer just about the kids, it was about the whole family. They went through a life-changing experience which they didn't expect. For me, I felt privileged to have been a part of making this happen.

Zita McAlister
Dublin, Ireland
Counselor

I had the honor and privilege of working with a cabin of 14 to 16 year old girls. They were collectively seen as a "tough nut to crack," but I saw nothing but potential. One camper, Eva, had a lot of baggage following her to camp. She was overweight which bothered her immensely, struggled with depression, lack of self-esteem, and wanted to rebel from societal norms any way she could, be it her clothes, hair, rules or choice of conversation topics. She was my favorite.

On the first full day, our cabin was assigned to the Low Ropes Course, the perfect way to get our girls to open up to each other, communicate better and start working together. The first activity was The Wild Woozy buddy walk. This is a tight rope but made for two people to work together as a team to walk down the wires, leaning on each other for balance and support. With each pair that went up on the challenge course, Eva got more involved, encouraging them and giving them tips on where to step. But she herself would not get onto the challenge course. As an overweight woman myself, I had a feeling I knew why she wouldn't do it: better to not try than to try and fail as a heavy person. I turned to my friend running the activity and said, "If you ask Eva to do the challenge course with you, I bet she will."

Watching Eva step up onto that tight rope and grab hands with my friend was incredible. With each step they took down the line, I saw her fear turn to determination turn to excitement turn to complete joy. Eva made it farther along the tight ropes than anyone else that day. Every girl cheered for her along the way and shouted congratulations when she made it so close to the end. She was now the camper that had tried and accomplished something she had previously determined she couldn't do. I knew in that moment we had turned a corner with our cabin and Eva.

Hilary Craw
Los Angeles, CA
Counselor

Chapter X

WELCOME HOME

Slugs on the sidewalk and dew on my shoes
and not knowing any American news.
The path to the barn, the path to the lake,
the path from the back gate when no one's awake.

Stealing precious moments in the garden alone,
then Bulmer's in town and priceless walks home.
Playing Jenga with kids and Redarse with the staff,
each moment bringing new reasons to laugh.

Banoffee Pie and chocolate profiteroles,
stubborn kids who ate nothing but dinner rolls.
Rhubarb yogurt, croissants, hot tea,
stashing Ribena's - what? who? not me!

Ten different languages, somehow it works
once you get used to the cultural quirks.
Watching kids open up, seeing kids make new friends,
hearing kids say they can't wait to come back again.

Unexpected connections and soft conversations,
A lesson each week in a new kind of patience.
Cottage Chat nights that leave you with chills,
sunsets over camp from atop Bishop's Hill.
Sheep at my window, sheep in the distance,
a beautiful life, a perfect existence.

Rosie Thede Potter
Louisville, KY
Counselor

A Hug to Last a Year

I was in the dining hall talking about the upcoming session of camp with some fellow counselors. We were all a little nervous, but very excited about the campers coming to play. I couldn't wait to catch up with the returning campers that I had met during previous summers. The other counselors and I were exchanging stories when we all heard my name shouted at the top of someone's lungs. I turned around to see Melanie come running through the doors straight at me. It didn't look like she was going to slow down. Next thing I know, she had jumped. Luckily, my arms were open waiting for the hug that I knew was coming.

That hug was an amazing way to start the week. I hadn't seen Melanie in a year, and it was great to catch up with her. The question of whether or not your campers will remember you was answered in that hug. This is their home, and we are family.

One of the greatest aspects about coming back to camp is the possibility of getting to watch campers you have known for years grow up before your eyes. I had met Melanie six years before when she had first come to camp full of the same energy but in a much shorter frame. Watching her grow up at camp was an amazing experience. She reminded me that what I did as a counselor made a difference, and that it mattered.

Linh Nguyen, RN
Jacksonville, FL
Counselor

A Reason to Smile Again

In the spring of 2009, Katie and I were at one of her Doctors appointments when one of the nurses gave us a flier for camp. I didn't think much of it, but when we got home, I noticed it had a website listed to take a video tour of the camp. So I did. I was so amazed that I hollered down the hall for Katie to come and look at this place. I read every single word about it and thought this place would truly take care of my daughter for me. We filled out the application and anxiously waited on pins and needles to see if she could attend. Finally we got the all-exciting email saying that Katie had been approved for her session.

The closer and closer we got, the more apprehensive I was. I'm sure Katie was too. We pulled to the front gate and were promptly welcomed by a King and Queen. They helped us unload Katie's bags and said not to worry about them. We were then escorted to the Well Shell. We walked into that building and saw nothing but happiness and excitement by every single person. We met with the nurse who would be in charge of Katie's medications and welfare. For many years, I was the ONLY one who took care of Katie's needs, day or night. Now I was leaving her with a stranger. I was nervous and scared that something would go wrong. But with the ease that this nurse took with us, listening to our concerns and letting us ask anything, I knew that this was the right place to be. Finally, Katie was all checked in. I got back into my car, turned on my music and headed home. I literally cried for 45 minutes.

At the end of the week, I was escorted to the Dining Hall where my gorgeous, happy child was awaiting. The best thing she brought home was a HUGE smile. I hadn't seen that smile in years. And I mean years. I am so glad that camp returned the brightness and cheerfulness back to me in my daughter.

Nancy Giertz
Bakersfield, CA
Camper Parent

Badges of Courage

My favorite part of camp has always been the pool. Not just because it's a highly anticipated, and a very necessary, respite from the 100+ degree heat in central Florida. But because it's one of those times when the magic of camp is palpable.

Each summer, my heart campers would race into the locker room, their tiny feet clapping on the tiled floor, as they wriggled out of their now-sweaty shirts and shorts, and into their High School Musical-adorned swimsuits. And as they lined up with their swim buddies, their eyes would start to wander to their fellow camper's chests and backs. For the first time, they were surrounded by little bodies that looked just like theirs.

Each camper had a scar from surgery peeking out from behind their suits, on their sternum, underneath their collarbones, or wrapping around their shoulder blades.

Tickled with excitement, they would trace their tiny fingers over their own chest scars – which were so often hidden behind carefully chosen shirts and blouses at school – and eagerly point them out. Once a symbol of difference, now a symbol of belonging and pride.

Every summer at heart camp, Mr. Spivey, the old man who lives across the lake, tells heart campers that those scars are nothing to be ashamed of, but instead are "badges of courage." And in the pool, everyone seemed to agree.

Alex Murphy
Anna Maria Island, FL
Former Camper, Counselor

In the Fall of 2012, I was a senior in high school, and my sister, Jenny, returned from her first summer at camp. She was eager to share her camp stories and I was ready to listen. We would sit for hours upon hours as she shared story after story. Every word she spoke was with a passion so deep it compelled me to believe that camp was an extraordinary place filled with incredible kids.

In that moment, I felt a challenge placed on my heart to bike from Kentucky to Florida to raise money and awareness, so that more kids would have the opportunity to attend camp. We began raising money and then we were training. Before we knew it, it was July 4th, and we were on our way to Florida. We rode in the rain and the hot summer heat; we rode over Tennessee mountains and Georgia's rolling hills; and we rode with semi-trucks and slow moving tortoises.

After 2 weeks, 5 states and 725 miles, we turned on to Brantley Branch Road. We had made it. The journey was breathtaking, but no words can describe the moment I rode into camp and down cabin row. I was anxious and eager to round the corner, to see the kids who had inspired me to bike across the country. And when I did, it was like nothing I'd ever seen. The campers were crowded at the end of every sidewalk all shouting "Maggie! Maggie! Maggie!" There were signs that were written for me, campers waving at me. Just me. I felt the unconditional love before I even spoke a word. This was love my sister had raved about for countless hours. I had kids tell me, I was a hero. If only they knew, that they were my heroes. These are not just incredible kids, they are the world's greatest kids.

Maggie Abney
Owensboro, KY
Counselor

Camp is Love and No Judgments

One of our little boys needed to wear a catheter to bed. We tried to keep it hidden so none of the other campers would notice, and no questions would be asked that would cause embarrassment. Boys will be boys, and it didn't end up that way.

As we were putting the boys to bed, one of the boys saw it and said, "What is that?" Well, the counselors and I all looked at each other not knowing whether we should redirect or let it play out. We decided to let it play out and boy are we glad we did. He jumped up on top of his bed as if he was about to make this grand proclamation and proudly exclaimed, "Well, this right here is the COOLEST thing ever. While all you guys need to get up in the middle of the night to go to the bathroom, I don't have to. I can just stay laying in bed and this thing collects it."

With all their jaws dropped, the little boys started circling around asking us where they could get one and how they didn't want to be getting out of bed in the middle of the night either and that was the coolest thing they have ever seen.

Camp is truth and learning to accept who you are.

Camp is love and no judgments.

Stephanie Gilman
Miami, FL
Counselor

I attended a Diabetes family weekend and didn't really know what to expect as I had only worked with camp during the summer when families aren't too involved other than for drop-off and pick-up. We entered the dining hall for our first meal, and I noticed a menu on each table. The menu listed all the food options for that meal AND important details like number of carbohydrates. My family sat down at their table and, for the first time in a long time, they didn't have to restrict food from their son with diabetes or worry about counting carbs or calories. A weight was lifted, and they were able to enjoy a meal as a "normal" family. Their son even got to have dessert!

The look on their son's face at lunch when everyone whipped out their monitors put a smile on my face. That was the first time since he'd been diagnosed that he felt "normal" again. They all took shots, tested their blood sugar, had experienced lows and highs... together.

At the end of the weekend, a older teen camper told me that it's been hard to find people that he can relate to since his diagnosis. He continued, "It's tough to feel like you're the only person in the world who has to deal with this, but then you go to camp. Camp, to me, is a place where I feel safe and people understand what I'm going through. When I'm here, everyone gets it, no one stares, and there's no explanation necessary. Camp has really impacted me and motivated me to take care of myself."

Sharisse Roberts
Casselberry, FL
Counselor

Embrace It, Relish It, Soak It Up

In the summer of 2011, I stepped off the plane in LAX international terminal to start my own camp journey. My first introduction to this world was through my roommate, whom had been both camper and "cairde" (which means counselor). I had only heard stories about the mayhem that is Silly-O, or no hands spaghetti, and stories never prepare you for the real thing.

During camp, I rarely ate food with a knife and a fork, and I would inevitably find myself in a dress, having lost a series of "bets" with campers. We would stay up well into the night to make sure everything was in place for the next day's fun-tivities (Disclaimer: 'Fun-tivities' is a new word created by me by smashing "fun" and "activities" together).

Our esteemed leader and all-around human wonder woman, April would talk at length that summer about the counselors being the backbone of the camp, the ones that kept everything running smoothly. In reality, it was the campers themselves who inspired everyone around them. Each week we would be surrounded by hundreds of campers, who refused to let an illness define who they are as people. How could you not be inspired!

My time at camp is something that will stay with me for the rest of my life. To all the campers, to all the staff and the families. To all the people who have or who will come to experience first hand the magic that is camp, I offer this one bit of advice: Embrace it. Relish every last morsel of it. Soak it all up. Camp is a symbol of courage, of willpower; it's a symbol of all the good we are capable of achieving as people. Most importantly, though, camp is a place to have FUN!

Stephen O'Riordan
Dublin, Ireland
Counselor

When Abigail was 7 years old, we sent her off to camp by herself, even though she had never spent the night away from us, not even at a sleepover. We had been there for a family weekend together, and each of us had fallen in love with the place, the people, the surroundings and that special magic felt there. We were nervous, but knew she was safe and would have the time of her life there. There is no other place on earth we would have been comfortable leaving her without us for a week.

Still, I worried, since I hadn't seen her face or heard her voice all week. We arrived at camp at the end of her week, went to the dining hall where we were to meet our kids, and didn't see her right away. We met her counselors who told us some of the fun things they had done, that she loved swimming and horses and that she had fallen asleep at the dining hall table the first night. One counselor told me that she had been sad the night before, and even cried a little. "Really?" I thought. "Poor girl must have gotten homesick." The counselor then gently told me that she had cried because she knew it was her last night at camp, and she didn't want to leave this place.

Finally, we spotted Abby playing in the far back of the dining hall, smiling and full of confidence and joy. I caught a glimpse of the young woman she has now grown into.

Camp is where she can be herself, challenge herself, stretch her imagination and spread her wings. It has shaped her perspective about her illness and has given her a touch-stone, a place to call "hers", a place to give back to, and a place to keep in her heart for the times when life is challenging.

Abby finally came over to us in the dining hall, that last day of her first week at camp, and greeted us with a hug and a question, "When do I get to come back here again?"

Kathleen Howell Fitzpatrick
Sacramento, CA
Camper Parent

Our son, Christian, has attended Heart camp for the past two summers and is looking forward to another summer week of unbridled fun! A trip to Disney World can be an anticipated joy to look forward to, but camp is a never-ending journey that is rooted deep inside his heart that brings a sense of fullness, peace, love, belonging, and so much more!

Christian began packing for camp including his tooth brush a few days ahead of schedule! Watching the GPS, he became increasingly excited when we were 10 minutes away from camp, then 8 minutes. At 5 minutes and counting, Christian wanted all the windows down so he could see the approach! When we drove through the security gate, I really believed he could run to the cabin faster than I could drive! However, he did stay in the car with us! We learned we were in Yellow 10. Eagle eyes, that he is, spotted the cabin first and was ready to leap from the car and sprint the remaining distance! The week was filled with excitement, energy, anticipation, PING PONG, dance, woodshop and so much love!

Eleanor Roosevelt once expressed that many people come in and out of our lives but only a handful leave their footprints in our hearts. Camp has left a permanent mark in Christian's heart as well as his family's! We are ALL very proud to be a member of the camp family!

Anna Daigle
Spring Hill, FL
Camper Parent

In 2008, my then 7-year-old was diagnosed with a rare blood disorder called ITP. The first two years were a blur of endless doctor appointments, blood draws, medications and multiple hospital visits. With the risk of bleeding, there were also many "no's." No more soccer. No wrestling with sisters. No more carefree childhood.

While at our Hematology office I saw a pamphlet for a medical camp. They were hosting a weekend camp for children with blood disorders and their families, free of charge. It sounded too good to be true. We filled out the paperwork, and the day finally came.

We were excited and nervous but soon realized camp was a very special place. The staff greeted us like old friends. Our counselors for the weekend were two caring and compassionate college students who treated our family like celebrities. To them, our daughter wasn't just "some sick kid." They were genuinely interested in her.

We were shown to the gym where the other campers and their families were assembling. Until that day, we had never met another family dealing with this illness, but here we found ourselves in the midst of a dozen. It was overwhelming to finally be with others who completely understood and spoke our "language."

There was a healing that weekend, something we will never forget. We saw our daughter open up and learn to laugh and be silly again. She met other kids her age battling the same disorder. Lifelong friends who could share in the good and the bad with her. We met some of the most beautiful people on this earth.

Each time we top the hill and see those blue roofs, there are screams of excitement and joy. The day we leave, there are tears. Camp has stolen our hearts, and we are grateful for all that they do.

April Loy
Austin, IN
Camper Parent

"We didn't realize we were making memories, we just knew we were having fun."

As soon as you step onto the camp, there is a breath of "this place is good" that washes over you. Take a few steps and you're bound to cross the path of the Blue Pride off to the horse barn, the Yellow Pride shuffling to arts & crafts, or the Red Pride in colorful costumes, at the theater. Big deep breath…this place is good!

Two days before the last day of camp, it became apparent to me that camp had become my camper's place to soar. While walking back from the evening's activities, Joseph asked "Can I stay here at camp after everyone leaves?" followed by a long monologue about how much fun he had had in just 4 short days. These feelings were reinforced during the last night at camp again, when Joseph changed the question to, "Can I stay here at camp forever?" I can still hear his voice asking these questions in my head and every time I replay it in my mind, the best part about his questions is that he was asking out of complete seriousness. I am sure Joseph is counting down the days until next summer when he'll be able to spend another week independent and free to discover new talents and abilities.

There is no question in my mind that this camp changes the lives of each and every one of these kids. It absolutely changed mine. At camp, you have fun. You give hugs and high fives. You do things for the very first time. You become empowered to do anything you want to do, find success, overcome challenges and be who you are. Campers and counselors take home many memories, and some of the strongest friendships are formed. At camp, we give tokens that read "good for a lifetime." Camp, indeed, is good for a lifetime.

Christopher Carter
Nashville, TN
Counselor, Pride Leader

That summer of 2005 was one of the best summers of my life. The campers, staff, and volunteers changed my life, and I made memories that will last a lifetime. It's a magical place, where "sick" kids can just be kids. It's a place where many "firsts" take place and so much love is shared. I have seen campers arrive so shy that they literally hid from sight, only to stand on stage, singing in front of the entire camp a few days later. I have seen campers trust enough to try swallowing their meds whole for the first time, no longer resigned to eating bitter, mashed up pills several times a day. I have seen a camper, formerly terrified of water, jump into the deep end of the pool for the first time after passing his swim test. Our campers have shown us what true bravery looks like and how to smile in the midst of adversity. I am overwhelmed by the changes that our campers have made and inspired by how they have changed us in return. From meeting my boating and fishing partner, Joey, until the last camper left, I will be forever grateful to the Best Camp on Earth.

Ashley Jenkins
Knoxville, TN
Activity Counselor

Like a Phenix

In June 2013, the Power House fire roared through Lake Hughes, which is where the camp is located. The fire devastated the community, and the summer and fall sessions at camp were cancelled for the health sake of the campers. It was a year and two weeks before camp resumed and we welcomed our first campers!

It was thrilling to be back at camp with so many eager campers at the Skeletal Dysphasia session. The Dining Hall was alive with laughter and music, the lake echoed with shouts of delight as fish were caught (and kissed and released!), and children smiled with new friends beside the new vegetation and emerging landscape. It was evident that the spirit of camp had returned like a phenix, stronger and more full of life than ever.

While I was helping one of the youngest boy campers in the woodshop he said, "Pops, I need help with a project. I want to make a boat. I missed camp last year because of the fire, and I have been dreaming of making it for two years!" So I told him let's see what we can come up with. We worked together and created his boat. Afterwards he told me, "Pops, YOU made my dream a reality!" I smiled down at him and put my hand up to high-five him but he looked up at me with a funny look. "Pops, a high-five is not good enough" and proceeded to give me a huge hug. This made my summer and it was only the first full day of the first session of the summer. This is why we do it; to help make kids' dreams a reality.

Pops and Sherry Immel
Lake Hughes, CA
Counselor

Before my first summer in 2012, when I was informed that I would be a cabin counselor for 13-year-old girls, my expectation was drama, drama, and more drama. Boy, was I wrong!

One moment, in particular, is permanently etched in my soul. As we were walking as a group to the Body Shop, Penelope made a comment, "I only act this way here and at home. This is me, and I am happy!" Penelope had no idea that her innocent comment had touched me to my core. When I thought it over after being with her for only 6 days, I realized that I knew Penelope's beautiful, caring, fun, outgoing spirit better than some of her friends at school, her teachers, her coaches, etc. How lucky can one counselor be?!

I learned that those girls have lived more in their 13 years than I had in my 25. Talk about humbling! That magic is with me every day. I thank the staff, volunteers and the campers for showing me the delightful enchantment of camp. I will never forget!

Sarah Charlick
Jenkintown, PA
Counselor

There's a rhythm to every summer camp session. Nervousness fills the air as we all learn one another's names and get settled on Cabin Row. Parents wave goodbye and busses arrive from far and wide. Counselors retrieve forgotten items at the Well Shell, a fortress of extra toothbrushes and turtle pillows. Cell phones are powered down in favor of an unplugged environment. The energy in the air is electric as we start the adventure of a lifetime packed into one week. The first campfire signals the beginning of it all as the sun sets, and our nostrils adjust to the scent of sunscreen and bug spray. Loud chants carry their way across cabin row, all the way up to the horse barn. Stars in the Sky is softly sung as the night comes to an end. This is the soundtrack to the moment just before everything changes, the moment where a bunch of cabins and paths and buildings become a home away from home.

Somewhere between the restless anticipation of those first few hours of camp and the slideshow at the end of the week, we become a family. A neon-wearing, no-hands-spaghetti-eating, random-act-of-kindness-promoting, Silly-Olympian, cha-cha-sliding-under-a-fire-truck family. For some it happens when they slide down the zip line for the first time, for others it is the empowerment of performing at Stage Night or the comfort of a cabin chat with new friends. It's impossible to pick one moment that defines camp for everyone. We all have moments where the impact of camp has grabbed a hold of us and changed our lives. As staff members, we treasure all of those moments and talk about them long after our campers go home.

We all count our lucky Stars in the Sky that we somehow crossed paths with the camp community. You are always in our hearts and we are honored to know you.

Kristin Friedersdorf
Costa Mesa, CA
Residential Life Coordinator

Packing and Unpacking

As I unpack my bag upon returning home from camp, I am immediately engulfed with the smell of bug spray, sunscreen and campfires. The smells welcome the memories of a summer that will forever be in my mind and my heart. I feel a little sad as I unpack what seems to be an arsenal of glitter-covered mementoes and sparkly headbands. As I reach the bottom of my bag, I can't help but shed a tear as I pull out and unfold my Spanish flamenco dancer cooking apron which had been proudly worn each session in the Kitchen of Dreams, a place where campers could experiment with different cuisines and cooking skills in a supportive community.

After unpacking, I sit at my computer looking at the hundreds of pictures that I took over the course of the summer. I see the story of true hope and love unfold in front of me. I see children who have been given so many limits in their lives run, dance, and play as if there wasn't a problem in the world; kids who have every reason to be angry with life laugh and joke with each other. Young men and women conquer tasks that normal people fear like climbing rock walls and a ropes course. All done knowing they have serious illnesses and questionable futures. I feel a sense of honor come over me knowing that I was part of a child's dream.

All I can think about is how much I take life for granted. How quickly things can change for the worse. How these kids have taught me that the worst thing in life is limiting yourself. Camp isn't limited to changing the lives of those children. I think I got the best lesson in life yet. Life is precious, and not just my own, but the lives of everyone around me. *"The time is short and there's so much to do/Don't waste a moment of what's given to you/Don't waste a moment 'cause you'll never see it return."*

Meera Ramamoorthy, MD
Cincinnati, OH
Counselor

Looking through my photo album of a summer at camp, I see...

...the camp director wearing a cowboy hat and a pink feather boa, holding the attention of hundreds gathered around the campfire as she tells the legend of the neighbor across the lake.

...kids huddled on the floor of the stage, eagerly writing a theatrical masterpiece, which comes to life in fantastic costumes.

...pinkies up and fancy dresses, as campers and counselors drink tea, eat sweets, all while talking in lovely English accents.

...not so sleepy sweethearts eating popsicles in their pajamas, after a sneak-out to the kitchen, and before tiptoeing back to their beds, just in time for the camp director's nightly rounds.

...happy faces at the pool, splashing and laughing together.

...cheeks, lips and chins covered in tomato sauce, a hazard of eating spaghetti with your face in honor of the Silly Olympics.

...masses of cheering youngsters, covered in red paint, waiting expectantly to give their counselors chocolate pudding facials.

...senior girls posing in their beautiful dresses before making a grand entrance at the dance.

...triumphant and exhausted smiles on a counselor and a camper who have just helped one another conquer the climb to the top of the ropes course and zip line back down to their cheering cabin-mates.

...rows of girls lying on pillows, cucumbers on their eyes, a mix of oatmeal and yogurt on their faces, a fresh coat of nail polish on their toes, in a state of total relaxation.

...hundreds of candles casting a warm glow as friends reflect, and remember, and share a moment of love and understanding.

Looking through my photo album, all these exciting, silly, touching, emotional, magical moments come right back to me.

Carly Robinson
New York, NY
Counselor

I was following two 14-year-old campers with Muscular Dystrophy down the hill from horses, one in a motorized wheelchair and one with crutches and leg braces. As they made their way slowly down the hill, one girl said, "I wish there was some magical and safe place that we could go, or could live, or could visit, where it didn't matter to anyone what our body looks like or whether we have disabilities or conditions that make us different. I wish we could just 'be' and everyone would love us for who we really are without judging us because of our being special needs."

The girl in leg braces, using crutches that wrapped around her forearms to enable her to walk, moved quickly to stand in front of her friend, causing her wheelchair to come to a stop...

"Look around, girl... This is that place! We have it right here!"

Tav Huffman, RN
Portland, OR
Camp Nurse

Emma was only 7 years old when her doctor told us about this new camp for kids just like her. We signed her up and less than a month later we were checking in at camp. As a mom of a sick little girl, I was very nervous about leaving her for a whole week. I wanted to protect my her, but I knew that through isolating her, I made her feel alone in her situation. My fears were gone as soon as we arrived. Volunteers were everywhere ready to help! Everyone knew who she was and welcomed her with open arms. A counselor came up and invited her to participate in a scavenger hunt. And boom, she was off and running, barely saying goodbye!

When we picked her up, we practically needed another suitcase for all the arts and crafts and woodshop projects she did, not to mention her turtle pillow and blanket. She couldn't wait to return. The sparkle in her eyes was back. The camp stories tumbled out with a kid's excitement. She took a new confidence and independence back to school with her. Camp was able to do what I was unable to do. They were able to give my little girl her childhood back. Camp made us all realize that we are not alone and that there is hope. It had been the best week of her life!

Kristen Sweaza
Orange, CA
Camper Parent

The Frog and the Princess

I believe in the magic of camp...to my core. I believe if a broken heart enters the gates of camp, it will return not only completely mended but beaming with joy. It happened to me. Many times.

I had the honor of being the camp photographer and work in a boys' cabin one of the years I worked at camp. Having only played in a girls' cabin my other years at camp, I knew that I was in for a new experience and that I would have to keep my bug fears and clean fingernails in my back pocket for another day.

We had youngest campers for Cancer week. "Babies" we call them, even though they are between the ages of 7-9. I was unpacking the suitcases with one of the kids when he looked at me, touched the mediport scar on my chest and said, "We're the same" as he showed me his mediport scar. I, of course, choked up and just said "Yep! We sure are" and excused myself to the porch to process that something so profound could come from someone so small.

I watched the bus stop in front of the cabin and went out to see if we had any kids arriving when I saw this tiny curly-haired kid with a painted green face step off the bus. He looked like a little frog, and had the deep scratchy voice to match. We introduced ourselves, and I helped him carry his luggage into the cabin.

This week would be my game changer. We had the most dynamic, fun, silliest group. They chased the magic, and I chased them. That's how camp works. You empty every bit of yourself into these kids. At the end of the day they hand your heart back, so full of joy, and fun and life that it doesn't fit inside your chest anymore, so you let it carry you like a giant balloon. When it was time to say "See ya later" to those special boys, my little green frog threw his arms around my neck and said, "I love you princess" and my heart melted.

Michelle Spencer Baranowski
Tampa, FL
Former Camper, Activities Counselor

The Happiest Place on Earth

It was Departure Day in the summer of 2010, and we were doing one of our usual, lively dances after breakfast. As I was called to get on my departure bus, I burst into tears of sadness at the realization that, in that moment, I was leaving the one place that I could honestly define as "The Happiest Place on Earth." From learning to sing camp songs and burn away calories dancing after meals, to wearing dresses and doing chants at the same time while walking to the dining hall, to throwing messy food and paint at all of my cabin mates and counselors, I would have done it all ten times over if I had gotten the chance to do it again. I didn't care that I ran back to my counselors with tears in my eyes to embrace them, for what I thought would be the last time I would ever be in contact with the best mentors and friends in the world.

For me, camp was truly life-changing; an experience that made me more outgoing, inspired, and motivated than I had ever been. I walked in the first day, scared that I would still feel alone and disconnected from the people around me, as I had mostly been for the previous 15 years. Less than one week later, I had gotten to know individuals who had gone through similar experiences as I did, carrying themselves with more joy and liveliness than I had witnessed in my entire lifetime.

Now that I've had the chance to become a counselor, I continue to happily reminisce upon the memories that tied me down to what will always be my home away from home.

Louis Tan
San Francisco, CA
Former Camper, Counselor

The Lessons that Camp Taught Me

To me, one of the greatest qualities about camp life is that it holds the potential to truly empower those who call it "home." No matter your role, there is just something about medical camps, that allows you to better understand that life is best spent laughing, getting messy, having fun, embracing the camp "bubble" and forming life-long friendships. Being a counselor has taught me to invest in others, to always give my best, to live life in the moment and to continuously believe in the potential of others. When you are blessed with incalculable moments to see children accomplish amazing things, you begin to see life through a different perspective. Camp changed me for the better, and I am thankful to have had the opportunity to fall in love with the beauty and magic of the medical camp world!

One of my favorite memories came from a week where my den was filled with older teenage campers who were able to form a "sisterhood" among themselves. That whole week, we experienced lots of special moments and genuine excitement about being in the moment and investing in each experience as it arose. We ended our amazing session by having a special oldest camper campfire, and it was so beautiful to see remarkable campers share stories, memories, tears and laughter together. It was also incredible to hear these campers courageously share how their lives include a life-threatening diagnosis but is not defined by a diagnosis. To hear such strength in their voices still resonates with me today.

Ultimately, at camp I learned to live life big and never take anything for granted. Being a camp counselor taught me that when you change a child's life, you also change your own life. I am thankful for that lesson and for the camp that I call home!

Lacy Harris
Campbellsville, KY
Counselor

The Universal Language of Camp

When I first arrived at camp, I did not know much about how it worked. I was selected as a Chaperone counselor so I got to accompany the kids from Spain to camp.

At the airport all the kids were so excited, and they got along very well from the first moment. We arrived very late at night and were taken directly to a girls cottage. Before we entered into the cottage, we were told that 4 Irish girls were already sleeping, so we asked the Spanish girls to put on their pajamas in the hall and go quietly to their beds in order not to wake them up.

The next morning I felt full of energy, and I was so excited to meet the Irish girls as well as the rest of the volunteers. Everyone was super nice to me and the girls were adorable! However, a little worry came to my mind when I realized that six of the girls were 12 years old while only two of them were under 8. Moreover, these two younger girls were from different countries. I wanted them to have a great week at camp but I was not sure if the smallest ones were going to fit in or not, due to the difference of ages and languages.

Fortunately, and to my surprise, these two campers became the best of the friends during that week. I could even see them holding hands when going to the dining hall or playing hide and seek during cottage time. They showed us that even if you do not speak the same language as another person, it does not mean that you cannot communicate with each other or share amazing and magic moments that happen at camp!

Maria Cabeza Castro
Oviedo, Spain
Counselor

Where I was Meant to be

After being diagnosed with a Medulloblastoma brain tumor at eight years old, I found joy in talking to others who had been through what I had, or something similar. This is one of the reasons that camp has had such an impact on me. It was a special place for me because no one was treated like they were different. I had something in common with everyone and could make friends so easily. Best of all, the camp didn't just focus solely on our cancer, but it gave us a chance to forget illness and just be kids.

One of my favorite memories of camp was my first camp dance. I didn't know about the dance, so I borrowed a dress from the older girls, and we all did each other's makeup. Everyone treated that night with importance and respect. It was a camp tradition. We had so much fun dancing and having a good time. It was amazing to see boys and girls who had cancer have a carefree night. I even watched a beautiful young girl dance in her wheelchair, and I was inspired by her courage.

At the end of the night, we went outside and sang Taps. It was so wonderful to hear all of the campers' and counselors' voices join together in a beautiful harmony. When we were singing, it was almost as if time had stopped. I couldn't help but think that night that it was where I was meant to be. It's the people you meet along the way that help you get through difficult times. If this had never happened to me, I wouldn't know all of the beautiful people that I know today.

Lauren Lam
New York, NY
Former Camper

Chapter XI

CELEBRATE LIFE

A Heart Hijacked by Camp

My memories of camp are locked away deep inside and, when I least expect it, they pop out and bring a real sense of belonging, warmth, love and happy days. I'll find myself singing "Stars in the Sky" at random moments and immediately flash back to nights around campfires or watching end-of-session videos; memories of eating s'mores or dinner without hands make my meals now seem dull; moments of giggles when I remember the ridiculous hair styles, the endless amounts of face paint or dancing after meals.

Even as time goes by, those who touched my heart continue to leave a lasting impression. The day when one camper described how being on a horse reminded him of what it was like to walk again; seeing the pure excitement of an incredible young lady who was on dialysis have the confidence to try swimming; cradling one boy in my arms as we swung on a zip-line as tears ran down his face with happiness as he had hardly been out of the hospital for years; being given the biggest hugs at the end of the week as one girl thanked me for "forcing" her to stay on camp after she had insisted on going home at the beginning of the week. The memories are endless.

In amongst those heart-warming moments, I can't help but remember the times that my heart felt like it'd been shattered as campers shared their deepest thoughts of treatments or their concerns for their future; to have seen conditions deteriorate and to have shared the last happy days of some inspirational young people. But, each one I have met has inspired me to live and to never take for granted the opportunities that I have available to me. The determination and positive outlook of those I have met at camp, camper, counselor, parents, and medical staff, continues to spur me on, each and every day, to overcome any challenge that comes my way.

Polly Sinnett-Jones
Bangkok, Thailand
Counselor

A Moment

If you were to ask me what is the most magical time that happens at camp, it would be when I get to witness "A Moment!" The light in their eyes when they talk about how much fun they had is the most amazing experience that you have to see to believe.

When campers arrive at camp, they have beliefs and fears of who we are and what they think will happen over the next five days. That perception quickly changes as we step into a very different reality. Who and what we thought we were in the "real world" does not matter and frankly, no one cares. As if on sacred ground, we all are together for one reason only: to give these wonderful special children a little bit of something more.

A moment!

You never know when or with whom it will happen. It is a different experience for every person. I just know that it will happen at some time at camp. A moment in time that transforms us. It is when we understand why camp matters. It reminds me of my favorite movie moment when the heart of the Grinch Who Stole Christmas grows three times its size. The most amazing thing about "a moment" is that it changes our lives forever. It is just a little bit of something more. We take it back to the "real world" and it makes life a little kinder.

Although a camp counselor doesn't get much for salary, the moments make it all worth it. Seeing the campers smile warms your heart. It was so easy to get lost with yourself when you are so invested in the camp. We got lost, we laughed, we cried, and we had a blast giving these kids the time of their lives.

Travis Durocher
Scottsville, KY
Counselor

A New Chance at Life

It was Transplant week and the second to last night of camp. Dance night. Every little girl's dream. We were having a pre-dance party in the cabin, helping everyone get ready when the camp director pulled up in the golf cart. She asked for a counselor and a camper named Ingrid to take a quick ride up to the office with her. When Ingrid returned to the cabin, her face was red and wet with tears. All of the other girls rushed to her, embracing her. It was amazing to see what, a few days ago, was a group of strangers reach out and blindly support this little girl in whatever it was she was going through.

When Ingrid finally broke her sobs to speak, I was only able to hear one line. "I got a kidney." After that every member of the cabin was both sobbing and cheering, and nothing else was audible through the celebration that was breaking out.

I've never been so touched by other's compassion. Some of these little girls had been on dialysis as well, waiting on that same transplant list for years, for that very same kidney that Ingrid was about to receive. Yet, they were able to put their worries aside for the moment to share in Ingrid's joy, knowing that her life would now be changed forever.

That was my very first week as a counselor, and it's safe to say that not only Ingrid's life was changed that week. I learned more from those young women than I could have ever imagined and every camper I've had the privilege of working with has made a lasting impact on my life for the better.

Devon Thomas
Paris, France
Counselor

One spring, a parent contacted our Head Nurse at camp saying that her son, Austin, had Duchenne's Muscular Dystrophy and that his illness had progressed to the point that he was now in hospice. She told us that he had gone to a nearby camp sponsored by the MDA for the past several years, but because he was now on hospice, they could no longer accept him. When the nurse came to ask me, as Camp Director, if I thought we could take Austin, my only thought was, "How could we not?" and so, we did.

One day while Austin was at camp, the costumed Shamu character from Sea World came to visit. Austin had spent some time with Shamu a few years prior for his Make-A-Wish experience, and he really loved Shamu, so we made certain that he got to get his picture taken with the character that day.

Because of the progression of his illness, Austin was taking morphine to help with the pain. When Dr. Sue went to administer his next dose of morphine, Austin, with his wry smile and dry sense of humor, said, "So Doc, how much morphine are you giving me anyway? Because I've been seeing dancing whales today!"

Austin had a great week at camp that summer, and he lived for several more months. After his passing his mom got in touch to tell us how much that week had meant to him AND to her. She noted that she didn't realize how much she needed the break she received that week, and in retrospect wasn't sure she would have had the strength to continue on through those next several months without it.

What we do not only for our campers, but also for their families, is a blessing – for us as well as for them. Stories like this are why we do what we do…keep doing it everyone!

Brandon G. Briery, Ph.D.
San Antonio, TX
Executive Camping Director

Enjoying The Moment

I was out in the middle of the lake on a paddleboat with one of my 7-year-old campers during a camp for children with cancer. Harper was fishing, patiently waiting for a bite, so I turned to him and asked if he wanted to play a game like I Spy while we waited. Harper turned to me ever so sweetly, reeled in his fishing line, put down his pole, and said, "Actually, let's just sit here and enjoy the moment."

So, we did just that. After a couple minutes passed, I turned to Harper and said, "This is the life, huh?" quoting a line he had said earlier in the week. He looked at me and simply smiled.

Camp allows us to experience pure moments such as this one. I thank this sweet boy for reminding me to enjoy the simple moments in life.

Erica Sokol
Miami, FL
Counselor

I was the camp photographer in 2006 and 2007. I loved my job because I could walk into someone's moment, take a few photos, and hopefully capture a small glimpse of their experience. Camp is such a perplexing place to me because everywhere you turn, there are opportunities for amazing photos. Anyone with a half-decent camera can take photos of kids having fun, but it takes a deeper understanding of camp and the theories behind how it works to really capture the magic in the moment.

When I think back to camp, I remember flashes of moments. Maybe that's part of the reason I enjoyed being the photographer so much. The floor shaking in the dining hall from pride cheers, the odd combination of dew and bug spray mornings at the tower, picking off dried paint flakes from silly O, late night cabin chats, the restrained silence during rest hour, the hiss and crackle from the campfire, gator grand prix fire car, feats of strength, sudden rain storms, silent bear tournaments, the relief of intersession, the best hugs in the world, tea parties, learning from a Mr. Spivey story, the hype of free choice, discovery zone rockets, the soothing creak of rocking chairs, sneaking out with the youngest, ooblek, the anticipation of a new week, surprised face photos, and bittersweet see-ya-laters.

I know there are still lessons to be learnt from camp and moments of magic left to be captured. Perhaps some of those magic moments, the ones that a kid may not even notice happening but that stop a counselor in their tracks with just how monumental they are, should be left uncaptured, ready for counselors and campers to experience without any warning. From my time at camp, the thing that stays with me the most is just how much a few days at camp can change these kids, and it never fails to take me by surprise.

Nigel Bibler
Grand Junction, CO
Camp Photographer

I worked at a camp for children from Ireland, Britain and all throughout Europe. In a given session, there could be children from ten different countries, all speaking different languages. As a Polish interpreter, I was often the first one who would hear the stories from campers. During my first summer, I met a beautiful, unforgettable 14 year old from Poland. As a result of chemotherapy, Nevaeh had lost all her hair, so she wore a bandana. She spoke about her experience with cancer in a positive manner. She was always smiling.

One day, Nevaeh asked me to help her put on her prosthesis. She then sat me down and asked me if I knew why she was wearing the same bandana for the whole week at camp. I said no, but if she wanted, I could get her different one. Nevaeh replied no and proceeded to explain that the bandana belonged to her friend who had died of cancer two weeks before she came to camp. He was scheduled to come to camp, and Nevaeh had been given his place. So, she brought a little piece of him to camp. He was here, with us, at camp. I was speechless.

Camp is an incredible place where magic happens. The campers teach us that life is simple, that happiness consists of eating ice cream with no hands, putting a frozen t-shirt on, being a little silly, and laughing till our face hurts. It's the best thing in the world. We, adults, sometimes forget what simplicity is. We always want something more. Stop for a second and look around. Take a look at all the kids' faces dancing in the dining hall after lunch or dinner. Look at the joy and fun they are having. There is no better feeling than seeing that..seeing them happy. I'm so grateful I witnessed those kids grow. Camp really does give them a chance to "kick back and raise a little hell."

Milena Sobesto
Krakow, Poland
Counselor, Interpreter

If You're Weird and You Know It

Like always, after the banquet and pride closing, we had our own cabin closing where we inducted our girls into our Royal family. We gave them each a key, allowing them the power to unlock all of the royal values they had embodied all week of courage, confidence, friendship, loyalty, happiness, strength, and beauty whenever they may need them. We ended with a cabin chat, where our campers shared what "Camp is..." to them, the theme of the summer.

As we were talking about how camp is a place where we can be ourselves without judgement, one of the campers grabbed the royal crown from the middle of the circle and said, "Why don't we all go around the circle and say the weirdest thing about us." And that is exactly what we did.

Ten teenage girls battling cancer went around and shared what they thought made them "weird." We laughed until we could barely breathe at all of the unique, funny, interesting, and beautiful quirks and talents we have. They were completely embracing exactly who they are. Skylar, a camper who had woken up blind from treatment two years prior, then said something that I will never forget. Skylar said that it is the people who stand out, the ones with the "weird" traits and interesting personalities, who are remembered and make the biggest impact on others. Those who try to blend in and be like everyone else are just another person in the world. Skylar told them to hold onto what made them "weird" and never try to change it, because it is what makes them special and powerful.

The night continued with fun slumber party activities, but my mind kept rewinding to the cabin chat. As Dr. Seuss once said, "Why fit in when you were born to stand out?" Camp is... embracing your imperfections and loving those around you exactly for who they are.

Jillian Roberts
Miami, FL
Counselor

Every year I look forward to what camp will bring. I love watching the campers dance, sing, play musical instruments, fall in love, disagree, laugh hysterically, share, cry, open up, become friends, become best friends, play pranks, respect, reflect and so many other illustrations I am fortunate to be a part of.

Last summer, a young woman arrived at our camp: long black wig, beautiful eyes, friendly, open and ready to participate in a week she really knew nothing about. She was brave too. She was a good listener and very open about what was on her mind. She was one of many, that made it okay for others to feel safe and unfold their stories. She made a lot of new friends that week.

By wonderful serendipity, Emily Rose lived 30 minutes from me. I was able to visit with Emily at home and the hospital. As her cancer progressed, her body became much weaker and she lost her sight, but the way she continued to see life was as enlightened and perceptive as ever.

Emily had so many wonderful friends and a loving family, but it was through camp, she was able to open up and laugh, cry, and share what was really going on, to others that shared some version of her story. They shared an empathy that was untouched.

The compassion that happens at camp makes me live my life better. I think often about the love and lessons these kids and young adults have taught me. My life would be different without them. I love them.

Patty McGinley
Newport Beach, CA
Counselor

William was 8 years old when he came to camp for the first time. He had been diagnosed with Brain Cancer less than a year prior. He had already had several brain surgeries, the most recent taking place just five days before he arrived at camp. He had undergone numerous rounds of chemotherapy and radiation. His head was half shaven, and he had 49 fresh stitches down the middle. His prognosis was poor. They warned us that William would likely be limited with energy and advised us not to push him too much.

But, William was the farthest thing from limited. William was determined. William got up on a horse faster than any other kid in the cabin, he threw buckets of water on his counselors during water fights, he ran across camp cheering day in and day out, spreading love and life around the whole camp. At 8 years old, he became a leader to those of all ages. By the end of the session, the whole camp was wearing a red bandana to be like William who wore one to cover his recent surgery site.

William passed away later that year, shortly after bringing his family to a family weekend where he got to show them the magic of camp. I was lucky enough to return the following summer to camp and be a counselor to many of the boys that were in William's cabin the year before. They picked up right where they left off, and carried William's spirit with them. Their love for camp shined, and I know William would have been so proud.

Even though William only got to experience camp for 7 short days, he experienced it fully. He loved, he laughed, he lived. And that's the magic of camp. Camp was lucky to have William, and his memory lives on in all those he touched that summer with his love for life and winning attitude.

Erica Sokol
Miami, FL
Counselor

On July 1st 2002, I took a bus to my home away from home, only I didn't know it then. This would be my first experience with camp, and I had no idea that it would mean so much to me so many years later. As I nervously got onto the bus and waved goodbye to my mom, I could never imagine that the week would change my life forever, I mean it's JUST camp, right?

While on the bus we made a couple stops to pick up more kids, and one of those kids from a stop at an IHOP soon became the best friend I would ever have. His name was Justin, and he was like my twin separated at birth and like no other person I had ever met before in my whole life. We made sure we picked the same morning manatee every morning, and at pride activities we were always together! When camp was over, we were sad to leave each other but, exchanged numbers and emails and kept close. The next summer was the same; we were inseparable, and this went on for many summers.

Towards the end of my freshman year in high school, Justin got really sick, and later found out he had prostate cancer. Being 14, I didn't really know a whole lot about cancer, but I knew Justin was strong, and he could get passed it. A few months later, it significantly got worse, and he stopped all treatment. I didn't know what that meant for Justin, or for me, but I tried to stay positive because Justin showed no fear. We talked over the phone everyday for two months, until our last phone call together.

On June 10th 2010, I got a phone call from Justin. I was happy to see his number on my phone, but my happiness soon turned into darkness when I realized what was happening. He had called to say goodbye. I had tears streaming down my face as he struggled to form a sentence and told me to look for a letter in the mail from him. I then heard him say "I love you guys," and then there was silence. A moment later I heard a loud beeping, and I soon recognized the sound. I had just lost my best friend, and all I could hear was the ear piercing beep from the heart monitor.

That was the only summer I didn't get into camp, but I didn't care because it didn't feel right going without my best friend beside me. I didn't know if it would ever be the same.

This summer, I got the chance to volunteer as a counselor. What made it even better was I had found something that I had forgotten about. I found something that filled me with so much happiness. I found my best friend.

One year at camp, when we had gotten a little older, our counselors had brought us to Sue Lila Hollow. We went there as a pride to reflect on our time at camp, to remember the good times, our fondest memories and our friends who had passed on. At the end of our time there, we all wrote on rocks. Justin and I wrote on a rock "Justin and Emily BEST FRIENDS FOREVER" and put it in a pile of other rocks and left Sue Lila Hollow together.

This summer, while the kids were at rest hour, I went to Sue Lila Hollow to sit and just reflect. While sitting there, I looked through some rocks, not expecting to find anything. I was just about to get up and leave when something caught my eye. I saw something familiar, something from my past that felt like deja vu. I found our rock! I found the rock that we had marked with our friendship so many years ago. I sat holding our rock with tears in my eyes, love in my heart, and Justin on my mind. I could see 13 year old Justin sitting beside me, as if he were still here with me. I knew then that my friend was with me, watching over me, and happy that I had made it full circle. I knew Justin was with me.

Emily Ragion
West Palm Beach, FL
Former Camper, Counselor

My Beautiful Children

That day, the sun beat down on cabin row as I anxiously awaited the arrival of my campers during the Immunology session for children with HIV. Their names in colorful chalk glistened on the sidewalk and handmade afghans and bears lined their beds. As a counselor, I felt prepared for their medical conditions and explanations of what we might expect to see and hear during the week.

Slowly, the campers began to arrive, and I excitedly introduced myself and helped them unpack their belongings. As more and more campers arrived, I suddenly had an enormous wave of emotion hit me. I knew all the children that came through the camp gates every session were seriously-ill, but I don't think it hit me until that exact moment. I had never viewed my campers as anything except what they were, which was my beautiful children, so my emotions came unexpectedly.

I excused myself to the counselor side of the cabin and sobbed like a baby for the first time in my life while being at camp. After I pulled myself together and dried my tears, it was time to get my head back in the game. Never in my life did I play so hard and love even harder. These kids brought the best of me, and I am grateful for that experience as it has changed my life forever. I had finally seen and felt the true meaning of camp deep inside my heart.

Charlotte Dang Kemp
Lake Mary, FL
Counselor

New Math

David, a camper sitting at the waterfront, asked me if we could do some math problems. I'm a teacher, so of course I said yes! He said, "I don't mean 2+2...I want to add up all the wonderful things you do at camp to see if it will fill my heart." David started naming all these things about camp, then just stopped and said, "My heart is overflowing! My heart is overflowing!"

We have all felt that goose bump-inducing feeling when you see a camper's nervousness shift to confidence, when unfamiliar faces become lifelong friends, and anticipation transforms into celebration. It's the moment campers accomplish something they are proud of, try something new, or build up a fellow camper that needs an extra boost of support. It's that camper who stepped quietly off the bus on Arrival Day, but left belting out the loudest version of their cabin cheer. It's the moment when campers reunite with parents and are beaming and talking a mile a minute.

These small but beautiful moments, and so many more, are why I volunteer my time at a camp that truly allows these kids, and their families, incredible, life-changing experiences.

Sarah Kersey
Columbus, OH
Counselor

No Regrets

One summer there was a courageous, young girl with terminal cancer who was counting down the days she had to live to make it to camp. When I saw Autumn on the first day of camp, I spent all day and night trying to figure out a way to control her pain. Fortunately, we did, and she had an amazing week until Friday when the pain could no longer be controlled.

When Autumn heard that she had to go back home to hospice, she did not complain. She said that she was at peace with dying. Her only regret was not getting to feed a giraffe before she died. How Autumn loved giraffes! Giraffe backpack, sheets, sleeping bag, etc. When I told our camp director, Patty, that story, she said, "We are going to fix that."

Patty arranged for a limo to pick up this young camper's mother and brother and drive them to the Santa Barbara Zoo where our ambulance had secretly taken Autumn. Once there, she fed lots of animals including her beloved giraffe! The picture of her smiling face with a smiling giraffe resting his head on her shoulder was cherished memory for her family and us! Autumn unfortunately died very soon after that adventure but with no regrets.

Mark Mogul, MD
Huntington, WV
Camp Doctor

Resilience

It was the summer of 2011 during Crohn's and Colitis week. In this group of young men, one of them was from Liver Transplant week. Anthony had missed his session because he was very sick in the hospital for most the year. Fortunately, he was able to come to this session since it was his last year as a camper. From fighting for his life and to get an opportunity to be back at camp where he belonged was a dream come true for Anthony. He couldn't stop smiling from the moment that he walked into camp till the day he left. The other guys in the cabin were very accepting and adopted Anthony as one of their own.

The courage of this individual was second to none and the appreciation he had for camp and the people that create it was infectious. Upon meeting Anthony, I asked myself a lot of questions. How did he do it? How did he accomplish more in his life than some people struggle to do so in their entire lives? How did he sacrifice his comfort for everyone else's happiness, even when it would be the most difficult thing to do? How did he make himself a role model amongst role models?

The answer was staring right at me in the face: Resilience. Anthony remained strong, and didn't let illness dictate who he would become. He is a person I will never forget.

Ben McMaster
Melbourne, Australia
Counselor

To talk about camp is a difficult thing,
What makes it so hard is where to begin.
For me and for many the magic is housed,
In a hall with long tables, a stage and a crowd.
Three times every day we all come together,
To share a hot meal over riddles and laughter.
The clinking of forks, the smell of great food,
Excited, happy children creates a magical mood.
Dancing after dinner sets the whole hall in motion,
Bewitching the place like a magical potion.
A sight for tired eyes, a balm for the soul,
Watching a child dance makes the small parts seem whole.
Those small parts make up the rest of our camp,
The buzz of activities, being told you're a champ.
The way that our staff can alight in each camper,
The courage to believe that they'd make a great dancer.
And it's these things together not any one instance,
That makes a child grow in confidence, self-belief and resilience
On the last day of camp when the great banquet starts,
The hall is transformed and beats like a heart.
The most magic of moments
Are seen over dinner,
Shared tales of success
Where each child is a winner.
To talk about camp is a difficult thing,
What makes it so hard is where to begin.
This place where we eat is a symbol to describe
Something so special, so magic, so alive.

Rebecca Egan
Dublin, Ireland
Counselor

The Camp Organ

Camp has always been a permanent fixture for me, like an extra organ. I imagine the spirit I carry within me shaped like the camp tree or the sun or a child's painted handprint, beating like a heart, always reminding me that I'm alive. Maybe it's like that for me because I grew up there. Its roots are embedded into my DNA like my mother's genes. It's situated somewhere between the brain and the heart but reaches all the way down to my toes. Invisible to the professional eye, unseen on a MRI or Ultrasound, yet lingering and visible to others with the same smiling organ, so vivid that you can pick it out in a crowd of strangers. It radiates like a light...a light that never dims...an inner beauty that can't be stifled.

And just like my drivers license declares me as an organ donor, I am always willing to give a little piece of my magic and donate my camp organ, beautiful and beating to those in need of a transplant. Because what is love, what is magic, what is this beautiful soul's real purpose if you don't share it with those who could use a little bit of magic themselves?

Michelle Spencer Baranowski
Tampa, FL
Former Camper, Activities Counselor

She arrived like most campers do-quite; reserved, looking down and twiddling her thumbs. As we began to talk about Taylor Swift, the Jonas Brothers, and her matching camouflage crocs, shorts, and jacket, Ellie started to tilt her head up as she spoke, making eye contact with us. Pretty soon, Ellie was smiling.

It was my first session of my first summer at camp, and this camper fundamentally altered the way I engage with other humans. By the end of the week Ellie was not just smiling, but also laughing, and making BFFs.

Like many campers that week, Ellie was in a wheelchair. Perhaps my favorite experience of the entire summer was spinning around in circles with her under the christmas lights at the dance. Later, at cabin chat, she snatched the cabin chat bear quickly from the ground after a counselor reminded the girls of the rules of cabin chat. Ellie tilted her head to the side, as she always did, and grew a small grin on her face. She shared that at the dance, she danced for the very first time.

I realize Ellie's story is not entirely unique. Many campers come out of their shells, make new friends, and seem to experience pure joy for the first time at camp. Yet, there will always be something special about Ellie's experience. When we danced and when I helped her smear a s'more on her face, I saw life in her eyes that I am sure was not there before, and I understood that camp is the gift of life.

Leah Glowacki
Austin, TX
Counselor

I met Garrett at camper check in- after reading his medical file several times, assuring our staff that he would miss as little programming as possible in between straight catheterizations, bowel regimens and needing to sleep in medical housing overnight to be hooked up to his ventilator. I knew he was going to have a great week. I didn't realize that I was the one who would be forever changed by this funny, smart and simply amazing young man that had to rely on others for everything except speaking as a quadriplegic. I can't even remember what had happened to Garrett because he made a disability seem so insignificant. He asked me about being a nurse and then promptly explained, with a laugh, that he was considering other career options now that professional wrestler was out of the picture. That's just who he was.

Garrett had never been on a kayak or swimming in a public pool since he required a special float, and we did all those things. I can still see how much his blue eyes lit up zip lining. We kept him cool. We kept him safe, respected and loved.

The last night of camp Garrett said, "This week is the best thing that's happened to me since getting sick. Thanks for taking good care of my body this week. I couldn't have done it without you." He cried, I cried. That's the awesome thing about camp: they think you help them but what they give you back is exponentially better. I am forever changed and a better person for working with kids and young adults like Garrett. That's the good stuff.

Faith Crozier, RN
Houston, TX
Camp Nurse

The Kitchen of Dreams

Legend says, it had always been an abandoned cabin. Many had heard or spoke of it, but no one had dared to enter…that is, until a beautiful and brave group of teenage girls arrived at camp. On that first night after lights out, they secretly made the long journey to the abandoned cabin, along with their faithful counselors. Yellow caution tape lined the old, log cabin, reminding those who bravely chose to enter, that a world of imagination and endless possibilities lay ahead. The girls looked at each other, smiled and linked arms. They had dealt with so many challenges in their short lives; Liver Transplant, Kidney Disease, HIV, Lupus, and Spina Bifida, respectively. They knew fear and hesitation had no place in their lives. They took a deep breath and crossed under the caution tape. As they entered the cabin, all 5 girls gasped.

To the naked eye, the cabin looked empty and dark. But the girls believed. They had faith. They saw a place to love and call their own. They saw a place where they could share late night snacks and laughs. And so, every night, as the rest of camp was entering dream land, they quietly snuck to a different dream land: The Kitchen of Dreams.

On the last night of camp, the girls invited the camp community into their home. Yellow caution tape no longer lined the cabin, as it was no longer abandoned. A waitress in a wheelchair spun by guests, offering hors d'oeuvres. *Beep!* Pizza was ready!

While the chefs were busy tending to the oven, a different piece of equipment connected to the Sous Chef captured the spirit of the night. Hardly a concern *that* night, the peritoneal dialysis machine usually symbolized isolation, no sleepovers, and no late night activities. But here, even an intense nightly process of dialysis could blend in, representing all that CAN be done. In the Kitchen of Dreams, it was about so much more: cooking and community.

Meera Ramamoorthy, MD
Cincinnati, OH
Counselor

The Most Beautiful Sunflower

It was only my second time of volunteering at camp, and I still wasn't quite sure what to expect! The weekend was for children with heart conditions, and I was assigned to a teenage girl. A million questions raced through my head, mostly hoping that a teenager would still enjoy camp. Thankfully, I was greeted by two huge smiles, from Abrianna and her best friend, Victoria. The two had met at camp years before and were a package deal. We did everything together! We danced to every single song never taking a break. As we ate spaghetti with no hands, we laughed at Victoria because she didn't like sauce and kept the cleanest face! During Stage Day, the three of us did a great rendition of Summer Love from Grease. At the time, I couldn't imagine the impact that weekend would have on my life.

Victoria had Pulmonary Hypertension and had received a lung transplant when she was 10 years old. Three years after meeting her, she was in the hospital awaiting a second transplant. Victoria's body went through organ rejection, and she was placed on a list for a third transplant. In our last conversation she told me she could not wait to go back and volunteer at camp.

On August 11, 2012, Victoria passed away. Her service was filled with sunflowers, memories, and many people who loved her. When I look back on why I volunteer at camp and people who have changed my life, I think of Victoria. I'll never pass a field of yellow flowers or hear Summer Love without smiling. Victoria taught me that our bodies may be weak but our spirit and hope can be strong, and even after death, we can continue to give, just as she did as an organ donor. I will always remember that heroes can be 21 year-olds with weak lungs but unwavering spirits and hope. Just like Mr. Spivey says, "We don't say goodbye, we say see you later." See you later, Victoria.

Amanda Taylor
Daytona Beach, FL
Counselor

The Power of the Small Moments

In 2008, at 17-years-old, I went to two weeks of camp for kids with Craniofacial Disorders. I was amazed at how camp could help a camper's self-esteem and confidence. I wished a camp like this had been available for me when I was younger, but I feel grateful that camp came into my life when it did. Just like it helped the campers build their confidence, it helped build mine, and more importantly, helped me realize what I wanted to do as a career. That next year I went to college already knowing I wanted to major in Therapeutic Recreation; it involves recognizing an individual campers' particular barriers and tailoring activities or challenges to help them grow.

One week, I asked the campers in my room if they wanted to learn how to make friendship bracelets during chill time. One camper knew what kind she wanted to make and got going on hers. The other camper, Juliette, wanted me to teach her how to make a particular one. Juliette did not have full ability of her left hand, and her left arm was significantly shorter than the other. This particular style of friendship bracelet would require two hands, so she asked me if she could borrow my left hand. I thought it was the sweetest question ever. This proved to be an even better way for her to learn how to make this bracelet.

During that week, Juliette and I made bracelets each day during chill time - me with my left hand and her with her right hand. I admired that she chose a bracelet that was harder than some of the others options and determined how to adapt on her own.

At the end of the week, Juliette was so excited to show her mom the ones she had made. These moments during chill time were simple, yet so much came out of it; learning something new, stretching comfort zones, social interaction, creativity, confidence in adapting when working with a physical difference, and more.

Paige Mackintosh
Duvall, WA
Former Camper, Counselor

Wonderful Words of Wisdom

It is funny how camp and the kids we meet can help and heal those who have never been to camp or know what it is like to have a serious illness. Earlier this year, my friend had a death in her immediate family. As I was thinking of ways to comfort my friend, I was reminded of this past summer. I had been sitting with Morgan, a camper, at campfire, and she was just staring up at the sky. I asked Morgan what she was looking at. Her response was delayed:

"I just can't think of that word...that word that brings you down. Ugh, what is it? Oh yeah! Ju-ju!"

"Ju-ju?" I was confused.

"Yeah, there is good ju-ju and there is bad. Even though the bad ju-ju brings me down, I look up at the sky and remember I am alive. So I fight that ju-ju with happiness. The happiness I find here, with the people who I love."

Such a simple yet wise statement. I passed those words of advice off to my friend and reminded her that although there are great struggles in life, whether it be an illness or a loss of a family member, the people who love you will always help you get through the bad ju-ju.

By the end of the week at camp, Morgan never talked about the ju-ju again. I wish we would have because I don't think she realized what an impact her words had made.

Becca Rose Wagner
Canfield, OH
Counselor

A few days within our weeklong camp, I had to take one of our campers, Avery, to the nurse's station for her treatment. She had primary immunodeficiency disease (PID) and, as a result, had to have an infusion of Hizentra every week. For the very first time in my life, I saw a ten year old girl lay out all her materials, assemble them together, and stick herself with needles. Avery was focused, efficient, and cautious. But what I saw in her face resonated within me: bravery. Avery was mature for her age. I wondered if this was maybe a byproduct of having to deal with her condition at such a young age. It showed me that there can be good brought out in even the most difficult situations.

Avery made animal noises when her infusion started in order to cope with the burning sensations. She later explained to me that a lot of animal noises simulated that of "ow!" These included the cat (me-OW) and wolf (OWW). When the infusion was in full swing, Avery made string bracelets, read her book, and practiced for her performance of the song "Gold."

That day, I learned about resilience. A ten year old girl taught me to live fearlessly. She taught me that any obstacle could be overcome with the right attitude. I had never heard the song Gold before, but since leaving camp I have recognized it playing around me. Each time, I have thought about Avery, her bravery and felt thankful for it.

"This, this is for all the girls, boys all over the world
Whatever you've been told, you're worth more than gold
So hold your head up high, it's your time to shine
From the inside out it shows, you're worth more than gold"

Sama Imran Ilyas
Orlando, FL
Counselor

A Letter to the Editor

Dear Meera,

When I went to camp for the first time I was sure of one thing: these campers would make a lasting impact on my life. Their strength, their courage, their resilience, their spirit, their silliness, their love - they would show me the sometimes brutal, overwhelming beauty of life.

What I wasn't prepared for was a group that would become known as my "camp friends." They were my peers - fellow counselors - who challenged me, encouraged me, and believed in me. They saw me  at my absolute best and my finest worst, loved me, and helped me discover the best version of myself.

Of all my camp friends, I was least prepared for you. I was instantly drawn to your passion for camp. I knew early on that you were a positive force of camp spirit and when we were matched in the same cabin group for the summer, I was grateful for the opportunity to work with you, to learn from you, and to build our friendship. What I didn't know is how hard I would have to work.

Creating camp magic with you is a serious business. I learned quickly that you had a deep understanding of the power of camp, you dreamed big dreams for what campers could accomplish and stopped nothing short of making everything possible - and perfect - for our deserving kids. Working with you meant being at my best, and I wouldn't have wanted anything less. I will always remember creating a new dance to "Reach for the Stars" until 4am in the arts and crafts building because we knew we loved the original dance so much but we just couldn't remember any of the moves. I loved that a simple idea for an act of kindness became "Operation Butterfly," complete with a secret mission map and with more butterflies, happiness, and love than we could ever bottle up. And everyone who visited the "Kitchen of Dreams" will forever remember how we turned an 'abandoned' cabin to a place where teenage girls could share late night snacks and many laughs. Along with creating delicious food, they created a community of support, friendship, and hope.

By summer's end, I knew you well enough to know camp wasn't limited to those 282 acres or that summer. You live camp every day.

Now serving as a representation of your camp friends, your community, we have been blessed to learn from you, grow with you and are inspired by your passion. You were among the first to fundraise for camp programs in India - at the ripe age of 20. You committed to volunteer at as many camps as possible and, in the process, introduced countless others to the magic of camp when you supported them to volunteer alongside you. You have brought together individuals connected by camp to celebrate friendship, often while wearing goofy mustache glasses or Santa suits in public. You have designed t-shirts and fundraisers inspiring us to believe there is good in the world and to be that good. And now you have connected all of us, along with the thousands of campers and all those that will read this book in the years to come, through your dream of sharing camp's story, our story - your story.

Thank you for welcoming us all to your heart's mission.

You are loved.

April Uyehara
Pukalani, HI
Camp Director

Epilogue

Inspired by these stories?

Come join the fun and make a positive impact on children with serious illnesses. Whether you have a day, weekend, week or an entire summer, our camps offer a variety of volunteer and paid opportunities. An integral part of making camp happen all around the world, our volunteers make up more than 50% of the adults that help run our camps; they come from all walks of life and defy all age, race, social, economic, and professional boundaries.

Cabin counselors: Through this volunteer or seasonal position you'll be actively involved in the supervision, guidance and motivation of campers for the entire session. They encourage friendships and teamwork within the cabin, role model camp spirit, and help campers to get the most out of their camp experience. From ensuring campers have brushed their teeth to helping them prepare for stage night, cabin counselors do it all!

Medical professionals: The number one concern is the safety of the children, from patching up a scraped knee to making sure campers receive medications on time. In addition to the full-time Medical and Nursing Directors, camps require other medical professionals such as doctors, nurses, pharmacists, nutritionists and psychologists to support the programs both on a weekly and seasonal basis.

In addition to these main opportunities, camps often have other needs, including kitchen and maintenance support, photographers and musicians.

Index of Contributors

Thank you for sharing a piece of your heart. You are loved.

And if by chance you should be going there
Please take this message that I hope you'll share
Please take this message to the ones to young to have learned
The time is short and there's so much to do
Don't waste a moment of what's given to you
Don't waste a moment 'cause you'll never see it return

Stars in the sky, stars in the sky
To bring the summer right back to me
Tell me you'll try, tell me you'll try
To think about me whenever you see those

Stars in the sky

44465170R00168

Made in the USA
Lexington, KY
01 September 2015